Childhood and Youth Studies

This book is dedicated to Coleman Everett Myers and our two children, Jonathan and Rosanna, from whom I have received both unrequited love and inspiration – to each, my gratitude and admiration.

Childhood and Youth Studies

Edited by

Paula Zwozdiak-Mayers

Los Angeles | London | New Delhi
Singapore | Washington DC

First published in 2007 by Learning Matters Ltd.

British Library Cataloguing in Publication Data
A CIP record for this book is available from the British Library.

ISBN 978 1 84445 075 6

The rights of Paula Zwozdiak-Myers, Neil Burton, Will Coster, Paul Gardner, Tina Harris, Andrew Hope, Andrea Raiker, Ian Roberts, David Stewart, Geoff Tookey, Rob Toplis, Martin Ward Fletcher and Amanda Wawryn to be identified as the Authors of this Work have been asserted by them in accordance with the Copyright, Designs and Patents Act 1988.

Cover design by Phil Barker. Text design by Code 5 Design Associates Ltd.
Project management by Deer Park Productions, Tavistock
Typeset by Pantek Arts Ltd, Maidstone, Kent
Printed and bound in Great Britain by CPI Group (UK) Ltd, Croydon, CR0 4YY

Learning Matters Ltd
33 Southernhay East
Exeter EX1 1NX
Tel: 01392 215560
info@learningmatters.co.uk
www.learningmatters.co.uk

Los Angeles | London | New Delhi
Singapore | Washington DC

Learning Matters
An imprint of SAGE Publications Ltd
SAGE Publications Ltd
1 Oliver's Yard
55 City Road
London EC1Y 1SP

SAGE Publications Inc.
2455 Teller Road
Thousand Oaks, California 91320

SAGE Publications India Pvt Ltd
B 1/I 1 Mohan Cooperative Industrial Area
Mathura Road
New Delhi 110 044

SAGE Publications Asia-Pacific Pte Ltd
3 Church Street
#10-04 Samsung Hub
Singapore 049483

MIX
Paper from
responsible sources
FSC® C013604

Contents

Part 3: Difference, diversity and multidisciplinary perspectives

Part 4: Researching childhood and youth

Introduction

The substantive content of this text reflects many components of the BA (Hons) Childhood and Youth Studies degree programme offered at the University of Bedfordshire that aims to provide a sound knowledge and understanding of both the scholarly inter-disciplinary study of childhood and youth and, the multi-agency practice of professionals who serve the needs of children and their families such as teachers, social workers and health visitors. These broad aims have been translated into the following strands of approaches to childhood and youth for the purpose of structuring this text:

● Social and cultural perspectives of childhood and youth;
● Childhood and youth development;
● Difference, diversity and multi-disciplinary perspectives;
● Researching childhood and youth.

Learning objectives and a summary of key points are featured at the beginning and end of each chapter, respectively, which enable you to identify the key concepts and themes incorporated within each. A range of approaches to teaching and learning about childhood and youth are embedded throughout this text as each chapter invites you to undertake focused, reflective activities that support the theoretical and conceptual underpinnings introduced. This enables you to practise, develop and acquire a number of cognitive abilities and practical skills which include: interpreting and evaluating evidence, assessing the strengths and weaknesses of rival theories and explanations, making informed and reasoned argument, perceiving the complex nature of diverse childhood and youth situations, accessing and synthesising information from different sources and being able to reflect upon and articulate your own learning experiences in order to become a more effective practitioner. Questions are raised to challenge your thinking and encourage you to enter into discussion and debate with colleagues, tutors and professionals working in a range of fields so that different views and perspectives can both be voiced and heard.

Multi-agency working is at the heart of the government's ten-year strategy to re-design children and young people's services. In 2004, the Children's National Service Framework (NSF) was introduced to tackle child poverty and inequality in order to improve the lives of all children and families. The tragic and untimely death of Victoria Climbié (www.everychildmatters.gov.uk) served as the catalyst for a radical shift in thinking about children's health and social care services and, of how services could be better designed and delivered around the needs of the child in an holistic way, as opposed to focusing more on the needs of organisations themselves. To reduce inequality and ensure that all children and young people gain access to the services they need, the government expects that by 2014, the education, health and social care services will have successfully addressed the standards embedded within the NSF, as detailed below. The eleven standards are grouped into three categories: Part I encompasses standards one to five that focus on the achievement of high quality service provision to all children and young people, their parents and carers; Part II encompasses standards six to ten that focus on children and young people, their parents and carers who have particular needs; Part III encompasses standard eleven that focuses on the particular needs and choices of women and their babies before or during pregnancy, throughout birth and during the first three months of parenthood.

The Children's National Service Framework (NSF) Standards

Standard	Description of criteria
Part I	
1	***Promoting Health and Well-being, Identifying Needs and Intervening Early:*** *The health and well-being of all children and young people is promoted and delivered through a co-ordinated programme of action, including prevention and early intervention wherever possible, to ensure long term gain, led by the NHS in partnership with local authorities.*
2	***Supporting Parenting:*** *Parents or carers are enabled to receive the information, services and support which will help them to care for their children and equip them with the skills they need to ensure that their children have optimum life chances and are healthy and safe.*
3	***Child, Young Person and Family-Centred Services:*** *Children and young people and families receive high quality services that are co-ordinated around their individual and family needs and take account of their views.*
4	***Growing up into Adulthood:*** *All young people have access to age-appropriate services that are responsive to their specific needs as they grow into adulthood.*
5	***Safeguarding and Promoting the Welfare of Children and Young People:*** *All agencies work to prevent children suffering harm and to promote their welfare, provide them with the services they require to address their identified needs and safeguard children who are being or who are likely to be harmed.*
Part II	
6	***Children and Young People who are Ill:*** *All children and young people who are ill, or thought to be ill, or injured will have timely access to appropriate advice and to effective services which address their health, social, educational and emotional needs throughout the period of their illness.*
7	***Children and Young People in Hospital:*** *Children and young people receive high quality, evidence-based hospital care, developed through clinical governance and delivered in appropriate settings.*
8	***Disabled Children and Young People and Those with Complex Health Needs:*** *Children and young people who are disabled or who have complex health needs receive co-ordinated, high quality child and family-centred services which are based on assessed needs, which promote social inclusion and, where possible, which enable them and their families to live ordinary lives.*
9	***The Mental Health and Psychological Well-being of Children and Young People:*** *All children and young people, from birth to their eighteenth birthday, who have mental health problems and disorders have access to timely, integrated, high quality, multi disciplinary mental health services to ensure effective assessment, treatment and support, for them, and their families.*
10	***Medicines for Children and Young People:*** *Children, young people, their parents or carers, and health care professionals in all settings make decisions about medicines based on sound information about risk and benefit. They have access to safe and effective medicines that are prescribed on the basis of the best available evidence.*
Part III	
11	***Maternity Services:*** *Women have easy access to supportive, high quality maternity services, designed around their individual needs and those of their babies.*

(adapted from DfES/DoH (2004) *National Service Framework for Children, Young People and Maternity Services: Executive Summary*, DfES/DoH, pp 6–7) – for more information visit: http://www.dh.gov.uk/PolicyAndGuidance/HealthAndSocialCareTopics/ChildrenServices/fs/en

The Children's NSF necessarily has implications for those of you preparing to work within the Children's Workforce. Following a period of consultation in 2004 the government introduced a Common Core framework of knowledge and skills that all professionals within the Children's Workforce should be able to demonstrate if they are to work effectively in multi-disciplinary teams with children, young people and their families. Appendix 1 identifies and positions the six areas of the Common Core of Skills and Knowledge.

- Effective communication and engagement with children, young people and families.
- Child and young person development.
- Safeguarding and promoting the welfare of the child.
- Supporting transitions.
- Multi-agency working.
- Sharing information.

alongside the government's *Every Child Matters* and *Youth Matters* Outcomes Framework of:

- being healthy;
- staying safe;
- enjoying and achieving;
- making a positive contribution;
- achieving economic well-being.

to guide you toward relevant source material that informs you of some expectations placed upon you as you prepare to work in a range of professional fields and services within the Children's Workforce.

The Common Core of Skills and Knowledge and the *Every Child Matters and Youth Matters* Outcomes Framework are embedded within the qualification structure for all those seeking to work with children, young people and their families e.g. Standards for the award of Qualified Teacher Status (QTS) effective from September 2007 (www.tda.gov.uk) have been revised to embrace the government's ten year strategy and vision. To ensure that you remain abreast of developments it is imperative that you adopt an approach of continuous professional development to your work by monitoring changes and initiatives to national and local policy and practice, on a regular basis via such websites as www.everychildmatters.gov.uk; www.info4local.gov.uk and those related more specifically to your own profession.

Paula Zwozdiak-Myers

Contributors

Neil Burton – MA Education programme leader at the University of Bedfordshire – has written several texts focusing on Educational Management and Leadership issues for Paul Chapman, Sage and Peter Francis publishers. He also edits *Science Teacher Education*, a journal aimed at those working in initial teacher education, for the Association for Science Education. Most recently he has written papers on inclusion in secondary schools in Tel-Aviv; the role of teaching assistants in both primary and secondary schools; training non-teachers for school headship; and the use of ICT to support trainee primary teachers in gaining a better understanding of science.

Will Coster received his DPhil in History from the University of York in 1993. He has published extensively on the history of religion and childhood, including *Family and Kinship in England 1450–1750* (2001) and *Baptism and Spiritual Kinship in Early Modern England* (2002). He is particularly interested in changing attitudes to children and disability since the medieval period. He is a Senior Lecturer in Education at the University of Bedfordshire.

Paul Gardner is a Senior Lecturer in Education at the University of Bedfordshire, formerly De Montfort University (Bedford). He has worked in a variety of educational contexts during a career spanning 30 years and has published several books. His areas of interest are multicultural education and inclusion, drama, film and English. Paul is a core member of the teaching team on a BA in Childhood and Youth at the University of Bedfordshire.

Tina Harris graduated from Brunel University, formerly West London Institute of Higher Education, with a BEd Hons degree in Special Education. She has worked across a range of settings including the primary and secondary sector for pupils with severe and moderate learning difficulties, including complex communication difficulties. Tina was Special Needs Officer in Hillingdon and gained valuable insights into the statutory and multi-agency facets of working with families with additional needs. Tina currently leads the County Inclusive Resource based at Beacon Hill School, Suffolk that provides a county-wide service for mainstream pupils with Autistic Spectrum Disorders, acknowledged by Ofsted as: *Outstanding in providing a very successful outreach service*. The school is part of the government's Leading Edge Partnership, placing it at the forefront of the new role for special schools.

Andrew Hope is a Senior Lecturer in the Department of Sociology at Manchester Metropolitan University. His current research interests include the sociology of risk and surveillance, social aspects of the internet and educational cultures. He co-edited the book *Risk, Education and Culture* (Ashgate Publishing) in 2005 and more recently has published articles on risk and the internet in the *British Journal of Sociology of Education*, the *British Educational Research Journal* and *Discourse*.

Andrea Raiker has followed a varied career in teaching, the Civil Service, business administration and designing/manufacturing, and joined De Montfort University as a tutor in mathematics and ICT. Her experiences as Project Director for the Midlands Consortium, an organisation delivering training in ICT to practising teachers led to a role introducing and developing e-Learning within the university. Recently, Andrea has developed a BA Honours/Foundation Degree for Teaching Assistants and other educational paraprofessionals. She now works in the fields of student personal development planning and increasing student employability as a Fellow at the University of Bedfordshire.

Ian Roberts has a BEd in Physical Education and an MA in Education. Having been Head of Physical Education in a large Hertfordshire secondary school, he is now Senior Lecturer in Physical Education at the University of Bedfordshire. His principal academic interests concern strategies used in schools to support students in serious danger of permanent exclusion and coaching processes used to empower athletes in elite track and field athletics.

David Stewart graduated with a BEd in Human Movement Studies from Bedford College of Higher Education in 1981. He was recently awarded an honorary MEd for his work in Special Education

Needs. David is currently Executive Headteacher of Beacon Hill School (Moderate Learning Difficulties) and the Suffolk County Inclusive Resource, an outreach service for children with Autistic Spectrum Disorders. Previously David worked in a mainstream high school in the field of Physical Education and then moved into SEN PE and Leadership. Beacon Hill School and the Outreach Service were awarded 'Leading Edge Status' in 2003.

Geoff Tookey works as a Senior Lecturer at the University of Bedfordshire and following the completion of an MA in Social Work had a protected caseload with a childcare team to develop preventive group work. He has worked in juvenile justice and education social work, for a large child protection charity and directly with families where the children's names were on the child protection register, and has chaired child protection conferences for over nine years. He has also been a senior childcare trainer in a local authority and a freelance trainer in child protection.

Rob Toplis joined the School of Sport and Education at Brunel University in 2005, having previously worked as a PGCE Science Tutor at De Montfort University and the Open University. He taught secondary science in inner-city, rural and suburban secondary schools in Yorkshire, Hertfordshire, Devon and Buckinghamshire for over 25 years. His research interests include practical work in science education, modelling in chemistry and ICT use in science education. He serves on the Research Committee of the Association for Science Education and is an editorial associate for *School Science Review*.

Martin Ward Fletcher is a teacher at the University of Bedfordshire. He specialises in the social psychology of education and has a particular interest in disability and special needs education. He has previously worked in mainstream secondary and all-age special schools. His MEd dissertation explored the experience of disabled children in an inclusive environment.

Amanda Wawryn has worked within the social care profession for Bedfordshire County Council for almost 20 years. Her varied roles include home carer for the elderly, community support worker for individuals with Alzheimer's and residential social worker for children and adults with spina bifida, muscular dystrophy and cerebral palsy. Amanda completed her BA Honours degree in Health in 2002 and is nearing completion of a further honours degree in Social Work. She admires the bravery and resilience shown by those she has supported and considers that effective working relationships must be based upon mutual respect and trust.

Paula Zwozdiak-Myers is programme leader for the BA Honours degree in Childhood and Youth Studies at the University of Bedfordshire, having led the development, writing and validation through to its launch in September 2005. She has particular interests in the psychosocial aspects of human behaviour and development, movement studies, communication and qualitative approaches to research. Paula also leads the professional studies component of an ITT programme for secondary students preparing them for entry into the teaching profession. She values difference and diversity, promotes potential and entitlement, and wholeheartedly supports the inclusive agenda.

Part 1

Social and cultural perspectives of childhood and youth

1   Social constructions of childhood

Will Coster

Learning objectives

By the end of this chapter you should be able to respond to the following questions:

- **Is it possible to have children without childhood?**
- **Is childhood a modern invention?**
- **Why does society construct childhood?**
- **How does society construct modern childhood?**
- **How do constructions of childhood differ?**
- **What factors influence our current view of childhood?**

Introduction

Each of us has experienced not one, but two childhoods: the first as a biological state of growth and development and the second as a social construction, which is to say as an institution that has been socially created. If this is true, then it follows that childhood is dependent on the nature of a society into which an individual is born and will vary from place to place and time to time. In the last half of the twentieth century a number of thinkers and writers in a variety of fields began to consider the ways in which this process of constructing childhood has been carried out, both in the past and today, and what the implications are for our experience of childhood and for current and future generations of children. If we accept this thesis then it follows that we can understand childhood only if we comprehend how it has been formed and how it varies and changes. These themes are explored throughout this chapter.

Children without childhood?

If childhood is constructed then it must be possible for there to be children without childhood. The idea may seem extraordinary, but it is possible. We take it for granted in modern western societies that there is a state we call 'childhood'. It is a commonplace of our language about the young and enshrined in law, both national and international, where special protection is offered to persons usually under the age of 18. In part, such persons need these legal protections because they do not have the full rights of a citizen: the right to own property, to be a legal entity who can go before the courts and to participate in such events as elections. But what of societies where these rights were not given to all adults or even to none? In such a world the distinction between child and adult might seem less important. Such a view is dominant in a large part of the modern world where citizens have limited or no active rights in the accepted sense.

It is worth considering that this is also a good description of most societies in the past: even the relatively recent past. Democracy, in the accepted modern sense of participation in free elections, was extended to all women in Britain only as recently as 1928, and civil and legal rights have retained elements of a society run by men and by a small social elite until within a few decades of the present day. The very concept of human rights is also relatively recent in historical terms, dating largely from the late nineteenth century, and has been incorporated into British law only within the last two decades. As a result we should not be surprised if the extension of protection to children was not a major concern in most of our history. The very idea of children's rights was not clearly formulated until the 1980s. With few rights for most citizens, the rights of the child, now so widely accepted, were hardly considered an important issue by anyone.

This appreciation of the relatively recent changes in ideas about children raises a number of important issues. Most important of these is the suggestion that if the nature of childhood is linked to changes about the nature of rights for adults and children, it is possible that childhood as a state is a very recent construction. If that is the case perhaps then it is a mere 'invention', much as we have invented democracy, capitalism or even, some would argue, the motor car. It is this possibility that led a number of investigations into the past of childhood in the twentieth century.

REFLECTIVE ACTIVITY *1.1*

Children and rights

Consider what rights modern children have in law under the following headings.

- *What types of laws protect children today?*
- *What rights do adults have that children do not?*
- *At what age do children begin to gain rights?*
- *At what age do they lose the protection that laws give them?*

Now consider how this makes childhood a different experience from adulthood. Do these differences mark childhood from adulthood as a distinct and clearly defined state?

The invention of childhood

The issue of whether modern childhood is an invention began to occupy a number of historians from the 1960s onwards who, for the first time, began to seriously consider the history of children and childhood. The most important of these thinkers was the French medievalist Philippe Ariès whose investigations led him to state that in *medieval society the idea of childhood did not exist* (1962: 125). While infants had to be cared for by parents, nurses or servants, Ariès believed that the evidence suggested that once they were old enough partially to fend for themselves, children were simply treated as if they were smaller adults. Thus childhood, in the modern sense of a separate and protected state, did not exist. He argued it was not until the modern period that this idea of 'childhood' came to be significant.

At the time, this thesis was widely accepted and built upon, partly because it fitted with the prevailing view of the past, particularly the distant past, as a cruel and unpleasant place. In particular Lloyd de Mause in a survey of the development of childhood stated that *the history of childhood is a nightmare from which we have only just begun to awaken. The further back in history one goes, the lower the level of child care, and the more likely children are to be killed, abandoned, beaten, terrorized, and sexually abused* (1974: 2). Perhaps the most eminent historian of the family in this period, Lawrence Stone (1977) added to this view by arguing that the very high mortality rates among children in the past until very recently meant that parents could not 'invest emotional capital' in their children. As a result, he argued, they did not show affection for their offspring and consequently avoided the worst emotional damage that such attachment would inevitably involve if or when the child died.

It was not long before a number of historians began to challenge this view of attitudes to children and towards childhood as a state. Linda Pollock (1983) and Ralph Houlbrooke (1984) demonstrated comprehensively the abundance of evidence of affection for children and suffering at their loss by parents in the sixteenth and seventeenth centuries. Shulamith Shahar (1990) perhaps provided the best counter to the Ariès thesis by demonstrating just how distinct and important childhood was as a state in the Middle Ages. Ariès seems to have been largely unaware of just how much was written about children and their natures in the period and his argument revolved around assumptions about the depiction of children in medieval art, where they are usually shown as smaller versions of adults dressed in adult clothing. Such a view makes some sweeping assumptions about both art and society, and such depictions, even if accurately described, may reflect artistic convention and ability as much as social norms.

However, this is not to say that the childhood that existed in the past was the same as modern childhood: it clearly was not. The fact that different societies in different times have distinct ideas about childhood indicates the ways in which childhood is contingent on the nature of a society and that the idea of childhood can be changed and reconstructed over time. What is important is to understand what those conditions were, how they came about and what forces led to that construction.

---

*REFLECTIVE ACTIVITY **1.2***

The conditions of childhood in the past

Read the following extract from an interview with John Birley from the Ashton Chronicle on 19 May 1884, recalling the working conditions of his childhood.

> Our regular time was from five in the morning till nine or ten at night; and on Saturday, till eleven, and often twelve o'clock at night, and then we were sent to clean the machinery on the Sunday. No time was allowed for breakfast and no sitting for dinner and no time for tea. We went to the mill at five o'clock and worked till about eight or nine when they brought us our breakfast, which consisted of water-porridge, with oatcake in it and onions to flavour it. Dinner consisted of Derbyshire oatcakes cut into four pieces, and ranged into two stacks. One was buttered and the other treacled. By the side of the oatcake were cans of milk. We drank the milk and with the oatcake in our hand, we went back to work without sitting down.

Now consider the following issues.

● *Why might small children be useful in running an industrial cotton mill?*

● *What were likely to be the effects on a child of this life in terms of education, physical development and mental health?*

● *Until the late nineteenth century most people accepted that this was a normal life for the children of the poor. How might they justify such attitudes?*

● *Could such children be described as having a childhood in the modern sense?*

Why childhood is constructed

Examining the exploitation of child labour in the past is a reminder about why childhood might be constructed in a particular way. The key issue is who has to gain by regarding children from a perspective that makes useful their employment for very little or no wages, just as some might wish to be able to exploit the labour of women and the poor in general. The origins of the idea of social constructionism lie in observations about how a minority who made up a ruling elite were able to contain and exploit a majority. This issue concerned Karl Marx who pointed to the importance of 'ideology' as a force for maintaining the status quo. He and subsequent writers observed the ways in which a series of ideas that suited the aims of the ruling classes was spread and popularised among the population in general. They were often presented as 'natural', 'fixed' or 'traditional' even if they fitted circumstances that we know were relatively new or novel (Marx and Engels: 1970).

In nineteenth-century Britain a series of laws was passed aimed at improving the working conditions of children. Most of these limited the hours which children could be forced or allowed to work, backed up by a series of inspections of workplaces. In a debate that resonates with modern arguments over the exploitation of labour in the developing world, a frequent reason for objecting to such acts was that industry could not function without child labour. Thus radical change to the exploitation of child labour was impossible without bringing down the British economy. Such a view suggests how the exploitation of children could be linked to an ideology that supported the status quo. There was also an attempt to enlist support from the parents of these children by arguing that they provided vital income for their families and that the children were gainfully occupied and thus made a useful part of society. It seems that many of the poor, who might struggle on the edge of economic survival, accepted these arguments. In Marxist terms they had absorbed the prevailing ideology. It might be added that the same ideology also gave them absolute authority over their children in a world where they had authority over very little else.

In the formulation outlined by Antonio Gramsci, they had accepted the prevailing hegemony that presented exploitation as 'common sense' (Gramsci, 1971). In the nineteenth century it was 'common sense' that children should be exploited, just as it was 'common sense' until the early years of that century to support the system of international slave trading and it remained 'common sense' to facilitate the exclusion of women from political life and parts of education. As a result, the fight to change the law to protect children was a long and exhausting battle because the social reformers who tried to change this situation were struggling against what seemed to many obviously necessary. In such circumstances the eventual triumph of those who argued for reform seems all the more remarkable and can be understood only if we appreciate how ideologies are developed and constructed.

REFLECTIVE ACTIVITY 1.3

Law and labour

Look at the list of some of the legislation passed in nineteenth-century Britain concerning child labour.

1802 The Health and Morals of Apprentices Act limited work of children in textile mills to 12 hours per day, prohibited night work and set minimum standards of accommodation; some elementary education was to be provided.

1819 The Cotton Mills and Factories Act prohibited children under nine years of age from working in cotton mills and restricted those over nine to a 12-hour day.

1825 The Cotton Mills and Factories Act limited the hours of children under 16 years to 12 per day between 5:00 a.m. and 8:00 p.m., with half an hour off for breakfast and one hour off for lunch.

1831 The Cotton Factories and Mills Act limited the working day of people under 18 years to 12 hours per day, and no more than nine hours on a Saturday.

REFLECTIVE ACTIVITY **1.3** *continued*

1833 *The Mills and Factories Act (Althorp's Act) provided for younger children to attend school for at least two hours on six days a week, and holidays for children and young persons were to be all day on Christmas Day and Good Friday, and eight other half days.*

1834 *The Chimney Sweeps Act forbade the apprenticing of boys under ten years, and the employment of children under 14 in chimney sweeping (unless they were apprenticed or on trial).*

1840 *The Chimney Sweeps Act prohibited any child under 16 years of age from being apprenticed, and any person under 21 being compelled or knowingly allowed to ascend or descend a chimney.*

1842 *The Mines and Collieries Act prohibited the employment underground of women and children under ten in mines and collieries,*

1844 *The Labour in Factories Act reduced the age at which children could be employed from nine to eight years.*

1847 *The Hours of Labour of Young Persons and Females in Factories Act (Ten Hours Act) reduced the permitted maximum hours of work for women and children to ten hours per day and 58 hours in any one week.*

1872 *The Metalliferous Mines Regulation Act prohibited employment in mines of all girls, women and boys under 12 years of age; introduced powers to appoint inspectors of mines; and set out rules regarding ventilation, blasting and machinery.*

1874 *The Factory Act raised the minimum working age to nine; limited the working day for women and young people to ten hours in textile industry, to be between 6:00 a.m. and 6:00 p.m.; and reduced the working week to 561/2 hours.*

Consider the following issues:

- *On which industries would these changes have had the most impact?*

- *How did the ages at which children could be employed change between 1802 and 1874?*

- *How did the hours they could legally be employed change?*

- *How much do you think this would have improved the experience of childhood in this period?*

Consider what arguments might be used in support of these changes.

How childhood is constructed

If we accept that childhood is a social construction we have to consider how it is assembled. The term 'social constructionism' derives from the work of Peter L. Berger and Thomas Luckmann (1967). Building on the ideas of Marxist thinkers they investigated the ways in which individuals and social groups participate in the creation of the reality they perceive around them. This is often carried out by a complex process by which ideas are originated, spread throughout society, become accepted and institutionalised, and rapidly move to be seen as traditional and therefore unchangeable.

However, it would be a mistake to assume that the construction of childhood is necessarily a predetermined lie that has been carefully pushed onto an unwilling society. Even where new or changing circumstances force a significant change or re-construction of the idea of childhood, they often utilise existing ideological building blocks in social conventions and wider ideologies such as family structures and religious thinking.

There is no better example than the Industrial Revolution in Britain that, between about 1750 and 1800, necessitated a rapid move to organised child labour in large factories and mines over a relatively short period. Contrary to some assumptions about the pre-industrial past it was not some rural idyll in which children lived in happy extended families playing carefree in fields. We know from the tragic child deaths in coroners' records from the late medieval period that boys as young as five were often with their fathers working in agriculture or in small-scale industry such as mining and workshops. Girls in contrast tended to stay with their mothers but the prevalence of domestic tragedies suggests they were already helping in and around the house at a fairly young age. Perhaps more surprisingly it was extremely common for children as young as seven to be sent away from their parents. Perhaps two-thirds left their family homes to act as domestic servants, labourers and apprentices. It was relatively easy then to move from a system by which children were sent to live with employers to one where they were placed in factories or mines.

Many were also prepared to accept these circumstances because they were disposed towards the necessity and even the rightness of these lives for children by their prevailing religious ideology. Christianity has within it a strong tendency to depict children as likely to do wrong or even as being intrinsically evil. This is exemplified in the theological concept of 'original sin' that, since it was outlined by St Augustine in the early Middle Ages, has dominated the understanding of human nature (St Augustine, 2004). The argument goes that because of the 'fall of man' we are all born into sin. Sin and wrong-doing is 'natural'. It is only a step from this view to one that argues that children must be controlled, watched, punished and corrected, and this view may have underpinned much of the harsh treatment of children that has prevailed until relatively recently. It is also true that it provided an incentive to keep children occupied. If 'the Devil makes work for idle hands' as the saying has it, then an obvious solution is to ensure they are not idle. What better means to achieve that than to place them in employment that filled their waking hours?

REFLECTIVE ACTIVITY 1.4

Time in childhood

Think about your own childhood and consider the following issues.

- *What is your earliest childhood memory and why do you remember it?*
- *What event or memory do you think of as summarising your own childhood?*
- *At what age did your childhood end and what event?*
- *Do you think childhood has been getting shorter or longer since you became an adult?*

Now look back over the historical evidence so far. How different do you think childhood would have been in the past and would it have been a longer or shorter period within an individual's life?

Different constructions of childhood

It would be wrong to give the impression that religious ideas gave only a negative view of children. Christianity is no exception to the rule that religions tend to be complex, and contain within them tensions and sometimes contradictory pressures. Beside the view of children as potential sinners there has also been a powerful image that depicts them as innocents. It is no coincidence that from the late Middle Ages depictions of angels, particularly cherubs, showed the faces of young children.

Thus the contradiction that some commentators have noticed in more recent attitudes to childhood as the 'demon/doll dichotomy', by which children can be seen as either potential wrongdoers or helpless innocents, actually has its origins in an angel/devil dichotomy from at least the early medieval period (Pifer, 2000).

These two rival themes in attitudes to children can be seen running through the history of Christianity. Their significance was not merely academic. The major impetus of the social reformers of the nineteenth century who did so much to improve the conditions for poor children by the intro-duction of labour laws was largely religious in origin. So was the initial motivation for what would evolve into the National Society for the Prevention of Cruelty to Children (NSPCC), taking that name in 1889, the same year that lobbying by its predecessor organisations was largely responsible for the passing of England's first *Prevention of Cruelty to Children Act*. Since then the ethos engendered by positive views of children has done much to raise issues of child protection and welfare.

This dichotomy can be seen in a variety of attitudes to children and childhood up to the present day. The two dominant images of children – as innocents or potential offenders – have been spotted in nineteenth-century literature, most obviously in works like those of Dickens and exemplified by *Oliver Twist* (1838) and the contrast with the Artful Dodger. In American literature perhaps the quin-tessential literary depiction of male childhood in Mark Twain's *Tom Sawyer* (1876) and its sequel *The Adventures of Huckleberry Finn* (1884) show both sides of the characterisation of childhood. The freedom and pleasure of childhood friends is clearly shown, but Twain's characters are no mere innocents; they are highly manipulative of adults and other children.

In the late nineteenth and early twentieth centuries, positive images of children appear to have begun to win out over the negative. It is from this period that many classic literary depictions of children date, most obviously in works like J. M. Barrie's *Peter Pan* (from 1902) and A. A. Milne's *Winnie the Pooh* (1926). Both painted a picture of an idealised Edwardian childhood that still has strong attractions and can be seen as the dominant literary image of children in the first half of the twentieth century. The backlash is often seen as coming after the Second World War, with its obvious implications for perceiv-ing the evil of man. William Golding's response was a literary exploration of the danger of the 'Nazi inside'; its expression was in the *Lord of the Flies* (1954) in which a group of middle-class English schoolboys stranded on a desert island devolve into savagery. Yet Golding was only restating a previ-ously dominant image and was expressing no more than the same problem of original sin.

The two rival views continue to be important in both adult and children's literature. It is notable that Harry Potter, the most commercially successful series of children's books ever, does not rest upon a conflict between good children and evil adults, but imports Draco Malfoy as a negative childhood counterpart to the main protagonist. It is clear that both demonic and angelic views of children still abound in modern literature.

Rival constructions of childhood can exist within the same society and each might be dominant in turn. Such tension between views of childhood does much to explain why the social construction of childhood is so complex and seemingly subject to considerable change. It also needs to be stated that the continuity of rival views does not indicate that childhood is constant: the specifics of that con-struction vary greatly from era to era and place to place. What is drawn from the well of the angel/demon dichotomy may be very different depending upon the circumstances in which it is used.

REFLECTIVE ACTIVITY **1.5**

Children and representation

Think about a particular book or film you have read containing children as characters and then consider the following issues.

- *How important to the story is the child or children?*

- *How fully developed are the children's characters: are they rounded (with complex emotions and concerns) or two-dimensional (simply depicted with one set of characteristics)?*

- *Are the images of the child/children positive or negative?*

Now consider when the work was originally created. Do the depictions of the child or children fit within or work against the dominant construction of childhood at that time?

Deconstructing and reconstructing childhood

A key question from this view of rival processes is whether they can still be seen to apply to the construction of modern childhood, or whether they have been superseded by more rational debates. Recent controversies suggest strongly that is not the case. There is a long and depressing history of outrage at the killings and mistreatment of children.

In 1945 it was the appalling murder of 12-year-old evacuee Dennis O'Neil that led to the establishment of modern childcare systems in a social service framework within Britain. Sadly this did not spell the end of such cases, and a similar cause célèbre has occurred roughly every decade. The most notorious of these recent atrocities was the murder of eight-year-old Victoria Climbié who was tortured and starved to death after brutal treatment in North London in 2001. The result was a call for a major overhaul of social service provision. Depressingly Victoria's was only one of a long line of such deaths that have occupied the national consciousness through the news media roughly once every decade. The sad events illustrate the continued prevalence of the angelic model of childhood. Had these not been 'innocents', the events surrounding them would perhaps not have attracted so much attention.

There is a second strand to such high-profile cases that underlines the existence of the alternative model of childhood. In 1968 the 11-year-old Mary Flora Bell was convicted of manslaughter on the grounds of diminished responsibility after she strangled a toddler and killed, then mutilated, a three-year-old in Newcastle-upon-Tyne. The child as murderer exerts a heady mix of horror and fascination for modern society. It is often seen as a symptom of a system in moral decline and part of the frequently voiced 'death of childhood' thesis. Yet child murderers, like the tragedies of child victims, are not new. They are thankfully relatively infrequent, but sadly occur with some regularity and probably always have done. From a historical perspective, the constant reiteration that they are something new and shocking without acknowledgement of their past occurrence seems to suggest what Stanley Cohen (2002) termed a 'moral panic'. Such panics have flared up over children throughout the late twentieth century, partly driven by a global mass media, and such panics show no sign of ceasing to occur.

An exemplar of these competing tensions is the case of James Bulger, abducted from a shopping centre near Liverpool and murdered by Jon Venables and Robert Thompson in 1993. The tragic case is notable for demonstrating that two competing sides of our ideas about childhood can exist side by side. There was widespread horror at the murder of an innocent toddler, but perhaps greater outrage at the fact that it was carried out by two ten-year-old boys. The subsequent press coverage around the trial, sentencing, imprisonment and eventual release of Venables and Thompson, and what can only be described as the demonisation of the perpetrators of this act in sections of the popular press, is a sharp reminder of how much the angel/devil dichotomy still plays a part in our view of childhood.

REFLECTIVE ACTIVITY 1.6

The media and childhood

Examine any popular daily newspaper and highlight any stories concerned with children.

- *Consider how many show children in a positive light.*
- *How many stories show children in a negative light?*
- *What is the gender balance between these two categories?*
- *What are the ages of the children that fall into these two categories?*

Assess what this may tell us about attitudes to boys and girls and younger and older children.

SUMMARY OF KEY POINTS

If we consider childhood from the perspective of social constructionism we can gain a number of useful insights into the nature of childhood and how this affects the experience of individual children.

> Childhood and the lives of individual children are separate but related sets.

> There was a concept of childhood in the known past.

> However, this construction was not necessarily the same as the modern understanding of what childhood means.

> Childhood as an entity may be constructed by adults out of self-interest or because it fits into a prevailing ideology.

> The process by which childhood is constructed is complex, and is dependent upon a number of factors including economic, ideological, religious and social institutions and norms.

> Within a given society and even within a prevailing ideology differing and apparently contradictory views of childhood may coexist.

> At different times one view may dominate over another.

> Even in contemporary childhood, similar themes and dichotomies can be seen to exist.

> These tensions and the circumstances in which they exist help to create the prevailing construction of childhood in any society.

ERENCES

Ariès, P. (1962) *Centuries of Childhood*. London: Penguin.

Augustine, St (2004) *The City of God*, ed. G. R. Evans and trans. H. Bettenson. London: Penguin.

Berger, P. L. and Luckmann, T. (1967) *The Social Construction of Reality: A Treatise in the Sociology of Knowledge*. New York: Anchor Books.

Cohen, S. (2002) *Folk Devils and Moral Panics*, 3rd edn. London: Routledge.

De Mause, L. (ed.) (1974) *The History of Childhood*. London: Souvenir Press.

Gramsci, A. (1971) *Selections from the Prison Notebooks of Antonio Gramsci*, ed. and trans. Q. Hoare and G. Nowell Smith. London: Lawrence & Wishart.

Houlbrooke, R. (1984) *The English Family 1450–1700*. London: Longmans.

Marx, K. and Engels, F. (1970) *The German Ideology*, ed. C. J. Arthur. London: Lawrence & Wishart.

Pifer, E. (2000) *Demon or Doll: Images of the Child in Contemporary Writing and Culture*. Charlottesville, VA and London: University of Virginia Press.

Pollock, L. (1983) *Forgotten Children: Parent–Child Relations in England from 1500 to 1900*. Cambridge: Cambridge University Press.

Shahar, S. (1990) *Childhood in the Middle Ages*. London: Routledge.

Stone, L. (1977) *Family, Sex and Marriage in England 1500–1800*. New York: Harper & Row.

2 Living and learning in different communities: cross-cultural comparisons

Paul Gardner

Learning objectives

By the end of this chapter you should be able to:

- **recognise the complex semantics of terms such as 'race', 'ethnicity', 'class' and 'gender';**
- **understand how social constructs may interact with individual agencies in children's lives;**
- **understand how intra- and intercultural factors, together with individual agencies, are dynamic influences in children's lives;**
- **recognise how societal factors influence the way children live and learn in different communities within national boundaries.**

Introduction

In the previous chapter, Will Coster explored the changing constructs of childhood across time and place and how these might be represented through various media. In this chapter, I shall return to certain themes introduced earlier. The emphasis here, however, will be on comparisons of the lives of children and young people growing up in different communities, where variables such as social class, ethnicity, race, gender, culture and social policy are factors that influence how children learn and how their lives are shaped. Before defining the categories mentioned above, it is important to remember that, although the focus in the chapter will be on these overarching themes, we should not fall into the trap of social determinism. By that, I mean we should not assume children are entirely malleable and that their lives are inevitably constructed in one way or another, by any one social category, be it social class, race or gender.

Social categories are dynamic forces that operate to produce particular patterns of behaviour that influence the child. The child might be viewed as an autonomous being who, according to social constructivists, such as Vygotsky (1930) and Bruner (1996) who have dominated theories of learning in the West since the 1960s, interprets the world around him/her, in order to make sense of it. The child interprets the world through language, a socially constructed sign system. So, while the child operates within social parameters and a culturally bound system of meaning-making, he/she is, nevertheless, an agent who is able to make choices.

In this way, social patterns influence children's lives, but within these patterns each child is also a self-determining entity, to some degree. It is this self-agency that makes each life unique even within the same culture. I hope to exemplify this point further in the course of the chapter. A further important point to recognise is that the social categories listed above do not operate in isolation, but interact with one another to produce a complex web of influences within which the child develops. This notion will also be attended to in this chapter. By comparing the lives of children within national boundaries who grow up in different cultures, the reader should be taken on a journey in which the conceptual landscape is drawn in sharp relief.

REFLECTIVE ACTIVITY **2.1**

Defining key terms

Before reading the following definitions of race, ethnicity, culture, social class and gender, write your own definition of each term.

Definition of terms

Returning to the terms race, ethnicity, culture, social class and gender, it should be noted that the meanings of each are contested, which makes simple definitions seem thin and meaningless. Although it is not possible to give exhaustive definitions of each term here, it is important to briefly explore the semantic complexities of the vocabulary.

Race

Of all the terms we shall deal with, none is more contentious than the word 'race'. Many writers place the word inside inverted commas, as is the case here, to highlight its contested semantics. As with many words in any language, the term has meant different things in different historical periods and within different groups (Malik, 1996. p71). Initially, it referred to line of descent, in the genealogical sense. In the fifteenth and sixteenth centuries the term, allied to racist belief, became a justification for slavery (Jennes, 2001: 305). There emerged what is now referred to as 'pseudo-scientific racism', in which humanity was not only categorised on the basis of skin tone and physical features, but was ranked hierarchically and assigned different moral, intellectual, spiritual and cultural attributes, with race being the basis of such categorisations.

The work of Carlous Linnaeus, who devised the classification system in botany, provided a pseudo-scientific basis for the dehumanisation of non-white groups (Fryer, 1984: 166). However, the emergence of genetics and the social sciences of anthropology and sociology has discredited the notion that 'race' is a biologically determined phenomenon. Fenton (1999: 7) identifies three reasons for this. Firstly, genetics demonstrated there is greater variation within so-called races than between them. Secondly, anthropological and sociological studies showed that historical circumstance and culture account for differences between people, not apparent biological difference. Thirdly, by the mid-twentieth century it was evident that race was a redundant analytical tool since it had a history of misuse, such as justifying the unequal treatment of supposedly 'inferior' groups.

Having discounted the biological basis of race, definitions of the term in use today emphasise the social construction of perceptions of race. These definitions are usually focused around physical appearance, with skin tone being a strong signifier. Perceptions of race may be closely allied to racism: the belief that different races exist along a superordinate–subordinate continuum thus creating the concept of 'superior' and 'inferior' races. Consequently, the term race is often considered to be subsumed within racist ideologies and perspectives. Malik (1996: 71) asserts that the key to understanding race is to recognise the ways in which social inequality has been conflated by physical differences with social hierarchies being deemed to be the natural order of things.

Ethnicity

Jenkins (1997) makes the distinction between externally imposed identifications of a people as an ethnic group and an internal definition in which group members establish signifiers of membership. These signifiers are located around culture, history, ancestry and language (Fenton, 1999: 7). Although ethnicity is not a fixed entity, cultural boundaries act as markers of similarities within a group and differences from others. For Jenkins, both external categorisation and internal identification are important dynamics in the social construction of ethnic groups.

Within society, the words race and ethnicity are often used as if they were synonymous (Fenton, 1999). There is a tendency to use ethnicity as a more politically correct version of race, which may result from the latter's biological connotations (Miles and Brown, 2003: 92), as discussed above. The meaning of ethnicity is further confused by official descriptors within the British government Census, along with equal opportunity monitoring processes of many institutions, in which terms such as 'white' and 'African' are used to denote different ethnic groups. Neither term is semantically correct: the term 'white' relates more closely to the discussion of 'race' outlined above and 'African' refers to continent of origin, not ethnicity. The use of nationalities, such as Indian and Chinese, also do not constitute ethnicities, leading Alibhai-Brown (2001) to refer to these terms as crude classifications imposed by officialdom.

Culture

There are at least three definitions of the word culture in use. The first is derived from horticulture and refers to nurturing in the sense of cultivating growth. The second refers to artefacts derived from artistic representation – opera, plays, sculpture, etc. In this context one may refer to a person being cultured because they have a knowledge and appreciation of the 'Arts'. However, neither of these uses of the word helps to locate the definition required for our purposes. The third definition of culture, however, is appropriate for our purposes and refers to belief systems, values and customs that are shared within and between members of a social group and which influence common patterns of behaviour within the group, distinguishing it from other socio-cultural groups. In making a general observation of culture and individual identity, Thomas (2000) makes the point that cultures favouring individualism socialise children to be independent, whereas those favouring collectivism emphasise the need for close family relations and the 'sacrifice' of self-interest for the needs of the group.

Social class

Some have argued that we now live in a classless society, yet 69 per cent of people think that social class affects an individual's life chances. Social class is still considered to be the main influence in a child's educational attainment (Hickey, 2000: 163). The notion of a hierarchical social structure remains a persistent theme in social analysis. In Britain, social class is officially categorised in terms of one's general occupation, with unskilled manual labour representing the lowest category. Furthermore, social policy is often devised on the basis of this system.

Discussions of social class in sociological theory, however, extend beyond the descriptive element of occupational ranking and attempt to explain why social classes exist and how they become dynamic forces in social relations, reproduction and change. Two key thinkers dominate theories of social class: Marx (1974) and Weber (1958). While their theories share some commonality, they equally have significant divergence. For Marx, the basis of social class is economic, with one's position in the hierarchical class structure determined by one's relationship to the means of production, that is the means by which wealth is created. In classical Marxist theory, the means of production is owned by one class, the capitalists or bourgeoisie, but wealth is created by another, subordinate class, the workers or proletariat. The worker receives a wage, which is set by the capitalist, but the value of his/her productivity exceeds the remuneration received because the capitalist also sets the price of the product in the marketplace.

In this way, the capitalist class exerts power and control over the working class by means of its superior economic position in the class structure. Tension and conflict are inherent in the unequal relationship between the two classes, since it is in the interest of the capitalists to keep the working class in its place and it is in the interest of the working class to overthrow the social structure in order to create a more egalitarian one. According to Marxist theory, the creation of hierarchical class structures that provoke conflict caused by inequality between classes will result in an inevitable revolution. The theory continues that these revolutionary, new social structures are the driving force of history.

In the twentieth and twenty-first centuries, Marxist theory has been refuted on the grounds that the burgeoning number of non-manual occupations has created a large middle class and, consequently, blurred the relationship between the bourgeoisie and the proletariat. This calls into question the difference between objective and subjective dimensions of social class. For Marx, the class structure and unequal distribution of power, determined by economic differentiation, is an objective condition. However, he recognised that consciousness of one's class position was not a foregone conclusion and that individuals may be persuaded to believe they belonged to a class, if any, that differs from objective reality. This subjective position is perpetuated by the ruling class's ability to persuade sufficient numbers of subordinates to accept their status as part of the 'natural' order of things or to see themselves as a class above themselves.

For Weber, social stratification has three determining factors: wealth, power and status. His concept of economic class shares some similarity to Marx in that it differentiates common life-chances of a group in relation to advantage or disadvantage in the marketplace. However, Weber's theory differs from Marx's, in so far as it does not place economic differentiation at the heart of social stratification. Weber asserts that social status, the social value ascribed to a group by society, can be independent of social class, although he also acknowledges that, in capitalist society, higher social status is usually attributed to those with greater wealth. An exception to this may be the so-called nouveau riche, those who acquire wealth by means other than inheritance. This group is often attributed lower social status than their wealthy counterparts in the class to which they aspire. Thus people of different occupations, ethnic groups, religions and 'lifestyle' groups, irrespective of social class, may be ascribed varying social 'value'.

The third classification in Weber's theory, power, is the key element in his analysis of the social dynamic. Weber sees power in the form of groups with common interests forming to influence social policy and decision-making. Political parties represent one form of social power, but single interest groups, professional bodies and trade unions also compete in the quest for power. Parties may represent the interests of a specific social class or status group but equally may represent people across those divisions.

Hence, in Weber's theory, there is a complex interplay between class, status and power. These three elements operate as variables, causing us to analyse social stratification in terms of how these variables behave in specific societies at particular moments in history. For Marx, on the other hand, the economic stratification of classes in relation to the means of production is an unalterable fact. By combining Marx and Weber's perspectives, we might conclude that a person's social class is signified by their life chances, which may be dependent on economic status and the degree to which they can exercise social power.

Gender

Just as race and ethnicity are often considered synonymous, the terms *gender* and *sex* are frequently used interchangeably. In common parlance, men and women are often referred to as 'the opposite sexes'. This assumed dichotomy masks the fact that men and women have, in many respects, a shared biology, albeit with differences in terms of the production of hormones, internal and external sexual anatomy and other physiological characteristics (Wharton, 2005: 18).

A person's sex generally refers to their anatomical and biological features and classification as either male or female. Gender refers to the social meanings attached to male and female classifications. These meanings are imbued with differences in social power, often leading to inequality, which may vary between different cultures, social classes and historical periods (Kimmel, 2004: 94–5). Accordingly, behaviours associated with 'masculinity' and 'femininity' are socially constructed and culturally defined.

REFLECTIVE ACTIVITY 2.2

Reviewing key term definitions

Re-read your definitions from Activity 2.1 and compare them with the ones you have read.

Has reading these definitions altered in any way your understanding of the terms?

Would you agree that the terms are more complex than is suggested by their common usage?

Identity in childhood

We have begun to explore the social categories that influence the development of a child's identity as a social being. Each child belongs to many social groups, each of which influences who he or she is. In a class-based society, each of us has a social class; in a multi-ethnic society, each of us has an ethnicity. Similarly, we each have a gender. The interplay of these social constructs shapes our social experience, influencing who we are as individuals and how we see the world. We have argued that class, race, ethnicity and gender are social constructs that are, therefore, ascribed categories at the macro-social level. We are born into these groups that are defined by society and they inform our social self.

Societies, however, do not exist only at the macro-level. Between society and the individual is the community, which comprises key agents of socialisation such as school and family. Institutions at the community level mediate the influence of social constructs, leading to a communal self. As we develop through childhood to adolescence, we become more conscious of ourselves as decision-makers. The individual further mediates the influence of social categories, so we have a personal self. The process of mediation is represented in Figure 2.1.

The individual is not a passive recipient of these factors but rather is able to accept or reject, to some extent, particular social influences. This model shares similarities with Bronfenbrenner's Bio-ecological Systems Theory (1979), in which he explains how *macrosystems*, those factors at the societal level, influence individual development through a series of interrelated, nested systems. In his model, macrosystems affect *mesosystems*, which are social institutions at the community level. These, in turn, influence *microsystems*, such as the family or classroom. A further dimension to his model describes how microsystems interact with one another; these he calls *exosystems*.

REFLECTIVE ACTIVITY 2.3

Personal biography of development

Draw a timeline of your own development as an individual. Try to identify periods of significant change. Briefly note possible causes of those changes.

Can you discern any links between these causes and factors at the community or societal level?

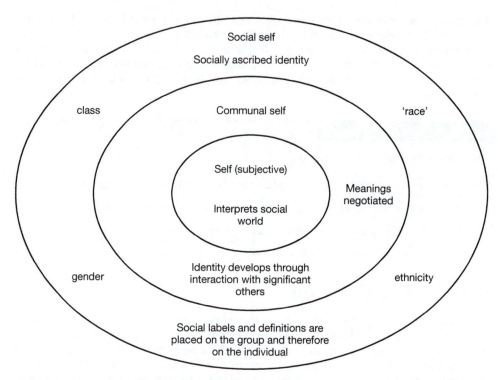

Figure 2.1 Concentric model of social reality and identity

In an attempt to combine the two models, the following conversation between four six-year-old British-Bangladeshi pupils and a visiting teacher illustrates how one societal construct, racism, can infiltrate the microsystem of the classroom and affect children's learning.

Ayesha: *They [white peers] call me 'Paki' in class, too. They were throwing books and puzzles. I got on the floor to pick up the puzzle and put it back in the bag. One of them kicked me. My teacher said she couldn't help, as they were being naughty to her. Then one of them tore my work and tried to cut my hair with scissors. I want to go outside the classroom to work. I don't want to come to school.*

Rafiq: *It makes me feel horrible inside when they call me 'Paki'.*

Ayesha: *When they call me 'Paki' I feel angry. I feel like hitting and kicking them. I say nothing.*

Iqbal: *I just try to take no notice. My mum says ignore them. Don't listen, that way I can cope.*

Rafiq: *They knock on my door and run away. They throw mud and stones at my house.*

Farzana: *They broke our upstairs window. They shout 'Fucking Paki' at my little brother when he goes out in the street. That's why he does not play out.*

Ayesha: *I took my auntie's baby to the park when she came. I put her in the baby swing. Then a boy came and threw a stone at the baby. I had to take my baby out quickly and very quickly run home with her and shut the door hard!*

(Gardner, 2001: 67)

By age six, these children were being ostracised by peers of a different race. In this case, the significant marks of distinction were a darker complexion (attributed to race), along with their clothes, lifestyle and language (features of culture and ethnicity). Unless we believe that children are born with prejudice, a much-contested assumption, the British-English children of this example had learned to undervalue their British-Bangladeshi counterparts. It appears that the tormenters felt empowered, and perhaps entitled, to victimise the other children not only in the classroom but also in the general community.

Where does this notion of power come from? A simple answer might be to say that the racist views and behaviour of the British-English children were derived from their parents. If this is true, then, the microsystem of the family can be seen to impact on the microsystem of the classroom. Beyond the family, the British National Party, a racist organisation with covert associations to international neo-Nazi networks, was active in the community. It could be argued, therefore, that the racist behaviour of the children was legitimated by attitudes that prevailed at both the communal and societal level. Might this be an example, as some argue, of the marginalisation of non-white British citizens, caused by ethnocentric perspectives perpetuated throughout history as justifications for aggressive policies, such as slavery and imperialism? This argument demonstrates how an ideology, in this case racism, can permeate society by being filtered from the macrosystem (society) through the mesosystem (community) into the microsystem (classroom or family) and, ultimately, the individual (children). In 1999, Sir William MacPherson perceived this relationship between society and its institutions, and published a report recommending the eradication of institutionalised racism in British society.

There is a sequel to the above discussion. Some ten years after the discussion of the children cited above, when they were in Year 11, a report about the local secondary school appeared in the press. Mounted police officers stood guard at the school gates to prevent warring gangs of British-Bangladeshi and British-English youths from attacking one another as they left school. It is uncertain whether the pupils in the conversation were involved in these fights but, irrespective of that, there is a symbolic element to this illustration. It would appear the British-Bangladeshi children had stopped 'shutting the door'; instead they had opened it and had fought back in an attempt to assert their right to belong in their community without harassment. By so doing, these children asserted their sense of self. However, in the absence of an effective counter to the protracted harassment meted out by the British-English children, there is a very real danger that racism may have criminalised both groups. 'Race', then, was a central feature of the social experience of both groups and had positioned them as distinct and separate.

Connolly (1995) made a similar observation in a case study of black working-class boys. He noted how the boys developed a strong group identity, as black boys, as a manifestation of their resistance to the racism they experienced from white peers. The boys had to appear 'tough' in order to defend themselves from physical assault. This type of behaviour caused teachers to view them as troublemakers, which inevitably consolidated their social identity as black boys. It can be seen that both gender and 'race' can coalesce to construct group identity and influence behaviour.

Living and learning with race, gender and social class

The need to create inclusive communities, in which children from different racial or ethnic groups can live and learn together, accepting both their commonality and differences, is a major challenge for our society. Pessimistically, Jones (2000) asserts that teacher education courses fail to prepare trainee teachers for issues of 'race'. Graduate teachers lack the knowledge to understand how children experience school and society differently as a consequence of racism, resulting in a teaching force that largely views children as a homogenous group.

In a significant study of children's educational attainment, Gilborn and Mirza (2000) draw on data from official sources to demonstrate how race, social class and gender may influence attainment within, and between, pupils of different ethnic groups. Recognising that local circumstances can influence outcomes, their findings suggest that ethnicity may contribute to educational inequality with British-Bangladeshi, British-Pakistani and British African-Caribbean pupils performing less well than their British-Indian and British-English counterparts. In the case of British African-Caribbean pupils, disparities in educational performance become *progressively greater as they move through the school system*.

Differences between social classes were also evident, with children from higher social classes significantly outperforming children from lower social classes, even when ethnicity was a constant. While gender played a less significant role than either ethnicity or social class, findings indicate that girls in all ethnic groups are likely to achieve five or more higher grades in GCSEs than their male peers (of the same ethnicity). However, British Bangladeshi-Pakistani and African-Caribbean girls performed less well than either British-Indian and English girls or British-Indian and English boys.

Bhatti (1999) also noted the complex interplay of race, gender and class in an ethnographic study of Asian children. A significant number of Asian children perceived that their teachers had low expectations of them and did not stretch them academically. Furthermore, Asian girls believed that their teachers held stereotypical views of arranged marriages. Girls tended to react in one of three ways to their teachers' perceptions: by exercising covert forms of rebellion, by exhibiting a lack of self-confidence or by actively asserting their 'Asian-ness'. This finding further demonstrates how the individual, as an active agent, can interact with a social category, in this case gender allied to ethnicity, to produce one of several possible responses.

Gender and ethnicity were found to interact powerfully in Shaw's (2000: 163) ethnographic study of a British-Pakistani community in Oxford. Shaw highlights how the concept of *izzat*, which can be defined as family honour, functions as an indicator of female behaviour within the family. As children, particularly girls, reach the age of puberty, the family's *izzat* becomes vulnerable unless strict codes of behaviour are adhered to. These codes govern forms of dress and contact between the sexes and are designed to ensure that girls remain chaste and pure. Under these circumstances the family *izzat* remains intact. Transgression from these codes can result in shame on the family, the weight of which is especially felt by the father, brothers and other related men. In some instances, retribution can be fatal.

In a separate study, Khanum (1995: 284) explains how, following racist comments by a Bradford head teacher which appeared in the national press, the city's Muslim community became increasingly insular and culturally conservative as a result of feeling its culture and religion to be under attack. This insularity was expressed through a stricter adherence to izzat and a demand for separate Muslim schools, particularly for girls. This example demonstrates the dynamic interaction of gender, ethnicity and 'race' and shows how Muslim girls were affected by internal cultural practices and the perception of an external social threat.

Some might argue that current global relations between the British-American axis on the one hand and parts of the Muslim world, following 9/11 and the occupation of Iraq, have fuelled greater Islamophobia, both within Britain and across Western Europe and North America. Observation shows an increasing number of Muslim girls wearing the hijab (head covering) and women wearing the burkah. Although for some women this will be an expression of self-assertion of ethnic and religious identity as a counter to Islamophobia, Khanum's study suggests that for others it is as a result of the continued threat felt by the community. The concentric model of social reality and identity (Figure 2.1), together with Bronfenbrenner's Bio-ecological Systems Theory, provide a basis for understanding how individual identity and behaviour may be influenced by factors functioning at a societal, or even international, level.

Individual agency

Part of the discussion, so far, may lead us to believe that individuals will inevitably respond in a uniform way to external social influences. Such a conclusion, however, disregards individual choice. While individuals have a degree of flexibility to exercise their will, they do so within a limited range of possibilities. In terms of ethnicity, Hutnik (1991: 134 cited in Kathane, 2000: 29) identifies four strategies an individual may use to position him/herself in relation to the majority ethnic group. The *disassociative strategy* occurs when the individual allies him/herself with the minority, rather than majority, ethnic group. Conversely, allegiance to the majority, rather than minority, is referred to as the *assimilative strategy*. If the individual relates equally to both groups, the *acculturative strategy* is at work. Finally, if neither group is considered important in self-categorisation, the individual has adopted the *marginal strategy*.

In a more complex version of individual agency and social positioning, Hall (cited in Marsh and Millard, 2000) refers to *cultural relativity*, in which society is made up of dominant and subordinate cultures. In such a society, the individual is able to 'mix and match' behaviour, attitudes and values by drawing on the different cultural groups to which he or she is affiliated. This complex web of cultural possibilities is illustrated in Figure 2.2.

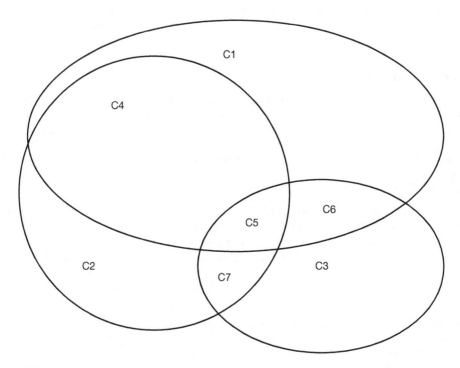

Figure 2.2 An interactional multicultural perspective

This model represents three cultural groups. C1 is the majority, or dominant culture. It is the culture of the most powerful group in society and the one that has the biggest influence over the general way of life in society. C2 and C3 represent other cultures that exist within a single society. C4, C5 and C6 represent other cultures that share aspects in common with the majority group and, thus, overlap with C1. However, the alternative cultures do not only interact with the majority culture, but also with each other, as shown in the figure at C5 and C7.

If we imagine individuals within this cultural web, they may adopt a variety of positions. Those in C1, C2 and C3 are furthest removed from the cultures of other groups and the most closely aligned with their respective cultural groups. This position might be exemplified by British-English children growing-up in monocultural communities with little or no exposure to the cultures of Britain's minority ethnic groups. It might also represent British-Chinese children who 'live in a cocoon within British society', staying within the security of family and maintaining clear boundaries between home and school (Yuen Mei and Woodrow, 1998: 223). On the other hand, those who adopt the position represented by C5 might be described as multicultural beings, as they share aspects of several groups.

During the course of a lifetime, an individual may adopt different social positions. For example, at birth a child may be wholly influenced by his/her own culture and be furthest removed from other cultural perspectives. By going to school, depending on the nature of school attended, the child may be introduced to other cultural perspectives and may, therefore, move to positions C4 or C6. Alternatively, as the study by Khanum suggests, some children and young people may realign with their cultural heritage as a result of external pressure. In this way, the model represents what Marsh and Millard (2000) refer to as socially constructed sites of shared discourses with fluid boundaries.

A more complex model would include multiple cultural groups, with greater potential for individual variation and cross-cultural influence. It would also require the mapping of social class, gender, race and ethnicity, which would provide an image closer to the complex profile of social identities in a pluralist society. It is within this complexity that children of different communities learn and develop.

SUMMARY OF KEY POINTS

In this chapter, we have explored the definitions of key terms and seen that the meanings of words such as race, ethnicity, gender and social class are more complex than may be suggested in everyday conversation. Each of these terms represents a socially constructed category able to influence the lives of children as they develop through childhood into adolescence. However, the categories do not act independently, but rather interact to form a powerful and complex matrix of influences. Within this 'web' of social forces, the individual child is an actor, who is able to position him/herself on the social stage, but only within boundaries prescribed by the community and society in which he/she resides.

A theoretical model has been provided to explain how social constructs are mediated from the societal level to the individual and thereby influence individual identity formation. Children and young people each experience their social world differently and this experience may be dependent upon their social class, ethnicity, 'race' or gender. These social categories may also influence the individual's life chances, through differing experiences of school and community, leading to varying levels of educational attainment between genders, social classes and ethnic groups. It has been suggested that racism functions as a conservative force on some minority ethnic groups, resulting in insularity and resistance to interaction with the wider community.

Societies comprise dynamic social forces and are constantly changing. Therefore the factors that complicate living and learning in different communities require continual ethnographic study. Such studies need to take account of differences within communities as well as between them since cultural pluralism allows for multiple identities both within and between different communities.

RENCES

Alibhai-Brown, Y. (2001) *Who Do We Think We Are? Imagining the New Britain*. London: Penguin.

Bhatti, G. (1999) *Asian Children at Home and at School*. London: Routledge.

Bronfenbrenner, U. (1979) *The Ecology of Human Development: Experiments by Nature and Design*. Cambridge, MA: Harvard University Press.

Bruner, J. (1996) *The Culture of Education*. Cambridge, MA: Harvard University Press.

Connolly, P. (1995) 'Boys will be boys? Racism, sexuality and the construction of masculine identities amongst infant boys', in J. Holland, M. Blair and S. Sheldon (eds), *Debates and Issues in Feminist Research and Pedagogy*. Clevedon: Multilingual Matters and Open University.

Fenton, S. (1999) *Ethnicity: Racism, Class and Culture*. Basingstoke: Macmillan.

Fryer, P. (1984) *Staying Power*. London: Pluto Press.

Gardner, P. (2001) *Teaching and Learning in Multicultural Classrooms*. London: David Fulton.

Gilborn, D. and Mirza, H. (2000) *Educational Inequality: Mapping Race, Class and Gender – A Synthesis of Research Evidence*. London: Office for Standards in Education.

Hickey, T. (2000) 'Class and class analysis for the twenty-first century', in M. Cole (ed.), *Education, Equality and Human Rights*. London: RoutledgeFalmer.

Hutnik, N. (1991) *Ethnic Minority Identity: A Social Psychological Perspective*. Oxford: Clarendon Press.

Jenkins, R. (1997) *Rethinking Ethnicity: Arguments and Explorations*. London: Sage.

Jennes, D. (2001) 'Origins of the myth of race', in E. Cashmore and J. Jennings (eds), *Racism: Essential Readings*. London: Sage.

Jones, R. (2000) 'Out of the abyss: the current state of multicultural education in primary education', *Education*, 3 (13): 60–4.

Kathane, R. (2000) 'Roots and origins: ethnicity and the traditional family', in A. Lau (ed.), *South Asian Children and Adolescents in Britain*. London: Whurr Publishers.

Khanum, S. (1995) 'Education and the Muslim girl', in M. Blair, J. Holland and S. Sheldon (eds), *Identity and Diversity: Gender and the Experience of Education*. Clevedon: Multilingual Matters and Open University.

Kimmel, M. (2004) *The Gendered Society*, 2nd edn. New York: Oxford University Press.

MacPherson, W. Sir (1999) *The Stephen Lawrence Inquiry*. London: Stationery Office.

Malik, K. (1996) *The Meaning of Race*. Basingstoke: Macmillan.

Marsh, J. and Millard, E. (2000) *Literacy and Popular Culture: Using Children's Culture in the Classroom*. London: Paul Chapman.

Marx, K. (1974) *Capital*, Vol 3. London: Lawrence & Wishart.

Miles, R. and Brown, M. (2003) *Racism*, 2nd edn. London: Routledge.

Shaw, A. (2000) *Kinship and Continuity: Pakistani Families in Britain*. Amsterdam: Harwood Academic.

Thomas, E. (2000) *Cultures and Schooling*. Chichester: John Wiley & Sons.

Weber, M. (1958) *The Protestant Ethic and the Spirit of Capitalism*. New York: Scribner's.

Vygotsky, L. S. (1930) *Mind and Society*. Cambridge, MA: Harvard University Press.

Wharton, A. (2005) *The Sociology of Gender: An Introduction to Theory and Research*. Oxford: Blackwell Publishers.

Yuen Mei and Woodrow, D (1998) 'Chinese children and their families in England', *Research Papers in Education*, 13 (2): 203–26.

3 Childhood in crisis?

Will Coster

Learning objectives

By the end of this chapter you should be able to understand:

- **the problem of childhood health and obesity;**
- **the issues of education and literacy;**
- **the debate over violence towards and by children;**
- **the 'sexualisation' of childhood as a threat to children;**
- **whether these factors have resulted in a shortening or fragmentation of childhood;**
- **whether these factors together amount to a crisis in childhood.**

Introduction

The archetype of the child from the early twenty-first century differs significantly from those images we tend to conjure for the preceding century. That period evokes images of evacuees, boys playing football in the street, girls with dolls in prams, participation in organised activities such as boy scouts or girl guides. These have been replaced with the picture of the 'computer game' or 'video screen' generation. In contrast to previous images, this child is sedentary, perhaps obese, uninterested in books and education, inured to violence and sexualised by games and television. In many ways this image sees a coalescence of many of the fears that have come to the fore in our ideas about children and childhood in the early twentieth century, and has led many to conclude that we have entered a period of crisis for childhood. This chapter will explore the perception and reality of these different aspects of childhood and examine whether they can be said to constitute a crisis.

Childhood health and obesity

In recent years the issue of childhood health and in particular that of childhood obesity (which is often seen to contribute to deteriorating general health among the young) has received considerable attention. This issue first became evident in the United States of America, where standards of living and availability of high fat food have generally been seen to have been higher since at least the end of the Second World War. Its effects have now also been noticed in European societies, particularly Britain, where fashions in food and entertainment (which are thought to have a direct impact on physical activity) most closely follow those in North America. The process may have been delayed by the recurring problems of the British economy and European views of food, but also by the habits enforced on a generation by wartime deprivation exemplified by civilian food rationing, which continued until it was finally lifted in 1954. These habits of frugality are often seen as having broken down completely after two generations, beginning in the 1980s, at the same time as the widespread introduction of fast and pre-processed foods into the country. The American Childhood Obesity Society states that 15.3 per cent and 15.5 per cent of children in America aged respectively 6–11 and 12–18 are technically obese above the 95th percentile of Body Mass Index (**http://www.obesity.org/ subs/childhood/prevalence.shtml**). According to the British Medical Association in Britain 5.5 per cent of boys and 7.2 per cent of girls aged 2–15 were obese in 2002. To put it in stark terms that is roughly a million obese children. This is a marked increase on previous years and it must be pointed out that these definitions include only the obese, whereas a larger number of children can be defined as 'overweight'. However, in Britain, and still more in most of Europe, levels of obesity have not yet reached North American proportions (BMA, 2005).

There can be little doubt that even if these trends are halted and perhaps even reversed, the long-term consequences of this growth of obesity will be profound. Attempts to reverse these trends, particularly where the state has some control over food consumption in state sector schools, have had a very high profile in recent years and have led to a rewriting of the guidelines and reconsideration of the budgets of British school dinners. However, it has to be hoped that this change is significant enough to actually reverse the trends in childhood food consumption through a re-education of children's expectations, as (rather obviously) school dinners, at best, only make up a small proportion of the food consumed by children (even assuming that they consume the dinners at all). Since obesity carries a greater risk of many potentially fatal conditions, most obviously coronary deficiencies, and a greater risk of debilitating conditions that might lead to disability, we can expect a heavy price to be paid by younger generations, both personally and in terms of health care costs in the future.

The consumption of food is, however, only part of the equation that accounts for an increase in obesity and overweight children. The other significant part of the explanation is the levels of activity carried out by children. This is in part where the alarming image of children slumped over a Playstation or Xbox comes into play and there seems little doubt that the default for contemporary children's play is interior, whereas for previous generations, particularly in the second half of the twentieth century, it was exterior. A number of reasons has been advanced for this including the reduction of physical education in schools (exemplified by the sale of school playing fields from the 1980s) and the growth of car-use (both in removing walking and cycling as means of transport and in preventing playing in streets or by crossing roads). But perhaps most significant are parental fears of danger to children, connected to worries over physical and sexual attacks on children. It is well known that such attacks are extremely rare and certainly no more common than they were in the past, but a change in climate towards them means that many parents and guardians, even if they are aware of that, cannot envisage allowing their children to play outside independently. Such activity is now reserved for older children and youths and here adult society is clearly contradictory, as congregations of youths in almost any location are seen as potentially threatening. So opinion combines a condemnation of the sedentary and indoor nature of childhood in modern Britain, but simultaneously fears the appearance of children in the 'adult', active and external world.

REFLECTIVE ACTIVITY **3.1**

Childhood obesity

Look at Table 3.1 and consider the following issues:

- *Is the problem of obesity and overweight children more marked among boys or girls in England?*

- *By how much did the problems of obesity and overweight children increase from 1995 to 2000?*

- *Which sex group experienced the biggest rises in obesity and in being overweight?*

Table 3.1 Proportions of children and adolescents (0–19) overweight and obese in England 1995–2000

Years	Percentage boys overweight	Percentage boys obese	Percentage girls overweight	Percentage girls obese
1995	18.6	3.7	23.5	5.7
1996	19.3	4.1	22.7	5.9
1997	17.7	4.0	22.9	5.8
1998	21.1	4.2	25.5	7.0
1999	23.0	5.9	25.3	7.1
2000	23.3	4.8	26.2	6.86

Source: National Statistics (**http://www.statistics.gov.uk/cci/nugget.asp?id=718**)

Education and literacy

It is often stated that the current generation of children is educationally deficient. There is a general assumption in some quarters that this is the result of failures in the (state) education system, which are variously timed as beginning in the 1960s or 1970s. Official literacy statistics certainly make for alarming reading. According to government reports one in seven adults is 'functionally illiterate': or to put it another way, more than one in ten adults cannot function fully in a literate society.

However, the key factor here is the term 'functional literacy'; that is not to say that these people lack basic reading and writing skills, but they may use them in a slow, grammatically incorrect or incomprehensible way. Thus they might have difficulty reading a book, newspaper or filling out a complex form. Of course, compared with some measures of literacy this may be a relatively high bar: the best measure of literacy for most of history is the ability of an individual to sign his or her name. What exactly this means in terms of functioning literacy is very unclear – self-evidently many making signatures may have been unable to do anything else but that. If we applied the same criteria to contemporary British society then almost everyone would be considered literate. It is evident then that literacy is not an absolute and fixed marker; it has moved because our expectations of literacy have increased. We should therefore avoid the trap of assuming that levels of literacy have fallen in recent years, placing the weight of our expectations on the current generation of children.

Arguments rage about the acceptability of subcategories of language, including 'street slang' and 'text speak'. Part of the problem is clearly that members of older generations (and we might add classes and regional groupings) simply cannot understand these forms of communication, and exclusion will always tend to create resentment. For many teenagers, their understanding of 'traditional' English grammar may be limited, but seen from their perspective they are functioning literates, since their ability to communicate with their peers through these mediums and idioms makes them so. There are two related problems here. One is that language, as has long been recognised in this country, is not fixed: there is no better example of this than the Oxford English Dictionary, which defines the 'meanings' of words, not according to some abstract value, but always by the way in which they are used, therefore if use changes so does meaning. The second issue is one that a number of thinkers from different disciplines have explored in recent years: the degree to which literacy is not autonomous or a set of discrete technical and objective skills that can be applied universally, but rather is a contingent measure, determined by the cultural, political and historical contexts of the community in which it is used. Literacy is therefore, in the technical sense, an ideology enforcing identity and values of the society that promotes it (Gee, 1996; Street, 1995).

This is not to say that any society can afford to abandon its language, and the communication, values and identity that attach to it. It is difficult to discern what the effects of change in the 'literacy' of youth will be. However, this is hardly the first time that children have adopted their own language and linguistic tendencies: the same fears were raised over Rockers in the 1950s and Hippies in the 1960s, yet such assaults on the English language left it largely unfazed and possibly even enriched. It is also questionable to what degree children are immersed in such tendencies. Some who use texting as a substitute for 'Standard English' might find the adult world a particular shock. Probably many more are, like generations before them, culturally amphibious: that is to say they might use particular idioms and methods of communication but understand that for other purposes, for example in writing an essay or letter of application, they need to use a different form of language.

The much noted 'Harry Potter Phenomenon' from 1997 seems to give the lie to the idea that children do not read, or read fewer books. Assessments of statistics for the sale of children's books were very difficult and fraught with pitfalls. However, worldwide in 1985 sales of children's books were estimated at 336.2 million, but by 1994 they had reached 1,170.5 million (**http://www.underdown. org/sales.htm**). Perhaps the greatest evidence of a growth in childhood reading is the transformation of children's publishing from a rather genteel and small-scale profession to a worldwide industry over the last two decades. Such an event could not have happened if children's book sales were not increasingly lucrative. We might raise questions about which books and who bought them, but the trend is undeniable. More books are being purchased for, and by, children than ever before. Unless we assume that they are being read by the same or a smaller group of children (which seems unlikely), it is logical to assume that what we are seeing is not simply a generation of children whose world is interior, chained to the television games console, but one that is also expanding its interior world through the imagination. Many older commentators also make the assumption that computer games and the internet are intrinsically opposed to literacy. Certainly few would approve of everything on the internet, yet we have to adjust to the concept of a multimedia world where children absorb games, associated comics, books and fan-sites which can be both imaginative and literary. The indications are that the current generation is far more 'literate' than the preceding generations. The question will be what they do with their literacy and how society reacts to the small minority who are not able to develop and transfer literacy skills.

REFLECTIVE ACTIVITY **3.2**

Literacy and activitiy

Before reading further, estimate how much time you spend in literary or intellectual activity.

Now analyse your day for the past 24 hours before you began reading this chapter.

What percentage of your time did you spend engaged in the following.

A *Reading books, newspapers or journals.*

B *Writing either on paper or a computer.*

C *Watching television or listening to the radio.*

D *Playing games or other leisure activity that utilised literary or intellectual skills.*

E *Engaging in a non-intellectually demanding leisure activity.*

F *Working or engaged in unavoidable activity (for example, work, eating or sleeping) that will not allow you to do any of the above.*

REFLECTIVE ACTIVITY 3.2 *continued*

Subtract F from your calculations then work out the percentage of the remaining day that did not involve some literary or intellectual skills. Then compare the time spent on A–D and on E. Does this fit with your expectations of what you do with your time?

Children and violence

The subject of computers and the media also raises issues of children and violence. This can be divided into two major concerns. On the one hand there are increasing anxieties about violence towards children, which have spawned an intensifying industry of child protection in both the public and private sectors. As we have already seen, it has been argued that this is one of the major factors contributing to the interiorisation of childhood. The second and somewhat contradictory element is the increasing fear of violence by the young, which we have also seen as contributing to a wide-spread fear of groups or even individual children.

Examining violence towards children, the growth of institutions including the National Society for the Prevention of Cruelty to Children (founded in 1884 in London) and Children First (in Scotland), the United Nations Fund for Children (from 1946) and more recently the development of organisations such as Childline (from 1986) have been followed by radical changes in the laws governing child protection in this country. The introduction of Criminal Records Bureau checks for those gaining jobs with children under 18 years of age has been the most profound of these and is expected to expand in the future.

Public outrage at cases of violence towards children including Victoria Climbié, who died in 2000 aged eight after sustained abuse, has tended to fuel this interest and a general climate of fear over the protection of children from violence and, as we will see below, over sexual violence in particular (the Victoria Climbié Inquiry). Yet none of these concerns is new. Similar outrage was expressed over the death of Dennis O'Neil in 1946 and Maria Colell in 1974, both of which led to changes in institutions and laws aimed at preventing future tragedies. They may well have done so, but they have failed to prevent violence towards children, even where it was possible that it could have been prevented. Such a failure elicits a particularly strong response in most of us, not least because of our outrage at the destruction of 'innocent' children (as we generally view the victims to be).

This image of the innocent child is part of the reason that the other side of this concern, that of violence by children, also brings out such strong emotions. The signal case here is that of James Bulger, a two-year-old abducted and killed by two ten-year-olds in 1993. The act was brutal, caught in part on closed circuit television (CCTV) and one of those events so shocking that it has imprinted itself on the national consciousness. Part of the shock was the 'innocence' of the victim, but perhaps more so was the young age of the protagonists. A child killing is horrendous it seems, but a child killing by a child is all the more shocking. In part this can be seen as forcing us to re-evaluate our view of children as innocents, but the depiction of the two killers in the popular press carried many of the attributes of established ways of thinking of children, as 'tearaways' and 'delinquents'. The campaign to prevent the release of the two offenders and then to reveal their identities in the popular and local press supports this view (Davis and Bourhill, 1997: 45–6; D'Cruze et al., 2006: 76–7). However, yet again this is not the first child murder in British history. The case of Mary Flora Bell who, aged 11, killed two toddlers (returning to dismember one) led to her conviction in 1968 and a campaign over her identity once released in 1980 (Gitta, 1998).

Many individuals sought reasons for the killing of James Bulger. The popular press put forward a number of explanations. Most notable of these was the assertion that the perpetrators had had access to the film *Childsplay 3* (1991) which was said to show a murder that resembled the killing (but in fact no such killing appears in the film and there is no evidence that the children had seen it). Similar claims have been made for violent video games, in particular *Manhunt* which was associated with the killing in Leicestershire of 14-year-old Stefan Pakeerah by Warren Leblanc, 17, said by his father to be 'obsessed' with the game. As a result it was withdrawn by a number of retailers. However, again the actual connection was less than clear. The main motive for the murder seems to have been robbery, not a copycat killing, and rather bizarrely turned out not to be in the bedroom of the killer but that of the victim (Gauntlett, 1995). This is aside from the furious debates over whether the young are really influenced by violence on screen as is often assumed and the evidence that violent crime is less common than it has been in most of the past, perhaps because teenagers actually have less opportunity to commit such crimes.

REFLECTIVE ACTIVITY **3.3**

Experience, witness and violence

Find a small sample group of children and ask them the following questions (bearing in mind that the answers should remain confidential):

1. *Have you ever seen a violent film or TV programme, or played a violent video game?*

2. *Do you think that the act of watching made you feel more violent or that violence was more expectable?*

3. *Do you think that such an experience would/did make you feel the experience can be a means of 'getting violence out of your system'?*

4. *Have you found yourself wanting to go back to the experience to repeat the feelings you encountered?*

Such a brief survey cannot be scientific, but it is interesting to note whether those that felt that their experience made them feel more violent or less violent wanted to repeat the experience.

The sexualisation of childhood

The influence of the media is also at the heart of a debate about the sexualisation of childhood. Traditional perceptions of the fundamental differences between adults and children in most societies tend to focus on the removal of children from sexual activity and thought, although the points at which this demarcation between the sexual and non-sexual activity should occur vary widely. Problematically humans do not suddenly move from physical sexual immaturity to full development overnight or at some arbitrary date. Thus sexual attitudes towards the young are almost always problematic. They represent an area of moral and social negotiation and dispute. This dispute has become all the more intense in recent years because of the perception that children are being either depicted as sexual objects or encouraged to internalise a move to sexualisation at an early age.

This has been seen in the use by adults of childhood imagery for sexual purposes, of which, among the many stereotypes, the dress of schoolgirls is the most obvious in both soft sexual imagery shifting (at least in Britain) to even more extreme pornography. Some of this may not be entirely obvious, but even what seem relatively innocuous elements of such images, for example the use by models of 'children's' hairstyles such as 'bunches' or 'ponytails' can be seen as a direct borrowing from such imagery. The second issue is the employment or imposition on children of adult sexual images. Thus the use of adult and 'sexualised' forms of dress, such as short skirts or low necklines, have been increasingly noted among younger and younger children.

All these elements were exemplified in 1998 by the release and success of Britney Spears' single *Baby One More Time*. The lyrics themselves, which relied on a refrain that implied an invitation to physical violence, might have been controversial enough, but the video, including the singer dressed in a (Catholic) schoolgirl outfit, prompted outrage in some quarters. Yet the meaning of the imagery was unclear. Was the outrage because Spears, aged 17 at the time, was an adult pretending to be a child, or because she was a child pretending to be an adult?

Both of these possibilities – the use of childhood in sexual imagery and the possibility that young children might be sexualised at an earlier age – seem to carry with them a number of serious dangers. The most obvious is connected with the awareness and concern over paedophilia and child abuse that has come to dominate debates in recent years. There is firstly a concern that the conflation of childhood and sexual imagery might prompt some individuals to engage in such thoughts and activities where they might previously not have done so; although how exactly this might work is less than clear to many psychologists and it may be impossible to prove or disprove this hypothesis. The second is that children might be prompted to be sexually active at an earlier age. The growth of teenage pregnancy that has been observed in recent years, and which has become a major political issue because of its possible effects on wider social issues (such as poverty, exclusion, crime and education), seems to support this view. However, some experts have pointed to the earlier maturation of girls in western society, due in part to improved diet. The results of this change may account for earlier sexual activity among girls in a society where marriage is not maintained as a largely indisputable boundary between illicit and permissible sexual activity (Biro et al., 2006).

It is extremely hard to separate and properly understand all these factors and the chain of cause and effect. The rise of 'tweenies' or pre-teenagers as a marketing group from the 1980s onwards marked almost as great a wave of rebranding and remarketing as the rise of teenagers as an economic group from the 1950s. Undoubtedly the willingness to market what can be seen as 'sexualised' toys and clothes to this group has played a part in this process, but it could be argued that this was simply a response to changing sexual maturity at higher ages and greater economic prosperity.

These debates prompt a number of observations about the way in which childhood has changed and our perceptions of it. First of all it is important to note that the debate is almost entirely focused on the sexuality of girls – there are very few concerns over the issue of male sexualisation. Whether this indicates that the real debate is simply a restatement of the problem of the 'double standard' or that it is constrained by those standards is unclear. The second observation is that most adults wish to preserve childhood as a separate state from adulthood, free from the problems of sex, and perhaps parents want this most of all. Yet it is parents who most commonly participate in the commercial sexualisation of childhood by buying toys or other items for their children. There is a second double standard that means we are inconsistent as a society over what we aim for and supply to our own children.

REFLECTIVE ACTIVITY **3.4**

Elements of sexuality

Consider at what age you think girls should be able to do the following.

- *Wear makeup.*
- *Wear adult fashions.*
- *Listen to adult music (dealing, for example, with implied sexuality).*
- *Begin dating.*

Now go through the list again for boys where appropriate.

Compare your results.

Do you have the same standards for girls and boys?

Now go through once again and consider at what age you think boys and girls actually do these things.

How close to reality are your values?

The shortening of childhood

All these issues seem to suggest that the crisis of childhood is in large part about the truncating of the childhood experience. Most adults have a perception that childhood should be a separate and carefully guarded period, free from the worries of adults, in which children experience healthy and character-building activity, learn important skills, are protected from violence and crime and do not have to deal with the demands of sexuality. Yet such a view of childhood seems under threat on all fronts. As all these 'adult' concerns and problems seem to be brought to bear on children it seems possible to argue that childhood itself has steadily been eroded.

The problem here is that, although the issues raised by many of these areas of debate might be real, what we tend to measure their effect on childhood against remains an idealised view of childhood as a state. The image of the Edwardian childhood, carried in classic children's books, such as *Peter Pan* (1911), *Wind in the Willows* (1908) and a little later *Winnie the Pooh* (1926), is important here. This is childhood as a safe zone of imagination and play, what many wish their own childhoods were or wish it could be for the next generation. Yet it is manifestly a middle-class ideal, excluding the large numbers of working-class children whose schooling was fragmented and limited and whose childhood was already filled with economic and other concerns. It is also a very male world and in reality the assumption of patriarchy and of male superiority seriously limited the freedom of the childhoods of even middle-class girls. Finally, as a brief examination of any handful of considered biographies from this period will show, even for middle-class boys, reality rarely matched up to an ideal. Just like children of all ages, some suffered ill health, some anxieties and some abuse. In fact, it rapidly becomes clear that there never was a golden age of childhood, that it has never matched up to our current ideals and, sadly, almost certainly never will.

The issue of when childhood ends seems to show this very clearly. At the moment the recognition of the lines of demarcation between childhood and adulthood remains somewhat confused. We can leave school and pay taxes at 16 and begin to drive at 17, but not vote until 18 or become a member of Parliament (MP) until 21. British society has been unusual in lacking clear rituals that mark the boundaries between adolescence and adulthood, leading to some confusion and drift. Some elements of adulthood may have moved back into childhood, but others have moved forward. For example, it is still possible to marry with a parent's consent at 16 and legal to have sexual inter-course, but a film of such activity is legally child abuse. This is not to say that these contradictions are welcome, but that the boundaries of childhood are not certain, and never have been, and they continue to shift, causing confusion and concern, but actually only continuing a situation that has been current from as early as records begin.

REFLECTIVE ACTIVITY **3.5**

When does childhood end?

Try to think of the activity and object that best summarises your childhood experience.

Now consider when you stopped engaging in that activity or ceased to have the object (you may of course still do or have both).

Now consider what points in your life marked the transition from childhood to adulthood: this may include acquiring a right, skill or new sort of relationship.

Now analyse the range of ages this suggests for the end of your own childhood.

What is the earliest and what is the latest?

Is this earlier or later than you might have anticipated?

Is there a crisis in childhood?

To what degree then do these elements collectively mark a real crisis in childhood? The term 'crisis' is, of course, medical in origin and should denote an intense and limited period in which a patient, possibly painfully and uncomfortably, either conquers an ailment or suffers (perhaps fatal) the effects. Judged by these standards the idea that childhood is in crisis seems unsustainable. The changes that can be seen occurring in the lives of children may be real enough and many aspects of it may be regrettable, but an examination of these changes suggests that they are in fact rather slow and less universal than might be assumed. Changes in the health of children seem to be one area where social policy may actually have some impact on improving the lives of children, although whether wider social and cultural transformations can occur is difficult to decide with certainty. In education and literacy the changes are dramatic, but they are not necessarily all negative and some elements, such as the apparent expansion of childhood reading, may give us room for optimism. Violence to and by children is to be abhorred and as much as possible prevented and mitigated, but it simply cannot be proved that it is a new or even increasing phenomenon. The sexualisation of childhood is also an area that needs considerable vigilance, but it seems best to avoid knee-jerk reactions to the perceived threats and changes. It is clear that we cannot completely construct the world of children for them. If they are to enjoy the special nature of childhood that most adults desire for them, they must also be free to make some of their own choices along the way.

SUMMARY OF KEY POINTS

This chapter has raised a series of questions around oftentimes controversial issues and viewpoints to challenge the 'childhood in crisis' thesis. The themes we have explored include childhood health and obesity, education and literacy, violence, and sexualisation. We have examined whether these different aspects of childhood contribute toward a shortening or fragmentation of the childhood experience, and question whether our perceptions of childhood may differ from reality.

FERENCES

American Obesity Association – **http://www.obesity.org/subs/childhood/ prevalence.shtml** (31 January 2007).

Bogart, D. (ed.) (2005) *The Bowker Annual Library and Book Trade Almanac 2005*, 50th edn. Medford, NJ:Information Today.

Biro, F., Lucky, A. W., Simbartl, L. A., Barton, B. A., Daniels, S. R., Striegel-Moore, R., Kronsberg, S. S. and Morrison, J. A. (2006) 'Pubertal maturation in girls and the relationship to anthropometric changes: pathways through puberty', *Journal of Pediatrics*, 142 (6): 643–6.

British Medical Association (BMA) (2005) *Preventing Childhood Obesity*. (See **http://www.bma.org.uk/ap.nsf/content/childhoodobesity** (31 January 2007).)

Child's Play 3 (1991) Dir. Jack Bender. Universal.

Davis, H. and Bourhill, M. (1997) 'The demonization of children and young people', in P. Scraton (ed.), *Childhood in Crisis*. London: Routledge.

D'Cruze, S., Walklate, S., and Pegg, S. (2006) *Social and Historical Approaches to Understanding Murder and Murderers*. Cullompton: Willan.

Gauntlett, D. (1995) *Moving Experiences: Understanding Television's Influences and Effects*. London: John Libbey.

Gee, J. P. (1996) *Social Linguistics and Literacies: Ideologies in Discourses*. London: Taylor & Francis.

Gitta, S. (1998) *Cries Unheard*. London: Macmillan.

National Statistics (See **http://www.statistics.gov.uk/cci/nugget.asp?id=718** (31 January 2007).)

Street, B. V. (1995) *Social Literacies*. London and New York: Longman.

Victoria Climbié Inquiry (See **http://www.victoria-climbie-inquiry.org.uk/** (31 January 2007).)

4 Children and risk

Andrew Hope

Learning objectives

By the end of this chapter you should:

- **understand that risk is socially constructed and politically mediated;**
- **have a critical awareness of the risks facing children in contemporary societies;**
- **be able to identify some differences between risk perceptions focusing on younger children and those related to youths;**
- **comprehend that risk-taking can have positive outcomes for children.**

Introduction

It might seem from watching television news reports or reading daily newspapers that concern with risk is a depressingly prevalent feature of modern existence. Fuelling anxieties, children often appear in such stories, frequently as victims, sometimes as perpetrators. Arguably, no age group is more associated with risk than children. Yet there is often disagreement as to the exact nature of a risk or its relative importance compared with other dangers. Indeed, if you were to ask experts to describe the risks that face children at the start of the new millennium, it is likely that you would get some very different answers. With such differences in mind, this chapter explores some of the key social-cultural issues related to children and risk in contemporary societies.

Understanding risk as a social construct

In everyday life when people talk about risk, they are often referring to the chance of loss or the possibility of damage to themselves and what they value. This is not to deny that risk may also be positive (this is discussed in the penultimate section of this chapter). Yet, risk is used predominantly in contemporary cultures as another way of talking about danger. Western societies have become increasingly obsessed in recent years with the probability of damage, illness and death, with anxieties ranging from food production to global terrorism. Even mundane experiences such as using the internet, public travel or feeding children have been perceptually transformed into hazardous undertakings. Following the reporting of risks in the media there is often a deluge of opinion offered by experts as to the probability of a danger being realised. From this viewpoint not only is risk a negative label, warning of possible death and destruction, but also something that can be estimated through the use of scientific measures. Such an approach, where risk calculations are seen as 'absolute truths', has traditionally dominated in disciplines such as engineering, psychology and economics. From this perspective expert risk perceptions are labelled as objective, and disagreement with these views assumed to indicate 'irrationality' or 'hostility to technology'.

However, within the fields of sociology and social anthropology a different way of thinking about risk has emerged. This approach is broadly critical of claims that risk can be objectively measured, instead focusing on the manner in which 'risks' themselves are socially constructed. Much as defini-

tions of childhood are built up through social and political processes, so it is argued are risk perceptions. Therefore, any analysis of risk needs to understand the cultural context within which it is
generated. This might seem a somewhat strange assertion. Yet, people do not always agree on what
should be labelled as risky. Consider the example of teaching about homosexuality in UK schools.
Section 28 was a controversial amendment, enacted by the Local Government Act 1988, which some
people believed prohibited local councils from promoting gay relationships as normal. Until its
repeal in November 2003, many staff in local education authority controlled schools feared that discussing gay issues with students might lead to prosecution. The amendment was at least partly a
response to right-wing groups' fears that discussing homosexuality in schools might undermine
'moral values' and 'traditional family structures'. In this context, the risk was perceived to be the
threat to public morality and conservative values. However, opponents labelled this as a human
rights issue, suggesting that the amendment was tantamount to persecution. Here the risk was seen
to arise from the amendment itself, which it was argued threatened individuals' rights and liberties.

Such conflicts can arise not only from political and ideological disagreements, but also from broader
cultural differences regarding what passes for appropriate and acceptable behaviour. Indeed, the
social anthropologist Mary Douglas suggested that as knowledge is never value-free, debates about
risks always involve questions of cultural meaning and political position. In short, risk is always social
(Douglas and Wildavsky, 1982). This is not to deny that 'real dangers' exist but rather to suggest that
each subculture or society elevates some risks to a high point while depressing or ignoring others.
Therefore risks are not 'given' but rather selected through social processes. Decisions as to what
becomes labelled as a 'risk' and which risks then form the focus of concern are political. Indeed the
privileging of certain risks offers an indication of the sort of communities and societies in which
people wish to live. Being able to control what gets labelled as risk and encourage others to accept
this viewpoint is a position of power, especially as competing claims often exist.

REFLECTIVE ACTIVITY **4.1**

School dinners in the UK

*The battle for better school dinners in the UK was brought to public attention when celebrity chef
Jamie Oliver revealed the poor state of children's diets in the 2005 television series* Jamie's School
Dinners. *As a response to subsequent media coverage, public pressure and political concern, the UK
government sought from autumn 2006 to restrict the sale of 'junk foods' in state schools, while prom-
ising additional rules to encourage healthy eating among children (Department for Education and
Skills, 2005). In one school in South Yorkshire two mothers rebelled against what they saw as 'food
fascism', reportedly passing chips, burgers and fizzy drinks to children through the school railings.*

Now consider the following questions.

- *From the viewpoint of those campaigning for healthier school meals what risks might be posed
by 'junk food'?*

- *Why do you think the mothers in South Yorkshire reacted in the manner in which they did?*

- *The head teacher of the South Yorkshire school expressed surprise that this story attracted such
attention when he noted that at the same time there were people dying on the front line in Iraq.
What does this statement suggest about differing views of risk?*

- *Why do you think the UK government primarily focused on the risks posed by 'junk food' in
schools rather than at home?*

Children and 'danger'

It has already been suggested that risk can be defined as the possibility of damage or loss and that decisions regarding which risks to focus upon are political. Nevertheless, it is still essential to consider the risks that spring to mind when thinking about children and danger. It would seem sensible to start by suggesting that children might face those risks that threaten all people regardless of age. Yet, while certain risks such as poor diet, bullying or sexual abuse might affect adults as well as children, there is a tendency in contemporary society to see children who are subjected to these dangers in a different light from adults experiencing similar threats. This partly reflects the view of children as innocents who need protection from the adult world. Such a perspective lends itself towards treating children as part of a 'minority group', that is individuals who are excluded from adult activities and treated in ways that minimise their agency. Arguably, in conjunction with children's rights arguments, such views resulted in many countries signing the United Nations (UN) Convention on the Rights of a Child in 1989, to protect children's welfare. As there is a separate Universal Declaration of Human Rights built into the UN charter, it might be asked whether risks exist that are particular to childhood. A short answer would be that since risks are socially constructed, dangers might develop that are seen solely as endangering children. However, a more insightful observation might be that the important differences reside not in the actual risks but rather in the adult view of the nature of childhood in contemporary society.

While accepting that risks are selected through social processes it is still possible to think about dangers in terms of hierarchies. Thus it might be feasible to label injecting heroine as a greater risk than neglecting schoolwork. However, it is always necessary to think about who has categorised the 'risk hierarchy'. Indeed, a criticism that is sometimes levelled at social research into childhood is that much of what is written is an adult interpretation of children's social worlds. Here lies the danger of failing to understand children's actions from their perspective. Instead, a tendency may exist to interpret events from an adult viewpoint, adopting an 'adult-centred' outlook. Acts that might seem irrational in the adult world may well make perfect sense when seen through a child's eyes. Indeed it is worth noting that children often generate or moderate their own risk perceptions in response to their social environments. For example, research into internet use in schools has shown that while staff label a whole range of activities as 'risky' for children, including accessing pornography, using chat-lines and viewing race-hate sites, students are largely unconcerned about such things, instead focusing on the risk of been caught misusing the Internet (Hope, 2007). This suggests that it is necessary to privilege children's own worlds as real, distinct places and listen to their voices (the so-called tribal child approach).

Focusing upon risk-taking, Abbott-Chapman and Denholm (2001) carried out research among almost 1,000 school children in Tasmania, Australia, in an attempt to establish some form of risk hierarchy. The risks identified by students ranged from sharing needles to sunbathing without sunscreen. Students were subsequently asked to rank these risks and perhaps unsurprisingly those labelled as very high risk, such as hard drug use, were found to be activities that few students participated in. Some of the main research findings are listed in the following activity.

REFLECTIVE ACTIVITY 4.2

Children and risk hierarchies

Very high perceived risk/very low participation
Sharing needles, injecting heroin, snorting cocaine, taking speed/ecstasy

High perceived risk/low participation
Drunk driving, sniffing glue, starving / slimming

REFLECTIVE ACTIVITY 4 . 2 *continued*

High perceived risk/moderate participation
Sex with a partner not well known, hitch-hiking, leaving home (even temporarily), sex not on the pill, sex no condom, driving without a licence

Moderate perceived risk/fairly high participation
Drop out from school considered, speeding, shoplifting, body piercing, accessing Internet pornography, smoking marijuana, gambling

Low perceived risk/high participation
Watching X-rated videos, smoking cigarettes, binge drinking, sunbathing without sunscreen, wagging classes, drinking alcohol

(Abbott-Chapman and Denholm, 2001: 290)

- *Read through the various 'dangers' listed above and identify two risks that you would place in either higher or lower risk categories.*

- *Why would you re-categorise these two risks and what exactly do you think is the nature of the potential harmful outcome?*

- *This research was carried out among 15- to 17-year-olds. How do you think the risk hierarchy might change if the views of younger children were considered instead? What new risks might appear in such a list?*

Thinking globally about childhood risks

It is worth noting that being a child is a very different experience across cultures. While there may exist some common ground, the risks faced by children in western societies are not necessarily the same as those that threaten children elsewhere in the world. Sometimes this is a reflection of cultural differences, other times it is a product of economic exploitation and political unrest. Thus while child labour has largely disappeared in economically developed countries, it is estimated that there are 400 million children working in poorer societies. Although concern might be rightly expressed about the physical and social dangers faced by children working long hours under harsh conditions, it should be recognised that the possibility of starvation is often also a great risk. While poverty and starvation are risks that some children still face in western society it should be recognised that in countries subjected to famine, floods or war the scope of the problem is often much greater. In particular, armed conflicts have blighted children's lives in many parts of the underdeveloped world. It is estimated that globally half of the war refugees are children. In numerous countries, boys and girls are recruited as soldiers by armed forces. While the numbers recruited and used in hostilities are difficult to quantify, research suggests that around the world some 300,000 child-soldiers are exploited in over 30 conflicts. Lest the thought arise that these risks exist only in politically unstable societies it is worth noting that the UK has been criticised for allowing boys to join the armed forces at 16 and to fight at 17. After all, the UN Optional Protocol to the Convention on the Rights of the Child on the Involvement of Children in Armed Conflict (2000), which entered into force on 12 February 2002, sets 18 as the minimum age for direct participation in hostilities. Other risks to children have deep roots in cultural and historical traditions. Thus early marriages are pervasive in a number of countries in Africa and South Asia. Consider the following example:

Child marriage in India

While marriages of girls under the age of 18 and boys younger than 21 is illegal in India it is claimed by human rights activists that forced marriages of children, especially in rural areas such as Rajasthan, are not uncommon. Economic reasons are often cited for this activity with poverty stricken parents being persuaded to part with daughters, while richer ones seek to foster alliances with the intent of keeping property and money within families. It is argued that such marriages may protect children from unwanted sexual advances. Yet, child marriage can impact negatively on health, particularly through premature pregnancy and domestic violence, as well as restricting life opportunities, such as educational possibilities for girls.

Now think about the following questions:

- *Why might some parents in India not consider child marriage a risk?*

- *Why do you think child marriage may disadvantage girls more than boys?*

- *It is claimed that some police ignore child marriages, failing to arrest the parents responsible, especially in poor communities. Why might this be the case?*

From innocence to dangerousness

Historically there was no conception of childhood as a separate stage of the life course, with children simply being absorbed into the adult world as soon as they were capable of survival. It was only from the late Middle Ages in Europe, following moral pressure from the Church and the Protestant Reformation, that children came to be seen as either innocents and objects of affection, or odd moral creatures capable of evil disposition. This perceptual dichotomy of children as either innocents in need of protection or dangerous individuals in need of taming has persisted. In contemporary western society, competing discourses of children at risk and the 'dangerous' child have often been approached through a deconstruction of the concept of childhood itself and the reclassification of 'later childhood' as youth. While children are often defined in national and international law as those under the age of 18, a range of rights and responsibilities is enshrined in legislation for those who are younger. In the UK, it is widely assumed that under a certain age young people are not legally responsible for their actions. In England and Wales this age of criminal responsibility is 10 (8 in Scotland). Some social commentators have suggested that this age can be defined as the end of 'innocent' childhood and the start of youth. Yet others have defined the concept of youth in terms of 'teen consumer culture', suggesting that the age of 12 might be the end of childhood. Although there is value in such distinctions, it should nevertheless be recognised that they may neglect the actual life experiences of young individuals.

There is a strong association in public imagination between the concepts of youth and risk. While youths in modern industrialised societies may be seen as experiencing a range of dangers and opportunities unknown to previous generations (particularly with regards to education, employment and lifestyle) there is a tendency to focus on this group as engendering risk, a source of delinquency and deviant subcultures (Furlong and Cartmel, 1997). As criminologist John Muncie points out, while 'child' and 'adult' are largely neutral terms, 'youth' usually evokes emotive and troubling images of *uncontrolled freedom, irresponsibility, vulgarity, neglect, deprivation or immaturity* (Muncie, 1999: 3). Partly this is because of the perceived marginal nature of youths, no longer labelled as 'innocent' children but yet to achieve the assumed 'social maturity' of adulthood. Belonging to neither of these two supposedly 'stable' social groups, they are perceived as offering a potential threat to social order.

Despite a tendency towards the conceptual polarisation of 'innocent children' and 'dangerous youths' in the mass media, social reality is not so clear cut. With regard to internet use in UK schools, research has shown that staff who expressed concern about students accessing unsuitable material, including online pornography, hate sites, bomb/drug making websites and sex chatlines, did not always make interpretations as to who was at risk purely on the basis of age (Hope, 2006). Although there was some tendency to interpret younger students' risky internet practices in terms of the corruption of 'impressionable' minds, while the inappropriate online activities of youths were labelled as 'dangerous' to staff authority and school image, these viewpoints were not rigid. Indeed, in some cases, such as with websites providing instructions for bomb/drug production and the use of chatlines, youths were seen to be at risk. Factors other than age, such as life experience or prior knowledge of the students involved, influenced staff risk perceptions and in such cases youths were not always seen as a homogenous body.

Yet this is not to deny that there is a connection between youth and crime. Whether judged by official statistics or self-report studies, the peak ages for involvement in criminal activity predominantly lie in the teenage years. A significant proportion of such offences falls into the category of what is known as 'volume crime', that is everyday property crime and anti-social behaviour. Property crime, which includes domestic burglary, theft from a person or vehicle and criminal damage, is not just concerned with the event of robbery but also the distribution of stolen goods. In spite of concerns about young people and property crime it is the second subcategory of 'volume crime' that has caught media attention. As a backlash against perceived 'yob culture' Anti-Social Behaviour Orders (ASBOs), were first introduced in the UK by the Crime and Disorder Act 1998, later strengthened in England and Wales by the Anti-Social Behaviour Act 2003. ASBOs are civil orders made against a person who has been shown to have engaged in acts which caused, or were likely to cause, distress to other individuals. In practice the orders may prohibit any behaviour and can result in custodial sentences. Children's charities have expressed concern that almost half of all ASBOs are issued against juveniles (those under 18 years of age). Although ASBOs are often used in an attempt to combat serious deviant behaviour, it has been argued that the system can also make criminal the behaviour of youths that would otherwise be lawful. Consider the examples in the following exercise:

REFLECTIVE ACTIVITY **4.4**

Young people and ASBOs

There is little restriction on what a court may impose as the terms of an ASBO or what can be designated as anti-social behaviour. Occasionally this results in the somewhat bewildering criminalisation of seemingly mundane activities. For example, following the issuing of ASBOs, two teenage boys from Manchester were banned from wearing one golf glove, a 13-year-old was forbidden from using the word 'grass', while a 17-year-old was prohibited from using his front door. More recently ASBOs have been used to ban two brothers in Newport, South Wales from wearing 'hoodies' (hooded tops). While ASBOs have also been issued to deal with more serious anti-social behaviour, there is little evidence that they work and some researchers claim that youths view them as a badge of honour.

- *Charities have expressed concern that the use of ASBOs on children is becoming 'entirely routine'. What do you think are the risks of such a problem?*

- *'Hoodies' have created controversy after bans in some shopping centres, pubs and schools. Should the law be used to restrict the wearing of such clothing? Why? What is the perceived risk?*

- *What do you think is meant when researchers claim that ASBOs are seen as a badge of honour by some youths?*

- *Briefly consider whether juveniles should be treated in the same way as adults in the criminal justice system. Why?*

None of this is to deny that children do commit crimes. Indeed not only are they the victims of a range of crimes, but also upon occasion they are the perpetrators of offences against their own age group. Consider the form of physical assault, which became known as 'happy slapping'. This craze, which reportedly started in South London in 2004, involved physical assaults (initially slapping, although later incidents escalated to arson and murder) being recorded on video mobile phones. Teachers' unions pointed out that the name was inappropriate and that the attacks, which appeared to be predominantly perpetrated by and against children, should be considered as acts of bullying or physical assault.

Children and representations of risk in the media

In examining childhood, risk and the media, two issues are of particular relevance, namely how risk is presented to children through the media and in what manner those under the age of 18 are portrayed to audiences. Understanding how the mass media presents risk is an under-researched area, although there is recognition that some hazards are ignored while other more dramatic incidents are exaggerated. The sociologist Roy Boyne has suggested that the language of risk within the media is not rigorous, making it difficult to form judgements from the information provided (Boyne, 2003). This is especially true of magazines aimed at the youth market, which only tend to deal with risk in terms of manufactured and impossible dilemmas. This should hardly be surprising if one considers that magazines aimed at this age range are predominantly concerned with superficial entertainment rather than serious reporting. Most 'news' aimed specifically at the child market on television tends to be packaged in formats that include a variety of other non-news items. In part, this probably reflects the view that if children want to watch news they will watch the pre-watershed news programmes offered to adults. However, there are some notable exceptions in the UK such as *Newsround*, a long-running BBC news programme made especially for children. While attempting to inform younger viewers about current events this programme has not shied away from discussing risk stories and thanks to new technology, such as the internet, has sought to encourage children to offer their own views.

REFLECTIVE ACTIVITY **4.5**

Reporting risks to children

- *Visit the BBC Newsround website at* **http://news.bbc.co.uk/cbbcnews/default.stm**

- *What age range do you think this material is aimed at? Why?*

- *Select one story dealing with something that could be labelled as a risk.*

- *How does the coverage and discussion on this website differ from that on other sites dedicated to adult news coverage? Links to adult newspapers can be found at* **http://dailynewspaper.co.uk/**

- *How would you explain these differences?*

Relatively little attention is paid to children as media consumers; rather the focus tends to be on how they are portrayed and reported. Whether in television soaps or stories in tabloid newspapers, representations of children tend to be polarised around the child at-risk/'dangerous' child dichotomy. Sociologists have pointed out that older children are somewhat prone to be the focus of 'moral panics'. Sociologist Stanley Cohen, in his classic study of the reporting of bank holiday disturbances between rival gangs of young people, mods and rockers, suggested that the media exaggerated, distorted and sensationalised events, while making gloomy predictions about the future of society (Cohen, 1972). Central to Cohen's discussion of 'moral panic' and the various revisions of this theory that have emerged over the years is the concept of scapegoating. This is the process of unjustly projecting public fears and blame onto marginal groups. In Cohen's words, such groups become 'folk devils'. Douglas (1966) suggests that concerns about danger and impurity often focus around boundaries. These boundaries, both social and physical, are areas of unease, spaces filled with menace. As youths occupy such a threshold position, between childhood and adulthood, perhaps it is unsurprising if they become the focus of anxiety, with their behaviour or beliefs being 'demonised' by the mass media. In short, the 'moral panics' related to children reveal more about the fears and prejudices festering within adult society than they do about the actual risks posed.

Risk and pleasure

As the social anthropologist Mary Douglas notes, in early modernity risk was used in terms of calculable probability, allowing for the possibility that risks could be 'good' as well as 'bad' (Douglas, 1992: 23). While the concept of a good risk seems to have largely disappeared, with risk in contemporary society often acting as a synonym for danger, there nevertheless exists a counter-discourse, drawing upon social-cultural literature, which stresses the benefits of risk-taking (Lupton, 1999: 148). Additionally, there is a huge commercial market aimed at younger people that seeks to package and sell products glamourising or simulating risks, such as 'gangsta' rap music, action films, *manga* graphic novels and violent video games. Each of these issues will be considered in turn.

Social research that examines the perceived positive outcomes of children's risk-taking activities tends to stress emotional engagement, identity formation and skilled performance. Risk can be exciting, offering individuals a way to transcend the routine banality of everyday life. This argument finds resonance with writings within cultural criminology, which stress that some children engage in illegal activities, such as fighting in public, vandalism or under age drinking, to relieve boredom and engender an emotional rush (Presdee, 2000). Partaking in dangerous activities may also develop a child's sense of identity, through allowing experimentation that goes beyond the individual's everyday environment, developing a positive reputation as 'daring' or creating a 'communal spirit' among like-minded souls. As individuals start to realise their own sense of identity in childhood, it is unsurprising if some choose risk as a tool to develop their self-image. Essential to much risk-taking activity is skilled performance and the illusion of control. While young people may indulge in dangerous behaviour in private, if they wish to be acknowledged by their peers then they either need to relate entertaining stories of these events or, more likely, engage in public performance. Risk-taking before an audience of peers is likely to generate greater appreciation if the act itself or the presentation is skilful. Consider the example of 'backyard wrestling', where youths engage in theatrical staged fights, using highly dangerous moves which they lack the training to execute safely. Here the risky performances go beyond those friends watching the events, with footage of the fights often recorded and posted on specialist websites.

In recent years, there has been an increase in the commodification of risk. That is the (re)production, packaging and selling of goods or services that are intended to engender emotion through association with risk. As everyday life becomes less engaging for some individuals, daily excitement becomes an essential ingredient of consumer culture (Presdee, 2000). Many of the resultant products and services are aimed directly or indirectly at youth markets. From rap music glamourising extreme violence and casual sex, to video games allowing individuals to play the role of armed criminal (the *Grand Theft Auto* franchise), murderous death-row inmate (*Manhunt*) or assassin (the *Hitman* series), the packaging and selling of risk is big business. Another noticeable trend in recent years has been the glamourising of risk, hurt and humiliation though entertainment programmes such as *Jackass* and *Dirty Sanchez*. It is worth noting that children's consumption of some of the more extreme media may be age prohibited, yet there is a consensus that they still seem to be able to acquire such products. Neither does the merchandising stop there. It is possible, through franchising and advertising to wear, drink and eat items associated with risk. This is not to make a judgement as to the value of such products but rather to acknowledge their existence in child consumer culture.

SUMMARY OF KEY POINTS

In considering childhood and risk from a social-cultural perspective a number of useful insights can be gained regarding the nature of risks, the issue of who is at risk and whether all risks are merely negative. These include the following.

> In contemporary societies, risk is most commonly used to refer to danger, the chance of loss or the possibility of damage, but it may also have positive connotations.

> Risks are not 'given' but rather are selected through social processes, with decisions as to what becomes labelled as a 'risk' and which risks to focus upon being political.

> It is important to avoid an adult-centred view of the world and realise that children often generate or moderate their own risk perceptions in response to their social environments.

> Nevertheless, a consensus on risks may develop among children, making it possible to consider hierarchies of risk.

> Being a child is a very different experience across cultures, with young labourers, early marriages and child soldiers not uncommon in some countries.

> From the late Middle Ages, a perceptual dichotomy has persisted of children as either innocents in need of protection or dangerous individuals in need of taming.

> There is a strong connection between youth and crime, as the peak ages for involvement in criminal activity predominantly lie in the teenage years.

> Youths are sometimes 'demonised' in the media, providing the focus for the creation of 'moral panics' through negative reports that exaggerate and sensationalise risks.

> Risk-taking can have positive outcomes for children, including fostering emotional engagement, facilitating identity formation and providing opportunities for skilled performances that challenge boundaries.

> The commodification and marketing of risk to children is big business.

ERENCES

Abbott-Chapman, J. and Denholm, C. (2001) 'Adolescents' risk activities, risk hierarchies and the influence of religiosity', *Journal of Youth Studies*, 4 (3): 279–91.

Boyne, R. (2003) *Risk*. Buckingham: Open University Press.

Cohen, S. (1972) *Folk Devils and Moral Panics: The Creation of the Mods and Rockers*. London: MacGibbon & Kee.

Department for Education and Skills (2005) *School Dinners*. London: OPSI. (See: http://findoutmore.dfes.gov.uk/2005/11/school_dinners.html (last accessed 3 January 2007).)

Douglas, M. (1966) *Purity and Danger*. London: Routledge & Kegan Paul.

Douglas, M. (1992) *Risk and Blame: Essays in Cultural Theory*. London: Routledge.

Douglas, M. and Wildavsky, A. (1982) *Risk and Culture: An Essay on the Selection of Technological and Environmental Dangers*. Berkley, CA: University of California Press.

Furlong, A. and Cartmel, F. (1997) *Young People and Social Change*. Buckingham: Open University Press.

Hope, A. (2006) 'School Internet use, youth and risk: a social-cultural study of the relation between staff views of on-line dangers and students' ages in UK schools', *British Educational Research Journal*, 32 (2): 307–29.

Hope, A. (2007) 'Risk taking, boundary performance and intentional school Internet "misuse"', *Discourse: Studies in the Cultural Politics of Education*, 28 (1): 87–99.

Lupton, D. (1999) *Risk*. London: Routledge.

Muncie, J. (1999) *Youth and Crime: A Critical Introduction*. London: Sage.

Presdee, M. (2000) *Cultural Criminology and the Carnival of Crime*. Routledge: London.

United Nations (1989) *Convention on the Rights of a Child*. New York: United Nations. (See: **http://www.unhchr.ch/html/menu3/b/k2crc.htm** (last accessed 3 January 2007).)

United Nations (2000) *Optional Protocol to the Convention on the Rights of the Child on the Involvement of Children in Armed Conflict*. New York: United Nations. (See: **http://www.unhchr.ch/html/menu2/6/protocolchild.htm** (last accessed 3 January 2007).)

Part 2

Childhood and youth development

5 The origins of human behaviour

Rob Toplis

Learning objectives

By the end of this chapter you should be able to:

- **understand how behaviour contributes to survival;**
- **understand that behaviour patterns are complex and interrelated;**
- **recognise how an understanding of animal behaviour contributes to an understanding of human behaviour;**
- **be aware of some of the recent uses of technology in our understanding of learning and the brain.**

Introduction

This chapter explores some of the biological background to behaviour that may help to provide insights into the behaviour of human beings. In doing so it reviews some of the ideas and terms that arise from recent history and contemporary work in an attempt to answer questions such as the following. Do humans share similar behaviour to other animals? What is instinct? What is learned behaviour? What happens in the brain during learning? Can learning change? Although a study of animal behaviour may provide valuable insights into our own behaviour, the danger here is that it is sometimes tempting to use our own perceptions and human cultural values in attempting to explain our observations of animals. There may be common drives for these behaviours but the contexts and responses, mediated by different neural pathways, may be very different. For example, the wagging tail of a pet dog may be perceived as pleasure or friendliness to us but may have a very different meaning in the brain of the dog. Similarly, chimpanzees in the Gombe National Park in East Africa display various grinning expressions that we might think are signs of happiness but most of these signal fear or excitement (van Lawick-Goodall, 1971). As Hinde (1974: 4) points out: *No animal has a culture involving symbolic values, beliefs and norms of behaviour which even approaches that of our own species.*

Needs and survival

The theory underpinning animal behaviour is Darwin's theory of evolution (Darwin, 1968), often summarised as 'survival of the fittest'. It is based on the natural selection of those living things that are the best adapted for survival in their environments. Darwin's theory is in contrast to an earlier theory by Lamarck (Roberts et al., 1993) suggesting that characteristics acquired from life could be passed on to the offspring. The classic example is that of the evolution of the giraffe's long neck. According to Lamarck, the giraffe evolved a long neck because over the course of their lives they stretched their necks to reach the leaves at the tops of trees and this characteristic was passed on to their offspring. Using this same logic, dogs with docked (removed) tails would pass this characteristic on to their offspring so that all their pups would be tailless. However, Darwin's theory explains the long neck of the giraffe as being the result of animals that arose with longer necks that made them more successful at surviving and they then passed on these characteristics to their offspring.

Darwin's theory was based on his own extensive observations of animals and plants, and in subsequent studies of their structures and functions, observed both with the naked eye and through the microscope. However, as the science of genetics developed, our understanding about the genetic code of deoxyribonucleic acid (DNA) and its effect at the molecular level has provided a wealth of evidence to support evolutionary theory. Evolution can also explain the behaviour of different animals as that which enables their survival and consequent reproduction in their natural environments. The study of animal behaviour has not only contributed to our knowledge of the natural world but has also provided valuable insights into human behaviour and learning.

What do animals, including humans, need for survival? At the basic level is the need for food, water and shelter, needs shared by both humans and other animals. At another level is the need to be safe and to reproduce and rear offspring. Maslow's (1970) hierarchy of human needs (Figure 5.1) goes further and distinguishes needs in order of importance so that basic physiological needs form the broad base that must be satisfied before other, higher needs can be taken into account. The needs of concentration camp prisoners, for example, will focus first on the needs of food and warmth before they are able to think of higher needs of love and belonging or self-esteem. Similarly, children in school are unable to focus on the higher needs of understanding and knowledge or aesthetics if they are hungry or frightened.

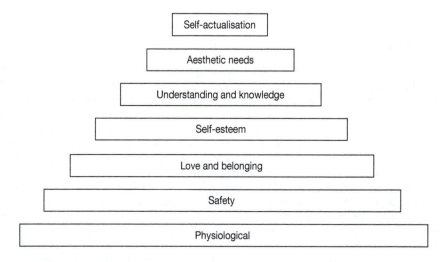

Figure 5.1   Maslow's hierarchy of needs

The need for self-esteem has two sub-sets (Child, 2004): firstly, the desire for strength, achievement and confidence and secondly, the desire for attention, reputation and appreciation by others. An individual moving into a new and unfamiliar area of the country usually concentrates on satisfying and consolidating their housing needs (safety) and their more immediate needs of the family, job and social life (belonging) before seeking the self-esteem needs of, for example, a desire for status and prestige by standing for a local election. The higher needs of understanding and knowledge involve the acquisition of information and the exploration of ideas and making sense of them, and those of aesthetics the appreciation of shape, order and beauty. Self-actualisation is the desire to achieve the individual's potential; clearly this involves the individual realising what their potential *can* be and this process may be helped by 'informed others' such as teachers, parents and friends. This highest need depends on satisfying all the needs lower down in the hierarchy; a realisation of this is important for anyone seeking to develop human beings.

Nervous systems and behaviour

Having discussed the evolution of behaviour and the needs of animals, including humans, it is now worth considering the biological systems that control behaviour. Animal behaviour relies on co-ordination of body activities via hormonal and nervous systems. An overall 'systems' organisation is shown in Figure 5.2 where a change in the environment, a stimulus, is detected by receptors. If the change is in the external environment, these receptors are often sensory organs that may detect sound, light, touch, smell or taste. If the change occurs within the animal's body, the receptors may detect chemical changes, pressure or temperature. Information from these receptors is then relayed to an integrator – usually the central nervous system – which processes the information and relays it in turn to effectors, often muscles, which in turn produce a response, resulting in an action.

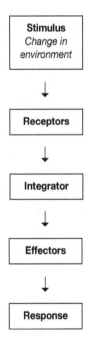

Figure 5.2 Stimulus–response system

Take, as an example, the aggressive behaviour shown by a domestic dog. In this case the change in the external environment may be an unusual noise, possibly made by an intruder. This noise provides a stimulus which is detected by the dog's acute hearing organs. This information, via nerve impulses, then travels to the brain where it is integrated. This integration may involve a match with familiar and memorised noises or the noise may be perceived as unusual and threatening. In the latter case, information, again via nerve impulses, may pass to the muscles of the throat, ears and hair – the effectors – which produce the familiar response of an aggressive dog with flattened ears, raised back hair and growling. This process is summarised in Figure 5.3.

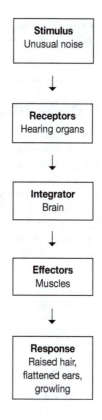

Figure 5.3 Stimulus–response system example in the domestic dog

With some actions there may be shorter pathways within the central nervous system that produce more rapid responses. These reflex actions are automatic, outside our conscious control and contribute to survival. In lower animals such as the earthworm the touch reflex causes the worm to retreat into its burrow; in higher animals reflex actions include swallowing, vomiting, coughing and blinking.

Instinct

The word 'instinct' is often used to describe inherited behaviour patterns that are genetically predetermined and do not require practice or learning. Using the idea of 'nature–nurture', instinct is the nature while environmental influences are the nurture. Instinctive behaviour has particular survival advantages for animals with short life spans or with little parental care, compared with those animals that need to learn new behaviours to survive in changing environments. However, the word 'instinct' is not a very helpful term in understanding animal behaviour because behaviour is a great deal more complex than a simple 'hard-wired' response; indeed, some psychologists prefer not to use the term 'instinct' at all (Smith et al., 2003).

There are three main problems with the term 'instinct'. Firstly, there is the influence of the environment on behaviour: growth and behavioural development are influenced by the external environment which provides food, water and experiences that may interact with genes to determine the exact course of development (Smith et al., 2003). The precise contribution of genetic and environmental factors in the nature–nurture balance varies from case to case. For example, hair colour is largely inherited whereas spoken language has a predominantly environmental input. The song of the chaffinch is an example where both components are at work. If young chaffinches are reared in isolation they still, instinctively, produce a song of about the right length and number of notes but lacking a melody that is recognisable from that of chaffinches recorded in the wild. Chaffinches reared in groups produce a song that is identical to all the others. This imitation, which serves as a social signal, is an example of an environmental contribution to behaviour. The example of the chaffinch song is limited to one species; it is 'species-characteristic' (Barnett, 1967: 172). Similar environmental influences have been seen with cross-fostering of two species of tits, blue tits and great tits, where the social rearing influenced the song-learning process (Johannessen et al., 2006). Other examples of environmental influences are evident with animals such as ducks, geese and deer where they will show *imprinting* by following their mother from shortly after birth or hatching. It appears that the following behaviour is instinctive but which mother to follow is learned. In his classic work with grey-lag geese, Lorenz (1970) demonstrated that newly hatched goslings would imprint on humans if they were taken directly into human care at hatching.

A second problem is that instinctive behaviour may not be observed at all unless there is the appropriate stimulus that can trigger the particular behaviour. In the case of the three-spined stickleback, the stimulus is the red belly of the male during the breeding season that triggers aggressive behaviour in other males; experiments using coloured models are also able to elicit this aggression (Hinde, 1974). In the case of a number of bird species, the gaping beak of the chick showing distinctive throat patterns provides the stimulus that triggers feeding behaviour by the adult bird. The third problem is that there may be some confusion between reflex actions and instinct: a young child may suck any object in its mouth or demonstrate a grabbing response of the hands. It is not easy to determine if these are reflexes or examples of instinctive behaviour.

There is some debate as to whether humans show instinctive responses, despite the use of phrases in our language such as 'acting on instinct'. Child (2004) reports the views of Lorenz that humans have a parental instinct where the sight of a doll elicits parental behaviour in female children. The cues that release this behaviour are thought to include the doll's short face, chubby cheeks and large forehead. Child (2004) also reports Tinbergen's (1951) views that patterns of locomotion, sexual behaviour, sleep, food seeking and parenthood are instinctive in humans.

REFLECTIVE ACTIVITY **5.2**

An experiment – logic or instinct?

Ask a friend to name a favourite example of an everyday food or drink. This should normally be something from a cup or bowl such as tinned fruit, soup, tea, squash, etc. Invite them to try some with you but just before they put anything into their mouth, get them to pause, as you need to stir the contents of the bowl or cup. If you stir with anything which is associated with toilets or bodily functions – such as a toilet brush or nail file but which not yet been used for the purpose, what is their response? Do they logically work out that the item, being as yet unused, is harmless or do they refuse the food and drink? Is a refusal an example of instinctive or learned behaviour?

Learning

So far there has been some limited discussion about the role of learning in terms of the contribution of environmental factors to behaviour and to the survival advantages for animals living in changing circumstances. Many animals survive by being able to learn new behaviours as a response to changing environmental conditions. Many of these changes in the environment influence access and availability to basic needs such as food, water and shelter. One example includes elephants learning and remembering information about sources of water and where to forage. Research into the domi-nance relationships in elephant groups in East Africa (Archie et al., 2006) shows that the groups are dominated by older, larger females rather than smaller, younger ones and that this competition may be because some resources that are critical for elephants are rare or can be usurped, including water, minerals, rubbing posts or high-quality foods. An older, dominant female is more likely to have learned and memorised the geographical location of these resources and can help maintain the sur-vival of the group in more difficult times. Other examples include rats learning about new or novel sources of food and early humans learning about the movements of prey animals during different seasons. Clearly, being able to learn new information about the environment and responding by changing behaviour can reduce the risk of death and even extinction. At this stage the discussion focuses on learning in more detail by looking at the ways in which animals learn by imitation, trial and error and insight learning.

Many animals learn by observing their parents or group members and imitating their behaviour. The previous examples of birdsong involve imitation, as do the responses of escape or crouching by many small and potential prey animals to the sight of a hawk in flight. The food preferences of some herbivores, and young cats observing their mother killing mice, may be behaviours learned by imita-tion. Manning and Stamp Dawkins (1998) mention the unique case of tits opening milk bottle tops by the 1960s as an example of imitation behaviour. However, behaviour is complex and observation and imitation behaviour can be indicated only with large samples where animal B observes animal A performing a behaviour which A has previously learned and B solves the same problem more quickly (Barnett, 1967). Imitation may also be seen in higher animals where simple tool use and grooming may be learned by imitation in chimpanzees. Imitation in human babies between the ages of six and twelve months is an important aspect of learning where they will copy adults' hand and mouth actions (Smith et al., 2003). A variation on learning by imitation is sometimes seen in young children where they may imitate their parents' responses to certain perceived threats such as dogs and spi-ders, even to the extent of the parent actively teaching the child to show caution or fear.

Trial and error learning relies on attempting alternative pathways until a successful one is chosen that offers a reward to reinforce the successful choice. Rats learning successful routes in mazes may build up a chain of right and left turn responses that finally leads to a reward. Unsuccessful routes are reduced over time so that achieving the successful solution becomes increasingly quicker. A child solving a number problem might have to make a number of unsuccessful trials before reaching the correct solution (Child, 2004). In some circumstances, a punishment such as pain may reinforce learning: children often learn to avoid picking up hot objects by trial and error.

Insight learning, sometimes thought of as 'intelligence' or the ability to think, is usually shown in the highest animals, the primates. This has been demonstrated with captive chimpanzees where they have shown insight in being able to stack boxes to reach bananas suspended from the ceiling, and in the wild with chimpanzees of the Gombe National Park in Tanzania with tool use and tool making. The Gombe chimpanzees were observed to form probes to obtain termites and to make simple leaf sponges to obtain rainwater (van Lawick Goodall, 1971). Under laboratory conditions, chimpanzees have shown self-recognition in mirror reflections and have demonstrated insight by practising decep-tion to obtain food. Again under laboratory conditions, a chimpanzee called Washoe was taught sign language; the researchers claimed she could string several signs together to convey meaning, an example being 'water bird' for a swan (Smith et al., 2003). Human insight learning, or the ability to 'think things through', has made us one of the most flexible and successful species on the planet.

Social behaviour

There is such a variety of social interaction in many species of animals from ants to gorillas that it would be impossible to cover even a fraction. As a result, this discussion will concentrate on the behaviour of primates (monkeys, apes and humans), and chimpanzees in particular, as they are one of our closest relatives and it is possible to draw both parallels and contrasts with human behaviour.

Social behaviour has been shown to be particularly important in the early development of young primates. Rearing under extreme conditions of social deprivation has marked consequences on the later development of behaviour. For example, young Rhesus monkeys, reared in the absence of their parents, develop abnormal behaviour such as panic when exposed to unusual sights and noises, clinging to inanimate cloth objects and unusual behaviour patterns with other young Rhesus monkeys. Clearly the lower levels of safety and love and belonging from Maslow's (1970) hierarchy of needs have not been met in these socially deprived monkeys.

Primates have been observed to show a rich set of social behaviour. Like humans, chimpanzees have a large repertoire of gestures, facial expressions and sounds. Van Lawick Goodall (1971) observed many of these over a long period and has been able to describe the precise expressions and calls, and the contexts in which this behaviour is exhibited. Grinning shows variation from a full open grin with upper and lower teeth showing, indicating fear or excitement during and after an attack where a high-ranking male displays close to a subordinate, to a full closed grin expressed when the individual is less frightened. Other facial expressions include a 'display face', a 'play face' and a closed grin that may be used when a low-ranking chimpanzee approaches a superior. Van Lawick Goodall (1971) suggests that this closed grin may have an equivalent in the human nervous or social smile. These facial expressions may be associated with a range of sounds from high-pitched squeaking, whimpering and screaming to hoots, barks and grunts. In addition, chimpanzees also exhibit the social behaviours of grooming, aggressive charges and sexual behaviour. Direct parallels in humans may not be obvious except that humans also rely on a range of expressions and sounds to communicate emotion.

What is the purpose of this advanced level of communication? At one level, communication can aid social interaction in helping to maintain cohesion and reduce internal strife within the group. Many animals exhibit a social ranking system where there is a hierarchy of dominance. Although this hierarchy may change from time to time, this is not a continual process and the ranking system helps to avoid constant group friction and anxiety by using a number of different body signals, such as grooming and facial displays, to maintain the hierarchy with the least amount of aggression. In addition, a hierarchy helps with the defence of the group and can ensure preferential mating with the dominant individuals. Aggression, whether initiated by physiological changes such as changing hormone levels or by external stimuli such as visual 'triggers', carries with it risk factors for the animal. One risk is that aggressive behaviour tends to use up energy which at times of poor food supply may be debilitating, a situation seen with some deer species where males may lose body weight due to constantly chasing away rivals during the mating season. Another risk is that of personal injury; this is frequently avoided by using signals rather than direct aggression. In chimpanzees these signals may be aggressive involving staring, head jerking, raising arms, hunching shoulders, swaggering, stamping, shaking branches, throwing rocks or vocal threats. Alternatively, submissive behaviour may include crouching, reaching out, whimpering, screaming or presenting the rump. With both aggressive and submissive behaviours, the risk of injury is greatly reduced and the social ranking of the group is maintained. Parallels with human behaviour are not easy as humans tend to be more complex with a set of social or cultural norms that reduce aggressive behaviour but animal behaviour studies point to human responses such as a reduction in proximity, frustration and fear (imagined or observed) as ways of reducing aggression (Hinde, 1974).

Observation of chimpanzee behaviour has yielded information about the importance of grooming, both between members of a family group and between members of different families, as a way of maintaining bonds (Van Lawick Goodall, 1971). Recent research (Mitani et al., 2002) indicates that strong social bonds not only develop between members of the same kinship group but also between unrelated male chimpanzees. It appears that these unrelated males develop and maintain alliances with members of the same age and rank, with one explanation for this behaviour being that the group structure and constraints limit the number of kin with whom male chimpanzees can co-operate: these alliances therefore develop between non-kin members. The alliances are themselves maintained by social behaviour such as proximity of individuals, grooming and meat sharing. Although it may not be useful to make direct comparisons with human behaviour, parallels may exist with, for example, the notion of 'personal space' in human cultures where familiar alliance members do not pose a threat to the invasion of personal space that strangers might. Although meat sharing behaviour has been suggested as a way of maintaining male group alliances, Gilby (2006), from observations of Gombe chimpanzees, did not find evidence that male chimpanzees swap meat for grooming or social allegiance. Gilby postulates that meat sharing is an example of 'tolerated scrounging' where the male chimpanzees observed chose to share rather than suffer the costs imposed by persistent beggars (Gilby, 2006: 961). Studies of animal models, such as chimpanzees, may provide useful insights into the origin of sharing in humans.

Obtaining meat by wild chimpanzees is one example of hunting behaviour observed at Gombe. Group members will actively communicate using a wide range of calls during the hunt where their target victims may be a number of species of monkey and even young bushbucks or bush pigs. Van Lawick Goodall (1971) has described this behaviour which is initiated by subtle body movements and slightly raised hair of one of the more dominant males that in turn causes the other chimpanzees in the group to stop resting and grooming and move to station themselves close to trees that would provide escape routes for the intended victim.

> The hunting seems to be a much more deliberate, purposeful activity and often at such times the different individuals of a chimpanzee group show quite remarkable co-operation.

(Van Lawick Goodall, 1971: 183)

Partially linked to hunting behaviour is territorial behaviour. Observations of chimpanzees show that they live in communities that contain adult males, females and immature individuals and that members associate in groups that vary in size and composition over time. Encounters between individuals of neighbouring communities are typically hostile with males defending territories by responding aggressively to intruders and patrolling the boundaries of their own territories and entering those of neighbours. Mitani and Watts (2005) report that there is considerable variation in the frequency of patrolling and that factors such as hunting activity, fruit availability, intruder pressure and the presence of females available for mating may affect patrolling behaviour. During these patrols, chimpanzees may kill or be killed by neighbours. Although patrolling may be advantageous in expanding territory size and with it food supply and reproductive success, these patrols are likely to be dangerous and costly. These costs are reduced by patrolling in large groups and by specific patrolling behaviour that differs from the normal group social behaviour of chimpanzees.

The social behaviour of non-human species, particularly chimpanzees, is often unique in maintaining their social order and using the survival advantages of this to obtain food and reproductive success. Although questions remain, there may be parallels here with human behaviour, including some of the more sinister aspects of our own species' behaviour.

REFLECTIVE ACTIVITY **5.3**

Thinking about aggression in humans

From your own experience, consider children's behaviour at the following stages: toddler (around 2 years), at nursery school stage (4 to 6 years) and early teens (12 to 14 years). What kinds of aggressive behaviours may be shown at these stages and how is this aggression reduced within the culture you are familiar with?

Observation of different types of animal behaviour has provided ways of understanding our own behaviour. We now turn to human learning, how the brain works during learning and how this learning can change.

Images of the working brain

The relatively new field of neuroscience covers the study of the nervous system and brain, and the biological basis of consciousness, perception, memory and learning. As such it is interdisciplinary in nature, drawing on information from biology, psychology and social and cultural studies. Some of the findings from neuroscience may be in conflict with some of our preconceptions, for example the notion of pre-determined learning styles. Firstly, the brain has three main regions: the *lower brain* that controls basic sensory and motor functions such as smell and movement; the *limbic brain* that deals with biological rhythms, memory and emotions; and the *neocortex* that controls thinking, reasoning and language use. Secondly, the brain is not a computer – it is not 'hard wired' and can change. Stroke victims provide evidence for this where they are often able to regain much of the speech and co-ordination they had before the stroke damage. Thirdly, the brain changes with use where mental concentration and effort can alter the brain's physical structure – if we consider the millions of nerve endings with their chemical transmitters it is possible to imagine the countless number of arrangements and connections.

With new developments in technology it is possible to map certain regions of the brain associated with different functions. Previously, the only way of being able to determine which areas of the brain were associated with certain functions was by using a 'deficit model': a polite reference to localised brain damage and its observable effects on behaviour and understanding. In addition, with the new technology it is possible to get a dynamic view of brain activity as it is working. The new technologies work externally to the brain and include electroencephalography (EEG), which records the electrical activity of the brain by using electrodes fixed into a scalp cap, and functional magnetic resonance imaging (fMRI) which is able to scan the brain and measure changes in blood flow to show which areas are active. Using these technologies, cognitive neuroscientists are able to investigate changes in the brain under experimental conditions that may involve memory, interest, attention, spatial awareness, language and mathematical reasoning. A number of examples is mentioned here to give some idea of the possibilities for this technology.

The first example is concerned with reading and dyslexia. fMRI studies indicate that certain areas of the brain are involved with reading but that these areas differ between young and adult readers. Correlations between brain activity during reading and reading ability ascertained from standardised tests show increased involvement of the left temporal and frontal regions of the brain, associated with phonology and semantics, as reading develops. However, studies with children with developmental dyslexia, those who fail to learn to read normally although of average intelligence and educational opportunity, show less activation of some brain regions when compared with typically developing readers. Remedial work on phonological skills and letter-sound conversion can normalise the situation but studies have been conducted only with reading English; there is some evidence of different brain areas being used with mature readers of other languages (Goswami, 2006).

A second example of the application of neuroscience is with understanding number and dyscalculia which occurs when a child experiences unexpected difficulty in learning arithmetic despite adequate schooling and social environment. Goswami (2006) reports an EEG study that showed that when five-year-olds perform a number comparison task (such as 'is 4 larger/smaller than 5?') they show similar effects to adults but that their reaction times show they were three times slower to organise their responses. This slow acquisition of calculation ability with this age group may have implications for primary education. Work using fMRI studies with children with dyscalculia is at an early stage but there is a suggestion that those with poor number processing skills may need to be assessed for damage to the parietal region of the brain (Dowker, 2004).

A third example of brain imaging concerns children with short attention spans, particularly those with attention deficit hyperactivity disorder (ADHD) who pose particular challenges in school classrooms. EEG results from 'attention trained' and control groups of four-year-olds are reported as showing a 'hint of an effect' (Goswami, 2006: 5) but this research is still at an early stage.

These limited examples illustrate some of the applications of cognitive neuroscience to learning; there are many more that deal with emotion, musical ability, spatial memory and social cognition. These examples also show that some areas of neuroscience are still at an early stage of research and development: much further work on brain imaging in cognitive neuroscience is needed. Some of those involved in education and educational policy have a tendency to jump on the bandwagon of new ideas if they perceive them to provide rapid solutions for improvement. Some current examples of these may be about the domination of the left brain over the right brain or the identification of preferred learning styles such as visual, auditory and kinaesthetic (VAK). There needs to be an increased awareness by educators of the importance of this evidence-based work in neuroscience if it is to be applied, and some of the popular but over-simplistic applications of neuroscience to education are to be viewed in a critical light (Geake and Cooper, 2003; Goswami, 2006).

Can learning be accelerated?

In recent years there has been an interest in *thinking skills* as an approach to problem-solving, verbal reasoning and critical thinking. Research in science education and later in mathematics and technology education has shown that using intervention strategies can accelerate learning. The cognitive acceleration through science education (CASE), cognitive acceleration through mathematics education (CAME) and the cognitive acceleration through technology education (CATE) (Kings College, 2006: online) are research and development projects informed by the theories of Piaget (Inhelder and Piaget, 1958) and Vygotsky (1978) on children's learning. The teaching strategies prepare pupils at the preliminary stage by introducing the problem and terminology (concrete preparation), challenge students' current level of thinking (cognitive conflict) and encourage them to construct knowledge together (social construction), think about their own thinking (metacognition) and transfer ideas and approaches to new problems or contexts (bridging). CASE intervention strategies at ages 11 to 13 have been shown to increase grades in examinations at age 16 in science, mathematics and English by moving children on from Piaget's concrete operational stage, based on description, to a formal operational stage that involves more abstract thought and reasoning. CASE materials, for example, include understanding variables, proportionality, probability, correlation, classification and modelling (Keele University, 2006a). Although cognitive acceleration or thinking skills approaches are not just limited to CASE, CAME and CATE as other schemes have been used, including philosophy for primary pupils, these have found favour in a large number of secondary schools and have been taken up by several local education authorities as part of their school improvement agenda (Keele University, 2006b). Unlike some initiatives in education, cognitive acceleration is firmly based on a body of research evidence.

SUMMARY OF KEY POINTS

In this chapter we have reviewed the survival needs of animals and the survival and social needs of humans. We have discussed the problems with defining behaviour that is genetic or instinctive and that which results from learning. In particular, we have considered the complex interplay between the effects of instinct and the environment. The area of social behaviour, so important to our own species, has been compared and contrasted in the context of other animals, principally our nearest primate relative, the chimpanzee. We have reviewed the contribution of neuroscience to understanding human learning and some of its current problems and, finally, have looked at ways in which learning can be accelerated.

Archie, E. A., Morrison, T. A., Foley, C. A. H., Moss, C. J. and Alberts, S. C. (2006) 'Dominance rank relationships among wild female African elephants, Loxodonta africana', *Animal Behaviour*, 71: 117–27.

Barnett, S. A. (1967) *'Instinct' and 'Intelligence'*. London: MacGibbon & Kee.

Child, D. (2004) *Psychology and the Teacher*, 7th edn. London: Continuum.

Darwin, C. (1968) *The Origin of Species by Means of Natural Selection*. Harmondsworth: Penguin Books.

Dowker, A. (2004) *Dyscalculia in Children: Its Characteristics and Possible Interventions*. Paper presented at OECD Literacy and Numeracy Network Meeting, El Escorial, Spain, March. Online: **http://www.brookes.ac.uk/schools/education/rescon/ocnef/dyscalculia.doc!** (accessed 27 September 2006).

Geake, J. and Cooper, P. (2003) 'Cognitive neuroscience: implications for education?', *Westminster Studies in Education*, 26 (1): 7–14.

Gilby, I. C. (2006) 'Meat sharing among the Gombe chimpanzees: harassment and reciprocal exchange', *Animal Behaviour*, 71: 953–63.

Goswami, U. (2006) 'Neuroscience and education: from research to practice', *Nature Reviews Neuroscience*. Online: **http://www.educ.cam.ac.uk/download/ug/Goswami-2006-NatureRevNeuroscience-online.pdf** (accessed 26 September 2006).

Hinde, R. A. (1974) *Biological Bases of Human Social Behaviour*. New York: McGraw-Hill.

Inhelder, B. and Piaget, J. (1958) *The Growth of Logical Thinking from Childhood to Adolescence*. London: Routledge & Kegan Paul.

Johannessen, L. E., Slagsvold, T. and Hansen, B. T. (2006) 'Effects of social rearing conditions on song structure and repertoire size: experimental evidence from the field', *Animal Behaviour*, 72: 83–95.

Keele University (2006a) *What is CASE?* Online: **http://www.keele.ac.uk/depts/ed/caseweb/whatis case.htm** (accessed 20 October 2006).

Keele University (2006b) *Why use CASE?* Online: **http://www.keele.ac.uk/depts/ed/caseweb/whyuse case.htm** (accessed 20 October 2006).

Kings College (2006) *Cognitive Acceleration*. Online: **http://www.kcl.ac.uk/schools/sspp/education/ research/cognitive.html** (accessed 20 October 2006).

Lorenz, K. (1970) *Studies in Animal and Human Behaviour*, Volume 1. London: Methuen.

Manning, A. and Stamp Dawkins, M. (1998) *An Introduction to Animal Behaviour*, 5th edn. Cambridge: Cambridge University Press.

Maslow, A. H. (1970) *Motivation and Personality*, 2nd edn. New York: Harper & Row.

Mitani, J. C. and Watts, D. P. (2005) 'Correlates of territorial boundary patrol behaviour in wild chimpanzees', *Animal Behaviour*, 70: 1079–86.

Mitani, J. C., Watts, D. P., Pepper, J. W. and Merriwether, D. A. (2002) 'Demographic and social constraints on male chimpanzee behaviour', *Animal Behaviour*, 64: 727–37.

Roberts, M., Reiss, M. and Monger, G. (1993) *Biology: Principles and Processes.* Walton-on-Thames, Surrey: Thomas Nelson.

Smith, P., Cowie, H. and Blades, M. (2003) *Understanding Children's Development.* Oxford: Blackwell.

Tinbergen, N. (1951) *A Study of Instinct.* Oxford: Oxford University Press.

Van Lawick-Goodall, J. (1971) *In the Shadow of Man.* London: Collins.

Vygotsky, L. S. (1978) *Mind in Society.* Cambridge, MA: Harvard University Press.

6 Social and emotional development

Paula Zwozdiak-Myers

Learning objectives

By the end of this chapter you should be able to:

- **recognise individual differences in patterns of attachment behaviour;**
- **understand how early experiences of attachment behaviour relate to feelings of (in)security across an individual's life span;**
- **understand how temperamental differences interrelate with attachment behaviours and parental (in)sensitivity;**
- **recognise how children come to understand, and respond to, the feelings of others and how to regulate their own emotions.**

Introduction

The first part of this chapter examines attachment theory and provides the basis for coming to understand how children's emotional worlds are shaped by their experiences. The influence of temperament on behavioural style and the relationship of temperament with attachment and parental (in)sensitivity are introduced. It then draws upon research findings from prominent theorists to explore how emotion is used to shape children's development of understanding and 'theory of mind' and how emotions can be regulated. The chapter presents Mead's theoretical perspective on the importance of children's play experiences in coming to develop a concept of self, along with the growth of social competence in coming to understand the perspectives of others.

Attachment theory

One of John Bowlby's goals in developing his theory of attachment was to position some of Sigmund Freud's insights about early childhood experiences and relationships in a scientifically defensible framework. He challenged Freud's assumptions that infants were totally dependent and organised their behaviour around purely instinctive drives, replacing them with notions that infants were competent, innately interested in their environment and could exercise some control over managing their behaviour.

Ideas proposed by theorists (e.g. Harlow and Harlow, 1969; Van Lawick-Goodall, 1968) as to how such animal behaviours as bonding, hunting, protecting and nurturing their young influence patterns of attachment, particularly those of primates, are also significant to Bowlby's theory. He believed that individual differences in the quality and quantity of care provided by caregivers would inevitably give rise to differences in development and to emergent secure or insecure control systems. Bowlby hypothesised that proximity of a young child to his/her primary caregiver or attachment figure was the principal function of this control system, one that is driven by the basic human need to form close affectionate bonds (Maslow, 1970).

Regarded by many theorists as the founder of attachment theory, Bowlby (1969/1982) describes attachment behaviour as a 'motivational control system' that aims to promote feelings of security and safety in early infancy and childhood through a child's relationship with his/her primary caregiver or attachment figure. Attachment behaviours such as clinging, shadowing, searching, calling and crying are observable outcomes of this inner system that is triggered and becomes activated in times of illness, tiredness, distress, danger and exploration: times when the young child will actively seek contact with and proximity to a specific caregiver. Attachment can therefore be viewed as a special type of social relationship that involves an affective bond; this is a major developmental milestone in the young child's life. Importantly, it is also the context within which the young child learns to regulate emotion (Sroufe, 1996).

Individual differences in attachment behaviour

Research suggests that how the primary caregiver responds to the young child in situations, as described above, rather than characteristics that are distinctive to each child (e.g. temperament), will shape attachment behaviours of the child as s/he develops along with expectations concerning future attachment relationships. Crowell and Treboux (1995), for example, report that the caregiver who is available, responsive, comforting and protective when danger or stressful situations present themselves promote attachment behaviour. This enables the young child to explore his/her environment, under normal circumstances, with confidence and security in light of the knowledge that the primary caregiver is there should the need arise. In broad terms, sensitivity by the caregiver in responding to the young child's needs results in secure attachment whereas insensitivity gives rise to insecure attachment.

Mary Ainsworth, also a prominent theorist and pioneer of attachment theory, observed mother–child relationships and documented their interactions and behaviours. With colleagues (Ainsworth et al., 1978) she designed the Strange Situation Procedure (SSP), detailed in Activity 6.1 to determine how much trust young children aged 12–24 months placed on the accessibility of their attachment figure. Observations were categorised in terms of how well the young child used the caregiver as a secure base for exploration and was comforted by the caregiver following episodes of separation.

REFLECTIVE ACTIVITY 6.1

The Strange Situation Procedure

Read through the following protocols and procedures for the Strange Situation Procedure (SSP). For ethical reasons a child can be withdrawn from the SSP at any stage if showing signs of extreme distress.

Key: M – mother or caregiver; C – young child; S – stranger

Approximately 20-minute session undertaken in a comfortably equipped room and divided into the following episodes.

1. *M and C in room, C explores for 3 minutes.*

2. *S enters, sits for 1 minute, talks to M for 1 minute and gets onto the floor to play with C for 1 minute.*

3. *M leaves, S plays with C then if possible withdraws, up to 3 minutes.*

4. *M returns, S unobtrusively leaves, M settles C and then sits down for 3 minutes.*

5. *M leaves, C is alone for up to 3 minutes.*

6. *S returns, attempts to settle C then if possible withdraws, up to 3 minutes.*

REFLECTIVE ACTIVITY **6.1** *continued*

7. M comes in, S unobtrusively leaves, M settles C and sits down.

Identify at least three potentially stressful components encountered by the young child.

Drawing from your own experience how do you believe a young child with whom you are familiar would interact in the above strange situation episodes?

Support your response with possible reasons.

Ainsworth et al. (1978) identified three different patterns of attachment behaviour and labelled these: *insecure-avoidant* (A); *secure* (B); and *insecure-ambivalent* (C). Some years later, studies by Main and Solomon (1990) recognised a fourth category: *insecure-disorganised* (D). Characteristic behaviours of each category include the following.

A Insecure-avoidant: *children who do not appear to be distressed and either ignore, avoid or pull away from the caregiver upon reunion.*

B Secure: *children who either actively seek proximity to their caregiver when reunited or acknowledge them from a distance with a wave or smile, openly communicate their feelings of distress and readily return to exploration.*

C Insecure-ambivalent: *children who combine strong contact (and often hostility) with resistant contact, or remain inconsolable and are unable to return to exploration.*

D Insecure-disorganised: *children who exhibit a range of undirected behavioural responses such as freezing, head banging and hand clapping and appear disorientated by producing conflicting motivations, e.g. even in the presence of the caregiver they demonstrate the desire to escape from the situation. Experiences of physical/sexual abuse and severe neglect are often associated with this pattern of behaviour.* (Cichetti and Beeghly, 1987)

Secure patterns of attachment are demonstrated when young children both seek and receive comfort, reassurance and protection in times of danger and distress. When the child reaches away to explore, s/he does so with confidence and knowledge that the caregiver will provide a secure base of protection.

Insecure patterns of attachment (avoidant, ambivalent, disorganised) are demonstrated when young children seek comfort, reassurance and protection in times of danger or distress and the response received from the caregiver is rejection or inconsistent, even threatening, behaviour. Feelings of anxiety arise as the young child becomes uncertain and confused as to the responsiveness of the caregiver should problems arise. To reduce this anxiety, young children frequently develop strategies to complement the behaviour of their attachment figure so that they can function within that relationship. In terms of the *insecure-avoidant* pattern of attachment (e.g. where the young child's attachment behaviour has regularly been responded to by rejection), when the child experiences a stressful or dangerous situation s/he will avoid looking at the attachment figure and does not seek contact. This particular strategy reduces the potential occurrence of rejection and feelings associated with distress (Main and Goldwyn, 1984). By way of contrast, the *insecure-ambivalent* pattern of attachment (e.g. where the young child's attachment behaviour has been responded to with inconsistency by the attachment figure) has been found to give rise to heightened attachment behaviour by the young child (Cassidy and Berlin, 1994).

To determine how secure the child feels with respect to attachment, narrative and story-stem approaches are frequently used. George and Solomon (in Howe et al., 1999) gave children a story line to complete and dolls of 'mummy and daddy' to use, to measure how the child feels about being left with a babysitter when parents go away for the night. *Insecure-avoidant* children acted as though everything was fine and that they were secure, not allowing feelings of anxiety or concern to show. *Secure* children were found to express concerns about being left that became readily resolved upon the parents return. *Insecure-ambivalent* children found difficulty in expressing emotional perspectives and recounted stories of what they do when their parents are away. Positive joyful experiences were often exaggerated as compared with negative distressing experiences that were frequently ignored. *Insecure-disorganised* children were apt to introduce an element of fear into their narrative, yet were unable to resolve the situation, as parents had been perceived as physically and emotionally unavailable.

Parental influence on attachment patterns

There is an assumption that, as the young child develops, the stability of the attachment pattern will be influenced by continuity or discontinuity of parental care. Bowlby (1969/1982) suggests that if an attachment pattern undergoes any form of transformation in childhood, it should reflect a corresponding change in the quality of child–parent interactions.

It could be argued that a mother has a natural bond with a child immediately following birth yet the father must establish a bond after the child is born. Research by Klaus et al. (1995) has shown that fathers who have early contact with their newborn develop a strong attachment with them in the months following birth. Early patterns of attachment observed between mother–child and father–child have shown some notable differences. Geiger (1996), for example, reports that, during mother–child interactions, the mother was viewed as nurturing and affectionate towards the child. During father–child interactions, however, the father was viewed as having a more physical relationship with the child, one that is associated more with affiliation and play. These observations raise some important questions, for example:

- To what extent does the gender of the caregiver/parent influence patterns of attachment with the child?
- To what extent does the gender of the child influence patterns of attachment demonstrated by the caregiver/parent?

The quality of marital relationships between parents has been shown to affect the security of a child's attachment to parents. Markiewicz et al. (2001) found that marital conflict or dysfunctional relationships influenced the attachment security of children and adolescents to the mother, in that the effectiveness and responsiveness of her parenting was significantly reduced, and to the father, in that his physical and emotional availability was lessened as he became marginalised within the family and distanced from the children. Some adults elect to stay together 'for the sake of the children' yet it must be remembered that children have their own issues as they develop that need to be nurtured. The loss of a parent can also disrupt parent–child attachment bonds that Furukawa et al. (1999) suggest could lead to future impairments in an individual's capacity to establish relationships.

A new way of approaching attachment is developed during adolescence. Allen and Land (1999: 319) suggest that attachment bonds between parents and adolescents are *treated by many adolescents more like ties that restrain than like ties that anchor and secure, and a key task of adolescence is to develop autonomy so as no longer to need to rely (as much) on parents' support when making one's way in the world.* It is important to note that the relationship between parent and child is not less significant during adolescence, rather it changes as the adolescent's goal is to seek more autonomy. Weiss (1982) notes that adolescents who show autonomy-seeking behaviour are usually those who have a positive relationship with parents and feel secure in their explorations as they have confidence that parents are always there for them. Adolescent development is explored more fully in Chapter 8.

It is beyond the scope of this chapter to consider in depth the wealth of research studies and literature that further understanding as to the innumerable determinants of caregiver/parent–child relationships and attachment (in)security. Belsky (1984), however, presents a process model that succinctly distinguishes between three important major influences.

1. Psychological resources of the caregiver/parent – the quality of 'working' models or internal representations of relationships (translated into sensitivity and responsiveness of parenting skills as opposed to child abuse and neglect); stability of mental health and personality traits (negative influences include aggression, anxiety, suspicion); and, importantly, their developmental history.

2. Contextual factors and sources of support – partner, relatives, friends and significant others; social, health and educational network of professional organisations; socio-economic status.

3. Characteristics of the child – temperament; maturation; emotional sensibility; individual learning and developmental needs.

Working models or representations of attachment relationships

A central developmental strand in attachment theory is the hypothesis that early child–parent relationships are prototypes for love and romantic relationships in later adult life. Building upon Freudian perspectives, Bowlby strongly argues that child–parent interactions are continuous in the sense that personal experiences gained are recycled and will feed back into the attachment behaviour system. For example, child–parent relationships not only affect the development of individual personality characteristics, but moreover play a central role in the translation of family patterns across generations (intergenerational transmission) and subsequent patterns of family organisation.

Working models, or representations, of attachment relationships can be viewed as affective/cognitive constructs that develop during behavioural interaction and communication between the young child and his/her principle caregivers. Individual differences, as identified above, emerge through the expression of attachment behaviour within the context of attachment relationships. Patterns of attachment initially reflect expectations about the principle caregivers' likely responses to various situations. The young, developing child abstracts from these expectations a set of assumptions as to how close relationships function and how they are used in stressful situations and everyday life.

An individual's model of attachment incorporates assumptions about the roles of both child and caregiver in relationships and *even when the models of self and other have become distinct, they represent obverse sides of the same relationship and cannot be understood without reference to each other* (Bretherton, 1985: 12).

Bowlby (1980: 55) considers that both the nature of the representational models a person builds and how attachment behaviour becomes organised are

> the results of learning experiences that start during the first year of life and are repeated almost daily throughout childhood and adolescence ... both the cognitive and action components ... become so engrained that they come to operate automatically and outside awareness.

Working models that develop as a result of recurrent experiences and interactions with attachment figures are presumed to act as a filter for later experiences and relationships. When expressed this way, they can be viewed as prototypes. Main (1991), for example, found that a protective strategy drawn upon in the case of insecure representations often involves the exclusion of certain information from awareness as an adaptation to attachment figures that were found to be inconsistent and/or unresponsive.

These affective/cognitive constructs provide the basis for action and behaviour in a range of situations. In principle they can be revised and reconstructed once significant attachment relationships have been experienced. Bowlby suggests that, in adult life, patterns of attachment can change when the development of *formal operational thought* (Piaget, 1976) is combined with the influence of new emotional relationships. Individuals at this stage of development should have the capacity to reflect upon and reinterpret the meaning behind past and present experiences (Crowell and Treboux, 1995).

Bowlby's conceptual metaphors (Bretherton, 1985) of *working models or mental representations* led to a shift in attachment research from earlier initial observations of young children's behaviour toward assessments that seek to identify cognitive and emotional underpinnings of the attachment behaviour system across an individual's lifespan. His constructs are important as they:

● help us to understand the effects of early experience on subsequent behaviour and development;

● provide a mechanism through which an individual's subjective view and experience can be seen to influence behaviour and development;

● help to explain attachment responses in new situations;

● provide a way of understanding attachment as a link that connects people across time and space;

● allow for a lifespan perspective of the attachment behaviour system to be realised.

Attachment theory provides a framework not only for understanding emotional reactions in young children, but also a framework for understanding loneliness, love and grief in adults. Ainsworth (1991: 38) suggests that attachment relationships between adults can function on a range of levels that incorporate companionship, sense of competence, sexual bonds and shared purpose or experience. Adult attachment relationships are distinguished between those that provide feelings of *security and place* (without which there is loneliness and restlessness) and those that provide *companionship or guidance*, opportunities to share common interests and experiences, feelings of alliance, assistance and competence and opportunities to feel needed.

Hazan and Shaver (1987) adapted patterns of childhood attachment to adult romantic relationships. They suggest a developmental programme in the acquisition of these elements across adolescence. In early adolescence, for example, close relationships are characterised by the desire for physical closeness or seeking proximity. This develops into relationships with the partner as a safe haven, characterised by seeking the partner in a time of need or emergency. In late adolescence, the partner is used more as a secure base (Crowell and Waters, 1994).

REFLECTIVE ACTIVITY 6.2

Measuring styles of attachment

Adult attachment is commonly measured through the Adult Attachment Interview and Self-Report questionnaires along two dimensions.

● *Anxiety – beliefs about self-worth and being accepted/rejected by others.*

● *Avoidance – beliefs about taking risks in avoiding or approaching others.*

Access and complete the online version of the Experiences in Close Relationships – Revised (ECR-R) questionnaire at: **http://www.web-research-design.net/cgi-bin/crq/crq.pl**.

How has this measure rated you in terms of secure, preoccupied, dismissive or fearful style of attachment?

Do you believe this measure accurately reflects your attachment style?

What has this research instrument actually measured?

Is this sufficient in determining your attachment style?

Discuss your views and observations with a colleague.

Temperament

Bates (1989: 4) describes temperament as *biologically rooted individual differences in behaviour tendencies that are present early in life and are relatively stable across various kinds of situation and over the course of time.* The New York Longitudinal Study (NYLS) of the 1950s focused on how temperamental qualities influence (mal)adjustment during childhood (Thomas and Chess, 1977). A nine-dimensional framework to describe temperament was designed for use with children from infancy to adolescence to examine how well a child fits in at home, school and with their friends. The particular behaviours associated with each trait incorporate the following:

- *activity level* – the amount of physical energy (high or low) a child displays;
- *rhythmicity* – the predictability and regularity of the child's biological functions (sleeping, eating, bowel movements);
- *approach/withdrawal* – the child's initial response to new people and new environments (positive or negative);
- *adaptability* – how the child adjusts to change (easily or with resistance);
- *intensity* – the energy levels of a positive or negative response (calm as opposed to excitement);
- *mood* – the child's general demeanour and tendency toward cheerful or stormy, happy or unhappy;
- *distractibility* – whether the child can concentrate and stay focused on a task or is easily distracted by what is happening in the environment;
- *persistence* – the child's ability to engage with a task for lengthy periods of time to finish it (attention span) or gives up easily when he becomes frustrated;
- *sensitivity or sensory threshold* – how the child responds to change within his environment from such external stimuli as bright lights, texture and loud noises.

Findings from the NYLS suggest that many infants (approximately 65 per cent) could be categorised into one of three distinct groups: *easy* (40 per cent), *slow to warm up* (15 per cent) and *difficult* (10 per cent). The remaining 35 per cent, however, were not easy to classify using this research instrument.

Easy infants were found to adapt readily to new experiences, have normal sleeping and eating patterns and generally display positive emotions and moods. *Slow to warm up infants* were found to adapt slowly to new experiences, yet gradually accept them after recurrent exposure, and demonstrate a low level of activity and a tendency to withdraw from new people and new situations. *Difficult infants* were found to have irregular sleeping and eating patterns, to be extremely irritable, fussy and emotional, and tended to cry a great deal. These broad patterns of temperamental qualities were found to be relatively stable throughout childhood and adolescence and were reflected across a range of different cultures. (To avoid negative connotations associated with the terms difficult and slow to warm up, children that display temperament issues are now referred to as *spirited*).

Recent research (Guyer et al., 2006) of children with extremely shy temperament or 'behavioural inhibition' reports heightened brain activity response to any prominent event, for example differences in base line levels of the stress hormone cortisol, heart rate and electroencephalogram (ECG) compared with children who do not exhibit this trait. The researchers suggest that this kind of temperament early in life is a risk factor for subsequent development of mental disorders. Adolescents in the functional magnetic resonance imaging (fMRI) study that had been monitored from infancy for temperamental characteristics associated with behavioural inhibition were found to be more fearful than others, have a more severe, constant type of shyness, have difficulty in adapting to social situations, are over-vigilant and hesitant in nature and react strongly to new experiences.

Although many researchers consider that genetic and biological influences (*nature*) are determinants of temperament, others advocate that environmental experiences (*nurture*) can also shape a child's temperament. *Easy infants* who adapt swiftly to family routines and respond well to siblings, for example, will encounter different experiences from those who display high levels of activity, irregular eating or sleeping patterns along with a low sensory threshold toward bright lights and loud noises such as the slamming of a door.

Interactions between children and their siblings and parents/caregivers can lead either to the creation of a harmonious household or to a stressful family life. *Goodness of fit* relates to whether there is a match or mismatch between family members and the child. For instance, a highly active child might frustrate a slow-paced parent or if both have high levels of intensity and physical energy this could result in conflict. Thus what might initially be construed a behavioural issue could be nothing more than a mismatch between the child's temperament and the parent/caregiver's personality.

It is vitally important to recognise individual differences in the behavioural tendencies of each family member so that strategies can be put in place to prevent or manage problems should they arise. A child who demonstrates inhibited behaviour, for example, with enough support can become less shy and withdrawn. Similarly, a child who is slow-paced can be given more lead time to get ready for activities or school. During the years that precede puberty, a child's temperament may undergo change, yet following puberty the importance of temperament is somewhat diminished as the personality of the adolescent becomes more fully developed.

REFLECTIVE ACTIVITY **6.3**

Using a temperament scale

Use the nine-dimensional temperament framework devised by Thomas and Chess (1977) in Figure 6.1 to estimate where a child (*) you know well and his parent/caregiver (^) are positioned along the scale.

Identify traits that match or are mismatched between them.

Discuss whether the occurrence of match and mismatch appears to influence the interpersonal relationship between the child and his/her parent/caregiver.

Emotion and 'theory of mind'

A series of observational studies undertaken by Judy Dunn (1987) in natural settings focused upon the family interactions of pre-school children to examine how emotion was used to shape children's development of understanding. Her major findings indicate the following.

- In emotionally charged family relationships (those wherein expressions of empathy, teasing, joking and humour are frequently conveyed) children gain social skills and interpersonal understanding.

- The ability of children to consider the feelings and perspectives of others serves both self-interest and empathy. By the age of 3, clear distinctions become evident in how children respond to a sibling in distress. For example, when the child is the source of a sibling's distress, he is likely to either ignore or exacerbate the situation further whereas if another factor caused the sibling's distress, he is more likely to provide comfort and reassurance.

- As language evolves, communication channels are extended. Language is increasingly used by children to question and comment on emotions, negotiate family rules, conventions and consequences, challenge boundaries and discuss issues related to blame and responsibility.

- Individual differences of how children use language to talk about their emotions and feelings appear to be related to their development of social understanding. Children who engaged in play and conversations about feelings and relationships, for example, were most likely to succeed in tasks that required perspective taking.

[Activity level]

High..Low

[Rhythmicity]

Regular...Irregular

[Approach/withdrawal]

Bold..Cautious

[Adaptability]

Rapid...Gradual

[Intensity]

Calm..Excited

[Mood]

Cheerful...Stormy

[Distractibility]

Rarely..Easily

[Persistence – attention span]

Lengthy..Short/intermittent

[Sensitivity – sensory threshold]

Non-reactive..Sensitive

Figure 6.1 Nine-dimensional temperament framework
Adapted from Thomas and Chess (1977)

Dunn's findings provide insight as to how emotional understanding and social development is embedded within families that are emotionally charged and exhibit intimate relationships. The concept of 'theory of mind', when applied to emotion, can provide an alternative explanation of how children come to understand, and respond to, the feelings of others: for example, to what extent a child can take account of another person's perspectives in terms of beliefs (how they perceive a particular situation) and desires (likes and dislikes).

Harris et al. (1987) conducted a series of studies to examine how children demonstrate their understanding of emotions. Of particular interest were the more complex emotions such as guilt, pride and shame that cannot readily be discerned through particular facial expressions or characteristic behaviours, as compared with more easily discernible emotions such as happy, angry and sad. It was hypothesised that an understanding of the more complex emotions requires quite sophisticated perspective taking. Children of different ages were presented with a range of simple (happy, angry, sad) and more complex (disappointed, relieved, grateful, guilty) emotion words and asked to write a story that reflected situations in which those particular emotions would be experienced. Findings revealed that for:

- 5 year olds – simple emotions (sad, angry and happy) could be recognised within the narratives (those associated with particular facial expressions);
- 7 year olds – more complex emotions (excited, grateful, guilty, jealous, proud, worried) could be recognised within the narratives (those not necessarily associated with particular facial or behavioural expressions);
- 10–14 year olds – in addition to all the above, such emotions as disappointed and relieved could be recognised within the narratives.

A notable extension to earlier studies (arising from the premise that judgements based solely on an individual's desires and beliefs can often be unreliable) was to encourage children to enter more deeply into the mind of the character within the story, in other words to take an *imaginative leap*. Harris (1989: 52) suggests that pretend play can act as a powerful agent in developing children's social perspective-taking skills, as it is *the key that unlocks the minds of other people, and allows the child temporarily to enter into their plans, hopes and fears*.

George Herbert Mead's (1863–1931) theory of play has significance here as it emphasises how, through play, children gain an awareness of who they are. In early childhood, for example, role-play is important for the development of self. In this play stage, children begin to form a self by taking such roles as nurse, teacher, parent or sibling and within these roles direct their actions toward him/herself. Through the experience of team games and wider social group membership in later childhood, children develop a mature sense of self as social beings, and the concept of the 'generalised other', *a generalized role or standpoint from which he views himself and his behaviour* (Mead, 1934, cited in Meltzer,1967: 11), comes to be realised. Harris (1989: 92) suggests this important development has arisen as the child needs to *switch from seeing people simply as agents to seeing them as observers of their own agency, observers who assess their responsibility in matching up to normative standards*. In other words, children need to extend their 'theory of mind' to embrace the standards of another individual alongside their own desires and beliefs.

REFLECTIVE ACTIVITY **6.4**

The cultural life of playgrounds

Opie (1993), Sluckin (1987) and Blatchford (1994) have undertaken research into the cultural life of playgrounds. Their findings suggest that playgrounds reflect a culture that:

- *is unique to children;*
- *mirrors that of adult society;*

REFLECTIVE ACTIVITY **6.4** *continued*

● *perpetuates negative behaviours associated with aggression, bullying and teasing, respectively.*

Examine each of these studies and consider the implications of their findings on children's social and emotional development as they interact with others in the playground.

Think back to your own experiences of life within the playground and consider how they relate to findings from the above research studies.

Regulating emotions

The expression of emotions is guided by *display rules*, or rule systems that serve as indicators as to what is, and what is not, considered appropriate to specific situations. Some display rules are shared between members of a particular cultural group within society, whereas others are more personal. The ability to use the display rules in order to regulate the expression of emotions develops both through maturation and socialisation. The former is demonstrated as children learn to temper the extremes of emotions experienced *as the spontaneity and volatility of the infant is displaced by a more measured and stable demeanour* (Woodhead et al., 1995: 169). The latter is demonstrated as children learn to channel their expression into socially acceptable behaviour and acquire coping strategies to deal with strong feelings. To better understand such strategies, reflect upon your own experiences as you work through the scenario in Activity 6.5.

REFLECTIVE ACTIVITY **6.5**

Regulating the expression of emotions

Scenario: It is your 15th birthday – family members have gathered and present you with a beautifully wrapped gift. Judging by its size and shape you already know it is not what you had asked for.

● *What are your immediate feelings and thoughts?*

● *Do you overtly express or covertly suppress these feelings and thoughts?*

● *How do you react when, having opened the gift, you realise that you actively dislike it?*

● *To what extent has your overt behaviour been influenced by:*

  – *socially approved display rules?*

  – *interpersonal relationships between you and members of your family?*

  – *your concern about the feelings and emotions of others?*

● *If you had opened the gift privately, would you have regulated your feelings and emotions in the same way?*

During any given day, children encounter a range of situations that might require them to *mask* their true feelings and *conform* to display rules that govern interpersonal behaviour within social relationships, for example interacting with parents, caregivers or siblings at home; a bus ride to school; time in the playground or queuing for lunch; lessons from a number of different subject teachers; peer activities within lessons that involve project work, role-play or small-group discussions. The extent to which children can function effectively within each of these situations will depend, in very large measure, upon how they interpret and understand each unique social situation. Research studies by Cole (1986) and Saarni (1984) into how children respond to disappointment, along with those of Harris et al. (1987) into how children distinguish between appearance and reality, have given rise to the following findings.

- Children can mask their emotions from an early age.
- Children actively search for clues within a given situation (social referencing) to work out appropriate responses (display rules).
- The association between expressed emotion and felt emotion relies upon a child's interpretation of a given situation.

Some situations, for example coping with the trauma of loss or separation from a loved one, can cause profound and enduring emotional reactions within children. Traumatic loss or separation from an early attachment figure can influence the child's inner 'working' model or mental representation of attachment relationships that in later life can affect the child's ability to form secure attachments with others. Burgoyne et al. (1987: 125) report that *separation and divorce are deeply disturbing as they demonstrate to a child that social relationships can end, even those as fundamental as the ones they have with their own parents.* The feelings of abandonment and powerlessness can make the child sad, depressed and angry. In this instance, *anger for a child is more complicated* as it might be accompanied *by the fear that to be angry with one or both parents may drive them away* (ibid.). This can give rise to feelings of anger within the child that become masked; also, there may *be a conflict between feelings of love and anger for a parent. Anger may lead a child to feel guilty for having bad feelings about their parents* (ibid.). Some children may project their inner hurt and feelings toward siblings and peers through aggressive behaviour. This further confounds the situation as it could result in heightened feelings of abandonment or solitude within the child as he drives others away. In some cases, the child might turn the anger inwards and endure a state of depression.

Psychoanalysts use such terms as regression, denial, repression and defence mechanisms to describe processes through which children manifest profound emotional experiences. During the upheaval of divorce, for example, some children regress *to earlier patterns of behaviour that they had already given up as they got older* (Burgoyne et al., 1987: 128). Older children may cope with the situation by immersing themselves in school activities; others have been shown to engage in sexual relationships and to enter marriage at an earlier age, as they prefer to escape the environment of *warring [or] depressed parents who seem totally preoccupied with their own problems* (ibid.). Clinical psychologists advocate using support groups and intervention strategies that encourage children to express their feelings and suggest that *it may be important to provide a child with a situation or a person with whom they feel safe enough to air their feelings and anxieties more freely* (ibid.). Children's artwork is another avenue that has great potential for bringing otherwise masked and hidden feelings and emotions to the surface. A vibrantly coloured drawing or picture of people close together with smiling faces, for example, can convey quite a different message from one that features darkened hues of individuals strategically distanced from one another and facial expressions of frowns, grimaces or bared teeth. Similarly, imagery of actions within a drawing such as skipping, swimming, hitting or hiding and events and situations as in a family picnic, the tsunami disaster or a patient in a hospital room can represent important messages. The current global climate that shows an increasing trend of immigration, refugee resettlement and the adoption of orphans across nations suggests that, when working with children for whom English is an additional language (EAL), children's artwork could be viewed as a vitally important medium for communication.

Child psychologists frequently encourage children to draw a picture about some situation or event that might appear to be troubling them and subsequently use this as a springboard for trying to engage the child in dialogue about that situation or event. When children and young people are traumatised, getting them to open up and to talk about how they feel can be an important step in helping them to rationalise how they are feeling and why. Importantly, this strategy informs us about the experience and view of the situation from the child's subjective perspective.

Although controversial, Nigel Parton (2004) provides a persuasive argument concerning cases of severe neglect and child abuse, suggesting that had strategies been in place to enable their 'voices' to be heard, the deaths of Maria Colwell and Victoria Climbié could possibly have been avoided.

SUMMARY OF KEY POINTS

In this chapter, we have reviewed attachment theory and considered how individual differences in patterns of attachment behaviour can influence the development of feelings and emotions associated with (in)security across an individual's life span. Some aspects of social and emotional development, prevalent in developmental psychology, have been explored and the role of temperament as a physiological and sociological construct in shaping behaviour has been introduced. How children come to understand and recognise the development of self and generalised other has been explored briefly. The quest to explain and understand why children, even within the same family, can be so very different from one another has merely begun!

FERENCES

Ainsworth, M. (1991) 'Attachments and other affectional bonds across the life cycle', in P. Harris, J. Stevenson-Hinde and C. Parkes (eds), *Attachment Across the Life Cycle*. New York: Routledge.

Ainsworth, M., Blehar, M., Waters, E. and Wall, S. (1978) *Patterns of Attachment: A Psychological Study of the Strange Situation*. Hillsdale, NJ: Lawrence Erlbaum.

Allen, J. and Land, D. (1999) 'Attachment in adolescence', in J. Cassidy and P. Shaver (eds), *Handbook of Attachment*. New York: Guilford.

Barnes, P. (ed.) (1995) *Personal, Social and Emotional Development of Children*. Oxford: Blackwell.

Bates, J. (1989) 'Concepts and measures of temperament', in G. Kohnstamm, J. Bates and M. Rothbart (eds), *Temperament in Childhood*. Chichester: John Wiley.

Belsky, J. (1984) 'The determinants of parenting: a process model', *Child Development*, 55: 83–96.

Blatchford, P. (1994) *Pupil Perceptions of Breaktime and Implications for Breaktime Improvements: Evidence from England*. Paper presented to the Annual Meeting of the American Research Association, New Orleans, April.

Bowlby, J. (1969/1982) *Attachment and Loss: Attachment*. New York: Basic Books.

Bowlby, J. (1980) *Attachment and Loss: Sadness and Depression*. New York: Basic Books.

Bretherton, I. (1985) 'Attachment theory: retrospect and prospect', in I. Bretherton and E. Waters (eds), *Growing Points of Attachment Theory and Research*, Monographs of the Society for Research in Child Development, Nos 1–2, Serial No. 209.

Burgoyne, J., Ormrod, R. and Richards, M. (1987) *Divorce Matters*. Harmondsworth: Penguin.

Buss, A. and Plomin, R. (1984) *Temperament: Early Developing Personality Traits*. Hillsdale, NJ: Lawrence Erlbaum.

Cassidy, J. and Berlin, L. (1994) 'The insecure/ambivalent pattern of attachment: theory and research', *Child Development*, 65: 971–91.

Cichetti, D. and Beeghly, M. (1987) *Atypical Symbolic Development. New Directions for Child Development*. San Francisco: Jossey-Bass.

Cole, P. (1986) 'Children's spontaneous control of facial expression', *Child Development*, 57: 1309–21.

Crowell, J. and Treboux, D. (1995) 'A review of adult attachment measures: Implications for theory and research', *Social Development*, 4: 294–327.

Crowell, J. and Waters, E. (1994) 'Bowlby's theory grown up: the role of attachment in adult love relationships', *Psychological Inquiry*, 5 (1): 31–4.

Dunn, J. (1987) 'Understanding feelings: the early stages', in J. Bruner and H. Haste (eds), *Making Sense: The Child's Construction of the World*. London: Methuen.

Dunn, J. and Kendrick, C. (1982) *Siblings: Love, Envy and Understanding*. Cambridge, MA: Harvard University Press.

Furukawa, T., Yokouchi, T., Hirai, T., Kitamura, T. and Takahashi, K. (1999) 'Parental loss in childhood and social support in adulthood among psychiatric patients', *Journal of Developmental Psychology*, 39, 387–404.

Geiger, B. (1996) *Fathers as Primary Caregivers*. Westport, CT: Greenwood.

Guyer, A., Nelson, E., Perez-Edgar, K., Hardin, M., Roberson-Nay, R., Monk, C., Bjork, J., Henderson, H., Pine, D., Fox, N. and Ernst, M. (2006) 'Striatal functional alteration in adolescents characterised by childhood behavioural inhibition', *Journal of Neuroscience*, 26 (24): 6399–405.

Harlow, H. and Harlow, M. (1969) 'Effects of various mother–infant relationships on rhesus monkey behaviours', in B. Foss (ed.), *Determinants of Infant Behaviour*, Vol. 4. London: Methuen.

Harris, P. (1989) *Children and Emotion*. Oxford: Basil Blackwell.

Harris, P., Olthof, T., Meerum Terwogt, M. and Hardman, C. (1987) 'Children's knowledge of the situations that provoke emotion', *International Journal of Behavioural Development*, 10: 319–44.

Hazan, C. and Shaver, P. (1987) 'Romantic love conceptualised as an attachment process', *Journal of Personality and Social Psychology*, 52: 511–24.

Howe, D., Brandon, M., Hinings, D. and Schofield, G. (1999) *Attachment Theory, Child Maltreatment and Family Support*. Mahwah, NJ: Lawrence Erlbaum.

Kagan, J. (1988) 'Temperamental contributions to social behaviour', *American Psychologist*, 44: 668–74.

Klaus, M., Kennell, J. and Klaus, P. (1995) *Bonding*. Boston: Addison-Wesley.

Main, M. (1991) 'Metacognitive knowledge, metacognitive monitoring, and singular (coherent) vs. multiple (incoherent) models of attachment: findings and directions for future research', in P. Harris, J. Stevenson-Hinde and C. Parkes (eds), *Attachment Across the Life Cycle*. New York: Routledge.

Main, M. and Goldwyn, R. (1984) 'Predicting rejection of her infant from mother's representation of her own experience: implications for the abused-abusing inter-generational cycle', *Child Abuse and Neglect*, 8: 203–17.

Main, M. and Solomon, E. (1990) 'Procedures for identifying infants as disorganised/disoriented during the Ainsworth Strange Situation', in D. Greenberg and E. Cummings (eds), *Attachment in the Preschool Years: Theory, Research and Intervention*. Chicago: University of Chicago Press.

Markiewicz, D., Doyle, A. and Brendgen, M. (2001) 'The quality of adolescents' friendships: associations with mothers' interpersonal relationships, attachments to parents and friends, and prosocial behaviours', *Journal of Adolescence*, 24: 429–45.

Maslow, A. (1970) *Motivation and Personality*, 2nd edn. New York: Harper & Row.

Mead, G. (1934) *Mind, Self and Society*. Chicago: University of Chicago Press.

Meltzer, B. (1967) 'Mead's social psychology', in J. Manis and B. Meltzer (eds), *Symbolic Interaction: A Reader in Social Psychology*. Boston: Allyn & Bacon.

Opie, I. (1993) *The People in the Playground*. Oxford: Oxford University Press.

Parton, N. (2004) 'From Maria Colwell to Victoria Climbié: reflections on public inquiries into child abuse a generation apart', *Child Abuse Review*, 13: 80–94. Online: **http://www.interscience.wiley.com**

Piaget, J. (1976) *Judgement and Reasoning in the Child*. New York: Harcourt Brace Jovanich (first published 1928).

Saarni, C. (1984) 'An observational study of children's attempts to monitor their expressive behaviour', *Child Development*, 55: 1504–13.

Sluckin, A. (1987) 'The culture of the primary school playground', in A. Pollard (ed.), *Children and Their Primary Schools*. Lewes: Falmer.

Sroufe, L. (1996) *Emotional Development: The Organisation of Emotional Life in the Early Years*. New York: Cambridge University Press.

Thomas, A. and Chess, S. (1977) *Temperament and Development*. New York: Brunner/Mazel.

Van Lawick-Goodall, J. (1968) 'The behavior of free-living chimpanzees in the Gombe Stream Reserve', *Animal Behaviour Monographs*, 1 (3): 161–311.

Weiss, R. (1982) 'Attachment in adult life', in C. Parkes and J. Stevenson-Hinde (eds), *The Place of Attachment in Human Behaviour*. New York: Basic Books.

Woodhead, M., Barnes, P., Miell, D. and Oates, J. (1995) 'Developmental perspectives on emotion', in P. Barnes (ed.), *Personal, Social and Emotional Development of Children*. Oxford: Blackwell in association with Open University Press.

7 Cognitive development

Andrea Raiker

Learning objectives

By the end of the chapter you should:

- **understand the distinguishing features of behaviourism, cognitivism, socio-cognitivism and multiple intelligence theory;**
- **know the principal proponents of each theory;**
- **understand the importance of language in cognitive development;**
- **be aware of their relationship to positive and interpretative paradigms.**

Introduction

Cognitive development can simply be defined as the structured growth of mind. The process begins before birth. Once a child is born this embodiment of a new generation is subsumed within the old, receiving and absorbing the past and present knowledge of its culture. The child learns facts, ideas, beliefs and behaviours. The production and use of signs, symbols and artefacts become part of the child's repertoire of individual and social accomplishments. How does this happen? Yes, the child learns systematically and formally as in school education, or unsystematically and informally, for example where children learn outside school from engagement with life, their family members and their peers. But how is this knowledge absorbed and retained by the mind? There are two major schools of thought on this, that of behaviourism and that of cognitivism. This chapter will focus on the latter and some of the theories encompassed by it. However, although behaviourism has been overtaken by cognitive theory, there are aspects of behaviourist theories that are still relevant to a discussion of growth of mind. Therefore this chapter will begin with a brief introduction to the work of four theorists in this field.

Behaviourism

Behaviourism is an approach to psychology based on the proposition that behaviour is of scientific value. It is based on the hypothesis that all learning, whether verbal or non-verbal, takes place through the creation of habits.

The roots of behaviourism go back to the Enlightenment, that period in British history during the seventeenth and eighteenth centuries when science dominated philosophical thought and it was believed that systematic investigation could be applied to all forms of human activity. Very simply, this approach maintained that the only information on human activity to be considered valid was empirical and measurable behaviours. By empirical, philosophers and scientists meant that which is the result of sensory experience. In other words, what was true about human behaviour could be determined through only sight, hearing, touch, taste and smell and not through just thinking about things.

The most famous of the early behaviourists are Ivan Pavlov (1849–1936) and Edward Thorndike (1874–1949). Pavlov had demonstrated through his famous experiment with dogs, bells and food that actions could be determined over time (Morris and Maisto, 1999). His stimulus–response theory, known as classical conditioning, was taken further by Thorndike. By using an elaborate cage with pulleys, levers and doors and the manipulation of which cats could or could not obtain food, Thorndike showed that responses that are followed by satisfaction will be strengthened and responses that are followed by discomfort will be weakened. This is known as Thorndike's law of effect. Thorndike concluded that animals learn solely by trial and error, or reward and punishment. Thorndike used the cat's behaviour in the cage, described by him as a puzzle box, to explain what happens when all beings learn anything (Hilgard, 1964).

You will note that there has been no mention of the cats or dogs thinking in these early experiments. Learning was regarded as mechanical, simply a stimulus resulting in a response, and directed through trial and error.

The founder of the behaviourist school of thought was John Watson (1878–1958). He applied the findings of experiments on animals to humans. Among these experiments was one where he tested stimulus–response theory on a child. This experiment could not be carried out today because it would be regarded as unethical for reasons that should become obvious. The child's name was Albert but he is known to history as Poor Little Albert. Albert, a child of not yet one, was given a white laboratory rat to hold. He was completely unafraid and happily played with the rat. Then a metal bar was hit with a hammer just behind his head. Albert, not unnaturally, began to cry. After a short interval, Albert was again given the rat, but this time just as he touched it, the metal clang sounded behind his head. This was repeated several times over a few weeks. Before long just the sight of the rat made Albert cry. In fact, anything furry – a stuffed toy, a fur coat, a Father Christmas beard – made Albert cry. Watson declared that this experiment successfully demonstrated the application of classical conditioning theory to humans. In doing so, he supported Pavlov's and Thorndike's view that mind did not have a place in learning. Watson proposed two laws (1928).

- *The law of frequency*. This stated that the more frequently a stimulus and a response are associated, the stronger the habit will become.

- *The law of recency*. This maintains that the response that occurs most recently after a stimulus is likely to be associated with it.

As you will read below, there is no doubt that mind has a significant role to play in learning in terms of what is learnt, how it is learnt and how deeply it is learnt. But there are aspects of stimulus–response theory that can be considered to be true. For example, a basic tenet of training is repetition and consistency. As a teacher, I took my class to weekly swimming lessons. The children were taught to keep head tucked between straight, stretched arms, and legs tightly held together when diving into the pool. They would practise this during the session and become quite competent. If they attended the next session, they would start at a slightly lower standard than that achieved the week before but would quickly make up ground and improvement would follow. Those, however, who missed the second session would in varying degrees have forgotten what they had been taught, and have to start again from a low level relative to their peers.

Skinner (1938), like Pavlov and Thorndike, worked with animals and food. Unlike them he came to the conclusion that the mind had a significant role in determining human behaviour. He is remembered for formulating two laws.

- *The law of conditioning*. This states that a response is strengthened when followed by a reinforcing stimulus so is likely to occur again.

- *The law of extinction*. This states the opposite.

Skinner is regarded as the founder of operant conditioning, as opposed to the classical conditioning formulated by Pavlov. The word 'operant' indicates that there is something functioning between the stimulus and the learnt response or conditioning. Unlike Watson, Skinner believed that the mind played a significant role in human learning (Skinner, 1938). From this point onwards behaviourism became replaced by cognitivism as the dominant theory of learning.

REFLECTIVE ACTIVITY **7.1**

Behaviours

The basic tenet of behaviourism is that through conditioning an event will be followed by a response that is predictable and measurable. Place yourself in a position where you can observe people. This can be at home, work, school or college or in a social setting. What predictable behaviours do you see? Examples are opening a door for another person, putting litter in a rubbish bin, queuing at the post office. Pick two or three and try to answer the following questions.

- *Where do you think these behaviours were learnt?*
- *How are they measurable?*
- *What is the value of these behaviours to society?*
- *What is the value of these behaviours to the individual?*
- *Did thinking come into the performance of these behaviours?*

Cognitivism

As has been discussed behaviourism incorporates a scientific approach. The scientific paradigm, or concept of reality, that embraces the scientific approach is positivism. Learning occurs through the senses being stimulated and responses being conditioned and thus controlled. The truths about learning are discovered directly through experiment. Events and activities that are to result in learning are created specifically for the purpose. Variables are reduced. Outcomes are the result of measurable observations. What is real and true is external, measurable and controllable and can only be accessed through the senses.

At the other end of the spectrum, the cognitive approach claims that learning is concerned with a person's internal representations of the world and how these are organised in the mind. The concept or model of reality that is applicable here is the interpretative paradigm. The truths about learning are discovered indirectly through observation and through what is becoming known about the structure of the brain. Learning is happening all the time. Events and activities that are created specifically for the purpose may or may not result in the intended learning outcomes. Variables are accepted as producing the richness of individual thought and action. Outcomes can never be more than interpretations. What is real and true is *internal*, immeasurable and uncontrollable and can only be accessed through the *mind*.

Jean Piaget (1896–1990)

Piaget is regarded as the foremost and most dominant cognitivist psychologist in the western world. Cognitive psychology involves the study of mental processes such as perception, memory and decision-making. When applied to education, cognitive psychology is concerned with the way children acquire, process and organise knowledge. His research centred on small samples of children, including his own daughter. Classic research practice would say that the findings from these studies, even though they were in depth, cannot be generalised because of the sample size. Piaget's work has, however, been tremendously influential because he was the first to link children's learning to stages of cognitive development. He identified schemata, cognitive structures or patterns of physical and mental behaviours, underlying acts of intelligence that appeared to correspond to specific ages. There are basically four stages, though some educationalists break the second stage into two, as exemplified below in Table 7.1 (Jarvis et al., 1998).

Table 7.1 Piaget's stages of cognitive development.

Age of child	Stage	Description of schemata
0–2 years	Sensorimotor	Children are learning that physical actions (motor) result in sensed responses, that is by one or more of the five senses. In this can be discerned the stimulus–response relationship of classical conditioning.
3–4 years	Pre-operational (Pre-conceptual)	During this stage children are egocentric. They see the world purely from their own perspective. They cannot 'decentre', that is see the world from another's point of view.
4–7 years	Intuitive	Children are beginning to perceive sets of things, similarities and differences. They are beginning to classify though this is not done deliberately, hence the term 'intuitive'.
8–11 years	Concrete operational	Children are beginning to think logically. They begin to understand that things and events can be ordered and that some can be reversed. They begin to classify deliberately and organise.
12–15 years	Formal operational	Children begin to move away from things that can be sensed, that is that are concrete, to abstractions.

A key aspect of Piaget's work was his belief that children needed activity in order to learn. Parents, teachers and other significant beings in their lives could give children information, but only when a child was 'ready to learn' would that information be learnt. Learning readiness would come through activity. For Piaget, the task of the parent or teacher was to set up activities that would give the child the necessary prerequisite information for learning. Only then would the parent or teacher be able to structure that information into a form that could be assimilated into existing schemata already established in the child's mind. The terms 'assimilation' and 'accommodation' are important Piagetian terms (1967). A child is assimilating knowledge by practising or repeating something learnt. When that knowledge has changed the existing schemata, then that knowledge has been accommodated. For example, learner drivers fully concentrate on their gear changes and manoeuvres. They are practising, assimilating what they already know but as yet the mechanics of driving have not been accommodated. When they have, these drivers will be able to hold conversations, listen to music or plan their holidays while still being in full control of their cars. Until new knowledge has been accommodated the mind, according to Piaget, is not in its preferred state of equilibrium. This provides the motivation for individuals to keep practising a skill or a task until it is mastered.

Piaget's perception that people construct their own learning was his great achievement. His structure of staged development explained, for example, why children aged four can count to five but have to count again if the five objects are rearranged, whereas children aged seven do not. The attraction of Piaget's theory was also that it gives learning consistency and predictability, particularly in terms of the age relationship with development. The development of numerical understanding could be tested and placed against the internal workings of the mind. But, as we have seen above, testing is an attribute of behaviourist theory. Critics of Piaget, including Margaret Donaldson (1978), demonstrated flaws in his testing methods. Influential educationalists such as Susan Isaacs (2000) cited examples of children as young as three demonstrating logical thought. A growing body of knowledge showed that children had difficulties with both the language and the contexts that Piaget used in his tests (Wood, 1998). Theorists such as Bernstein, Bruner and Vygotsky were putting emphasis on the fundamental importance of language and social interaction, including that of instruction. Nevertheless it must be remembered that these theorists built upon Piaget's work and are, in a sense, derivatives as well as developments of it.

REFLECTIVE ACTIVITY **7.2**

Piaget

A Piagetian test that is still valid as long as no 'age-relatedness' is attached to it is described below. It is Piaget's classic conservation test to demonstrate that children had moved from the intuitive to the concrete operational stage. Try it for yourself.

Find two glasses or bottles of different shapes and heights. Put some coloured water, say orange squash, in one of the glasses/bottles. In front of a child aged between 3 and 11, pour the coloured water from the first glass/bottle into the second. The water will be at a different height in this second glass/bottle than in the first. Now ask the child 'Was there more water in the first glass/bottle or in this one?' A child that says the amount of water is the same in each glass/bottle is in the concrete operational stage. A child saying that there is more water in one glass/bottle or the other is still in the intuitive stage. If a child can give the right answer without seeing you pouring between objects simply through your description s/he has reached the formal operational stage.

Take note: your question has to be very carefully worded!

Socio-cognitivism

Cognitivism is defined as the structured growth of mind. The prefix 'socio' denotes a cultural context. The most influential of the socio-cognitivists – Lev Vygotsky, Jerome Bruner and Basil Bernstein – believed that the development of reasoning and learning is the result of both formal, as in schooling, and informal social interactions mediated by language. Although the work of Bernstein and Bruner post-dates that of Vygotsky, the latter's ideas did not influence European and American psychology until 1984 when James Wertsch edited and published a collection of essays entitled *Culture, Communication and Cognition: Vygotskian Perspectives*. Therefore Vygotsky will be discussed last.

Basil Bernstein (1924–2000)

Basil Bernstein was an American sociologist who caused controversy when his views on the relationship between socio-economic class and language were published in 1960. He argued that differences in the means between test scores by children from different socio-economic backgrounds resulted from the way language was used and structured in those groups. Children from different backgrounds learnt and used language in different ways. These differences were brought to school where 'school' language was used. The outcomes of this were differences in academic achievement. So cognitive development in terms of measurable achievement was to some degree embedded in language (Bernstein, 1971).

Bernstein's ideas brought him into conflict with the theoretical theorists of the time, in particular with Noam Chomsky (1928–). The use and understanding of language in cognitive development is so important, particularly to Vygotsky, that some discussion of Chomsky's opposing theoretical stance is necessary.

Chomsky found resonance in Ferdinand de Saussure's (1857–1913) attempts to establish linguistics as a scientific discipline through systematic study. This places Chomsky firmly within the positivist paradigm. For Chomsky, the study of language meant the identification of the grammatical rules that humans use when they speak and listen. He also believed that human brains were 'hard-wired' to use and understand language (1988) through a cerebral mechanism termed the 'Language Acquisition Device'. For Chomsky, language acquisition is automatic and underpinned by innate mechanisms. The emphasis is on similarity, identity and repetition. At the heart of this approach to semantic analysis is the belief that the individual words in a language are endowed with a defined set of meanings. A set of rules is provided to combine them whereby the individual meanings of the words are merged to form the meanings of sentences. The meanings of these sentences are then combined to form the meaning of speech or text. Speakers use a fixed stimulus–response code to communicate whereby standardised grammatical forms are linked to fixed meanings such as those provided by dictionaries. Chomsky recognised that context and personal perspective provide a background to the way language is used and understood, but maintained that this background is too variable to be analysed meaningfully and should be disregarded.

This literal view of language is therefore objective, constant and makes little reference to context. It reflects the scientific and positivist approach that produced the behaviourists. Chomsky did not believe that cognition and language acquisition were connected and therefore did not accept a socio-cognitive approach to learning.

REFLECTIVE ACTIVITY **7.3**

Goodbye!

'Goodbye!' is a simple term we use frequently. Look it up in a dictionary and note the meaning given. Now think of how you would use this word

- *in your family home to your mother or father;*

- *in town to your friend after shopping;*

- *in a classroom to your teacher or tutor after a lecture or lesson;*

- *in a pub to your boy or girlfriend after a disagreement.*

Does the dictionary definition cover all the meanings identified through your consideration of these scenarios? Should context and personal perspective be considered as a background to the way language is used and understood?

Jerome Bruner (1915–)

Bruner's view of language was very different from that of Chomsky. He maintained that the transmission of meaning was rooted in pre-verbal communication which he called intersubjectivity:

> *Intersubjectivity begins with infant's and mother's pleasure in eye-to-eye contact in the opening weeks of life, moves quickly into the two of them sharing joint attention on common objects, and culminates a first preschool phase with the child and a caretaker achieving a meeting of minds by an early exchange of words – an achievement that is never finished.*
> *(Bruner, 1996: 57–8)*

The use of the word 'intersubjectivity' is interesting. It suggests the closeness of the being of mother and child. For the child, his/her reality is tightly bound up with that of the mother to the extent that for some time the child continues to think that s/he is still one with the mother. The development of the child appears to happen in parallel with a growing sense of separateness, of independence from the mother. At the same time the child develops language to bridge the gulf of separateness with the mother and also to create relationships with significant others, such as the father and siblings, and also other children and adults as his/her reality expands.

Bruner also points to the 'joint attention of common objects' for the 'meeting of minds' through words. This is important for an understanding of Bruner's contribution to cognitive development theory. Words are encapsulations of an individual's distilled experience, organised to varying extent by the patterns of grammar, and are situated, that is they have meaning according to the context in which they are used. The French philosopher, anthropologist and educationalist Pierre Bourdieu

(Grenfell and Kelly, 2001) termed the specific context where language is used at any given point in time as 'field', and the source of the distilled experience that manifested itself in words as 'habitus'. So each individual child's cognitive growth results from his/her diverse and varied experiences. There will be overlap with the experiences of others. But an individual's experience will build on those already integrated into his/her being and will therefore be unique. The words s/he uses in language to express those experiences in whatever form, be it rhetoric, mnemonic, explanatory, directive, descriptive, metaphoric, ironic or metalinguistic, will also have unique meanings reflecting his/her cognitive development.

That there is an overlap of meanings is undeniable. How is this achieved, given the individualism of language development discussed above? Of course the individual is a member of a socio-cultural group from the moment of birth until death. As has been discussed, the learning and use of language begins in the earliest days of infancy and involves interaction between the child and those caring for him/her and continues throughout life. This social dimension to the learning and use of language contributes to the transmission of the specific shared values, beliefs, goals and practices that define the culture within which the interaction takes place. Language and the cognitive development it constructs and by which it is constructed cannot be separated from the culture it describes.

Bruner (1996: 46) building on his own work (1976, also 1990) and that of Bandura (1977) contrasts the 'macro' dimension of culturalism as a *system of values, rights, exchanges, obligations, opportunities, power* with the 'micro' dimension which *concentrates on how individual human beings construct 'realities' and meanings that adapt them to the system, at what personal cost, with what expected outcomes*. Bruner argues that education – and for him that meant instruction – is an integral part of this process, writing of education as not being an *island but part of the continent of culture* (ibid.). This suggests that the impact of language in the classroom is not only on an individual's understanding of words, syntax and semantics but on other more subtle influences on the growth of that understanding in line with the socio-cultural norms with which s/he is familiar. This is the 'hidden curriculum', an essential component determining cognitive development.

Lev Vygotsky (1896–1934)

Vygotsky was a contemporary of Piaget but thought very differently about language and its effect on cognitive development. For Piaget, language did not have a role in structuring thinking. Vygotsky, on the other hand, maintained that social interactivity, which included written and verbal spoken language, laid down mental, culturally derived structures that determined how people constructed their worlds. Once language has been internalised it can be used to create personal constructs of reality, the world perceived by the individual. In this he was following Halliday's (1978: 24) argument that *The construal of reality is inseparable from the construal of the semantic system in which the reality is encoded*. This would suggest that an individual's perceptions of reality are incomplete or undeveloped before the mastery of the semantic system, in this country that of English, is achieved. Words are not simply verbal or written symbols. They form part of the thought process and their meanings evolve throughout life. Therefore adults and/or children will ascribe different subtleties of meaning, and communication could be adversely affected.

This has important implications for anyone working with children and young people. It would appear that the development of a shared language is crucial for teachers and youth workers to lead children through their Zones of Proximal Development, a term coined by Vygotsky (trans. 1987) to describe the difference in learning that children could achieve alone and with the support, or scaffold in Brunerian terms, of someone more knowledgeable. These zones vary in extent according to prior learning, genetic factors and environmental factors. Vygotsky and Bruner, particularly the former, have placed emphasis on instruction in the learning process. Unlike Piaget, they are emphatic that teachers can make a difference to the rate of children's learning. However, Balacheff (1980, cited in Hoyles, 1985) found that older children tended to judge the clearness of their explanation on the basis of *how clear it seemed to themselves* and not on the meaning perceived by their peers. In later work, Balacheff and Laborde (1984, cited in Hoyles, 1985) found that it was discussions about the ability of peers to 'decode' messages which tended to push them into a state of mutual understanding, not the teacher's discourse. In other words, there appeared to be a close relationship between learners' successful solution of a problem and the process of searching, testing and agreeing the meanings of appropriate words to use in explanation to their peers. It is important to ascertain if this is the case with teachers, youth workers and learners. Spoken language that appears clear to teachers and youth workers may not produce clarity in the minds of their learners.

REFLECTIVE ACTIVITY **7.4**

Vygotsky in action

Next time you are with a group of friends in a teaching session and you are asked to discuss some aspect of the lesson, sit back and listen. In most cases, the conversation will begin with someone either asking a question on or a restating in his/her own words of what you have been asked to discuss. Everyone in the group will have his/her own understanding of what is to be done although not all will articulate it. Watch the body language! Each person in the group will also bring differing accounts of experiences, ideas and observations to the discussion. By the end of the discussion there will be some level of agreement, some shared understanding, of the task and a group response. This is Vygotsky in action.

Multiple intelligence theory

The roots of Gardner's theory of multiple intelligences lay in his rejection of the concept of a 'g', a single general intelligence possessed by all individuals that can be assessed by means of standardised written intelligence tests. Such tests are examples of the positivist paradigm applied to education. They suggest that the cognition revealed by them is fixed and incapable of development.

Despite long-standing criticisms of IQ tests, their use was worldwide when Gardner's *Frames of Mind* was published in 1983. Psychometricians were still taking paper-and-pencil short-answer tests based on linguistic and logical abilities, originally conceived by Binet (Montagu, 1999) for a specific purpose with a specific sample, and applying them generally to large populations for a variety of purposes, principally social and culturally based. In contrast to this process, where an individual's intelligence was obtained *from* the results of the tests as a single score, a fixed intelligence quotient, Gardner looked at the totality of an individual. He considered intelligence from a neurobiological perspective, that is that intelligence comes from within the individual who brings it *to* the time and place of manifestation.

Gardner considered the flexibility of human development and the lessons from genetics in both individuals and in populations. In *Frames of Mind* Gardner argues a rejection of the concept of a general intelligence and its replacement by his own perceptions of intelligence. His definition of an intelligence at this time was *the ability to solve problems or to create products that are valued within one or more cultural settings* (1983: xiv) His approach was primarily that of a psychologist, his primary scholarly pursuit. A grant from a Dutch foundation, the Bernard Van Leer Foundation, and the accompanying brief to write a book about the then current state of knowledge on human cognition through discoveries in the biological and behavioural sciences gave rise to *Frames of Mind*. Gardner seized the opportunity:

> *To put in terms of my daily calendar, I was seeking to synthesise what I was learning in the morning from my study of brain damage with what I was learning in the afternoon from my study of cognitive development. My colleagues and I combed the literature from brain study, genetics, anthropology, and psychology in an effort to ascertain the optimal taxonomy of human capacities.* (Gardner, 2003: 3)

The outcome was the identification of seven intelligences: linguistic, musical, logical-mathematical, spatial, bodily-kinaesthetic, interpersonal and intrapersonal. Gardner acknowledges that he was not the first to attempt to identify different facets of human intellect. In *Multiple Intelligences after Twenty Years* (2003), Gardner refers to Thurston's seven 'vectors of the mind', Guildford's 150 'factors of the intellect' and Sternberg's three intelligences: the ability to order components of reasoning; the capacity to automate aspects of cognition to focus on the unknown or unfamiliar; and a practical intelligence. Neither does he claim that his seven intelligences are definitive and irrefutable. He recognises that *There is progress and regress, fit and lack of fit, but never the discovery of the Rosetta stone, the single key to a set of interlocking issues* (1983: 59). What Gardner does claim to be his unique contribution is that the intelligences he distinguishes are identified according to scientific process. He denounces a totally inductive approach and advises of the necessity of presenting a theory and then testing it (ibid.).

A question immediately arises – how does this approach differ from those of the behaviourists? How can Gardner justify the positivist, scientific process in relation to his own theory but reject that approach when connected with the identification and quantification of 'g'?

Gardner's basis for claiming a scientific approach lies in his *calling for ... sets of intelligences ... which meet certain biological and psychological specifications* in his *search for an empirically grounded set of faculties* (1983: 61). This is certainly redolent of behaviourism. However, the certainty of positivism in terms of discrete and identifiable outcomes is missing from Gardner's work. He recognises he might fail in his endeavour but believes *the effort should be made to find a firmer foundation for our favourite faculties* (ibid.). In the same work Gardner admits that *the selection (or rejection) of a candidate's intelligence is reminiscent more of an artistic judgement than a scientific assessment* (1983: 62). It appears that Gardner is nudging his theory away from scientific positivism and into the realms of interpretative rationalism. Much could be written about the apparent paradoxes in Gardner's work but this is outside the brief for this chapter. Let it suffice to say that Gardner's quest to widen the discussion of intelligence to embrace a wider range of 'smartness' demonstrates greater awareness of the strengths and depths of human diversity than do the narrow parameters of an intelligence quotient (IQ) test.

In his subsequent work *Intelligence Reframed* (1999), Gardner argued the identification of a naturalistic intelligence and postulated a spiritual, existential intelligence. His definition of an intelligence had also expanded to become a *biopsychological potential to process information that can be activated in a cultural setting to solve problems or create products that are of value in a culture* (1999: 33–4). In this latter definition in which the word 'activated' is used, Gardner is reflecting aspects of the work of Carl Rodgers (cited in Kirschenbaum and Henderson, 1989) and Abraham Maslow (cited in Wilson, 2002) on the value of intrinsic motivation. Applying their work to his own, Gardner believed that cognitive development would be enhanced if the appropriate intelligences and associated learning styles were used in teaching.

SUMMARY OF KEY POINTS

The definition of cognitive development used in this chapter is that of structured growth of mind. The generation of this structure and its capability of growth are viewed differently, depending on whether they are approached from a positivist or interpretative paradigm. Behaviourists until Skinner believed that the mind had no place in learning. The basic tenet of this theory is that through conditioning, an event or stimulus will be followed by a response that is predictable and measurable. Although this view of learning is now considered to be simplistic, many of the rules and regulations underpinning the way we act socially have their roots in behaviourism.

Cognitive development theory is concerned with a person's internal representations of the world and how these are organised in the mind. Like the behaviourists, cognitive theorists developed their thinking by considering each other's work. However, fundamental to all was Piaget's theory of developmental cognitive growth through activity. The age-related aspects of his theory have been largely discredited but his descriptions of various identifiable stages of cognitive growth have not. Bernstein demonstrated the importance of the socio-economic context and the language generated by it on learning. Vygotsky showed that language was not only the vehicle of thought but also laid down mental, culturally derived structures that determined how individuals constructed their worlds. Both Bernstein's and Vygotsky's approaches to language in cognitive development were at variance with that of Piaget and Chomsky. Vygotsky identified the Zone of Proximal Development as the difference in learning that children could achieve alone and with the support of someone more knowledgeable. Both Vygotsky and Bruner placed emphasis on the value of instruction. Bruner coined the terms 'scaffold' and 'scaffolding' to describe the support given by a more knowledgeable other to take individuals through their Zones of Proximal Development.

The chapter ended with a discussion of Howard Gardner's multiple intelligence theory. Gardner's latter definition of an intelligence as ... *a biopsychological potential to process information that can be activated in a cultural setting to solve problems or create products that are of value in a culture* enabled him to identify eight intelligences. The criteria by which he identified these intelligences and tested the cognitive development revealed by them has generated criticisms. These are similar to those brought against the positivist, behaviourist testing that his theory was established to refute. This demonstrates the difficulties encountered when attempting to create an overview of learning development from one particular standpoint or paradigm.

RENCES

Bandura, A. (1977) *Social Learning Theory*. London: Prentice-Hall.

Bernstein, B. (1971) *Class, Codes and Control*. London: Routledge & Kegan Paul.

Bruner, J. (ed.) (1976) *Play: Its Role in Development and Evolution*. Harmondsworth: Penguin.

Bruner, J. (1990) *Acts of Meaning*. Cambridge, MA: Harvard University Press.

Bruner, J. (1996) *The Culture of Education*. Cambridge: MA: Harvard University Press.

Chomsky, N. (1988) *Language and the Problems of Knowledge*. Cambridge, MA: MIT Press.

Donaldson, M. (1978) *Children's Minds*. London: Fontana/Collins.

Gardner, H. (1983) *Frames of Mind*. London: Falmer Press.

Gardner, H. (1999) *Intelligence Reframed*. New York: Basic Books.

Gardner, H. (2003) *Multiple Intelligences after Twenty Years*. Washington, DC: American Educational Research Association.

Grenfell, M. and Kelly, M. (2001) *Bourdieu: Language, Culture and Education*. London: Peter Lang.

Hall, J. S. (2000) 'Psychology and schooling: the impact of Susan Isaacs and Jean Piaget on 1960s science education reform', *History of Education*, 29 (2): 153–70.

Halliday, M. A. K. (1978) *Language as Social Semiotic*. London: Edward Arnold.

Hilgard, E. R. (ed.) (1964) *Theories of Learning and Instruction*. Chicago: University of Chicago Press.

Hoyles, C. (1985) 'What is the point of group discussion in mathematics?', *Educational Studies in Maths*, May: 205–11.

Isaacs, S. (2000) *Intellectual Growth in Young Children*. New York: Routledge.

Jarvis, P., Holford, J. and Griffin, C. (1998) *The Theory and Practice of Learning*. London: Kogan Page.

Kirschenbaum, H. and Henderson, V. (eds) (1989) *The Carl Rodgers Reader*. Boston: Houghton Mifflin.

Montagu, A. (1999) *Race and IQ*. Oxford: Oxford University Press.

Morris, C.G. and Maisto, A.A. (1999) *Understanding Psychology*, 4th edn. Englewood Cliffs, NJ: Prentice Hall.

Piaget, J. (1967) *Six Psychological Studies*. London: London University Press .

Skinner, B.F. (1938) *The Behavior of Organisms*. New York: Appleton-Century-Crofts.

Vygotsky, L. (1987 trans.) *Thought and Language*. Cambridge, MA: MIT Press.

Watson, J. (1928) *The Ways of Behaviorism*. New York: Harper & Bros.

Wertsch, J. (1984) *Culture, Communication and Cognition: Vygotskian Perspectives*. Cambridge: Cambridge University Press.

Wilson, C. (2002) *New Pathways in Psychology: Maslow and the Post-Freudian Revolution*. Chapel Hill, NC: Maurice Bassett.

Wood, D. (1998) *How Children Think and Learn*. Oxford: Basil Blackwell.

8 Adolescence

Ian Roberts

Learning objectives

By the end of this chapter you should understand:

- **how society redefines individuals as they enter adulthood;**
- **how the period of life we call 'adolescence' is a socially-constructed phase of life;**
- **the concept of social redefinition in adolescence across different cultures and societies;**
- **the concept of moral reasoning in adolescent development.**

Introduction

The adolescent is no longer a child, but by the same argument cannot be regarded as a little adult. According to Arnett (1999) it is within the nature of the adolescent to seek out new experiences, to find independence and to break new ground. There is also a desire to find a personality, make a mark on the world and become established as an adult. The adolescent is regarded as reactive and enthusiastic, passionate, full of curiosity and willing to take risks. In the days when there was a huge leap from the sheltered nature of life as a child to the challenges encountered in a hard and demanding adulthood, all of these elements of the adolescent personality were regarded as positive. In contrast, Arnett (1999) suggests that in modern contemporary society, for the teenager stuck largely in the world of the child, these character traits that traditionally enabled young people to embrace the challenges of growing up now make him awkward, argumentative, demanding, difficult and self-absorbed.

It would seem that the onset of a child's adolescence is no longer a cause for celebration. Parents, teachers and the media sometimes despair at changes that occur as young people make their journey through adolescence. Pre-teenage children are regarded as cute, amiable and eager to please. In contrast, their adolescent counterparts are sometimes considered problems waiting to happen. Traditional researchers frequently endorsed this point, and this period of life has been labelled as a time of storm and stress (Arnett, 1999). It is, however, not that cut and dried, and it must be stressed that the majority of young people pass into and through adolescence with few major problems, although some find this an extremely traumatic period of life (Arnett, 1999; Rutter and Smith, 1995).

One of the most important tasks of adolescents concerns the establishment of an identity. On a conscious level teenagers do not tend to consider the question of 'who am I?' Over the course of the adolescent years, young people integrate the opinions of significant others (e.g. parents, other caring adults, friends, etc.) into their own preferences. In an ideal world, the ultimate outcome could be individuals who have clarity in their values and beliefs, aims and expectations. It stands to reason that people with secure identities know where they fit (or where they don't want to fit) in their world.

Memories of adolescence

In groups of two or three, reflect on your own adolescent years and identify the events and feelings you went through to become adults, e.g. identify when and why you stopped feeling like a child and when you started feeling like an adult. What particular events do you remember?

Erik Erikson's stages of psychosocial development

Erikson (1968) considered the development of young people to consist of a passage through a series of incremental stages building upon one another, beginning in infancy and continuing through mature adulthood. If each stage is resolved successfully, the child moves on with strength to the next stage. If it is not, the child's behaviour in later stages will show consequences, albeit indirectly, of the instabilities of earlier stages. It would seem that it is analogous to building a house. If the foundations are unstable, then the consequences may be encountered in the future.

Adolescence is a crucial phase, but character development and identity does not begin or end there. In adolescence, development advances to the point at which individuals can begin to build an obvious route towards adulthood.

Trust versus mistrust (birth to 1 year)

Erikson (1968) suggests that infants' development relates to whether they can or cannot trust their world. If infants' needs are met, they will emerge from this stage considering the world a safe and dependable place. If, however, care is inadequate, inconsistent or harsh, children will emerge with a sense of the world being untrustworthy. These are important differences that may be later reflected in the ways in which children interact with others.

Autonomy versus shame and doubt (2–3 years)

The key challenge the child faces during the second stage relates to exerting independence. Toddlers have the capacity to move about and do a number of things on their own. If these skills emerge under judicious guidance from adults, a sense of independence will develop. This may be later manifested in children's handling of situations that require autonomy and confidence.

Initiative versus guilt (4–5 years)

Children who have the freedom to explore and experiment tend to develop initiative. Those who are restricted and find that their use of initiative is oppressed tend to develop a sense of guilt about pursuing their interests.

Industry versus inferiority (6–11 years)

During the pre-teenage years, children's behaviour is characterised by active curiosity and a sense of how they stand in relation to others. Children want to gain kudos through the things they do. If this occurs, usually through praise from a significant other, they will develop a sense of industry. The potential danger of this stage is that the child will not experience success and will develop feelings of inadequacy or inferiority.

Identity versus role confusion (12–18 years)

In the adolescent years, young people develop a desire for independence from parents, achieve physical maturity, and face the task of finding out who they are and where they are going. Even those seemingly most well adjusted will at some point experience some role identity confusion. Many young people, at some point, will experience elements of minor delinquency, rebellion and self-doubt.

Erikson (1968) suggests that during successful early adolescence, *mature time perspective* is developed whereby the young person acquires self-certainty as opposed to self-consciousness. Adolescents seek leadership and inspiration, gradually developing their own set of ideals. Erikson (1968) believes that adolescence affords a *psychosocial moratorium*, where young people do not yet have to 'play for keeps', but instead experiment, trying various roles, so maybe discovering the one most suitable for them.

It is at this stage that a solid sense of identity is developed or individuals are left with considerable role confusion, particularly about their social and vocational choices. In later adolescence, clear sexual identity is also established. If the adolescent explores the roles and arrives at a positive path to follow, it may well lead to positive identity. If, however, identities are forced onto adolescents, so disempowering them, they may not adequately explore alternative roles so leading to identity confusion. This will often manifest itself in the relationships established with parents, peers and school. Adolescence is often considered for many young people as a period of *identity crisis*.

Intimacy versus isolation (young adulthood)

During young adulthood individuals will often establish a close and committed relationship with another person. It could be said that failure to do this sometimes leads to a sense of isolation.

Generativity versus stagnation (middle age)

Erikson (1968) suggests that adults need to feel generative during middle age, witnessing their own offspring develop and sensing the contribution that they make to the good of society.

Integrity versus despair (old age)

Adults in their older years will often look back at their lives with pride and a sense of accomplishment. They may have developed a self-concept underpinned by satisfaction, experiencing a sense of integrity when they can. It could be suggested however if any of the earlier psychosocial stages have not been satisfactorily embraced, there are potential dangers. There may well be a sense of despair if they have no sense of satisfaction with their lives.

REFLECTIVE ACTIVITY **8.2**

Historical comparisons

Compare an average 16-year-old male growing up in the UK in 1950 to one growing up today. Identify specific ways in which these lives are similar and different? Repeat this discussion for an average 16-year-old girl in the two historical periods.

From your experience, discuss with a colleague the personality traits of two young people (you may wish to use characters from TV programmes): one who shows a healthy sense of identity and another who seems to be experiencing identity confusion.

What specific feelings, attitudes and behaviours might be demonstrated by each 'character'??

Autonomy as an aspiration

One of the principal issues facing young people concerns the establishment of autonomy. There is a naive assumption that autonomy is the idea of being completely independent from others, and with particular reference to this age group is the notion of teenage 'rebellion'. If one considers adolescence from a Vygotskian perspective it could be suggested that rather than severing relationships, the establishment of autonomy really means becoming an independent and self-governing person.

Phelan et al., (1994) suggest that young people making the transition between junior and senior school look forward to having more choices and making new and more friends. Mizelle (1995), however, although endorsing this point, suggests that they are also concerned about being picked on and teased by older students, having harder work, making lower grades and getting lost in a larger, unfamiliar school. As young people make this difficult transition into a new school, many experience a decline in grades and attendance (Barone et al., 1991). They also view themselves more negatively and experience an increased need for friendships (Hertzog et al., 1996). For many young people, including those who have been labelled 'gifted and talented', the transition into senior school can be an unpleasant experience (Phelan et al., 1994).

Autonomous young people should have the ability to make meaningful choices and the conviction to follow through with their own decisions They are principled with regard to right and wrong, and have become less emotionally dependent on their significant others.

The status of the adolescent

One of the key issues at this time is the change in status that young people sense. With changes in status, adolescents sense an increase in freedom as well as increased responsibility. There is, however, an expectation that adolescents will interact differently with their elders and with children as their 'role' in the family changes.

There may well be an increased expectation of service towards other people. Adolescence may bring the right to own property and control over one's income. Adolescents can obtain work positions that younger children cannot. Reaching a certain age allows young people to engage in certain 'adult' activities, such as driving and drinking alcohol. While children may experience serious offences, and adolescents may come into contact with the juvenile justice system, after a certain age adolescents who commit crimes will be handled by adult courts. Young people over the age of 16 encounter adult sanctions when they commit serious crimes. Courts will often rule in a way that is inconsistent with regard to the level of decision-making maturity of adolescents.

In the UK, the age of majority is set legally at 18, but the young person ceases to be a child many years before that. The law does to some extent acknowledge this, and children gradually assume legal rights and responsibilities from a much earlier age. A 13-year-old is only three years away from being able to marry, a 16-year-old can leave home and get a job and a 17-year-old can get a driving licence. Most teenagers are physically capable of becoming parents, yet society, school and family may treat them largely as children. Although they yearn to become independent, many young people will also continue to need the acceptance, love and support of their family for many years to come. Inevitably, frustrations, resentment and confusion arise for teenagers and their parents, and family life can become a battleground.

The concept of intimacy becomes important during the stages of adolescence (Erikson, 1968). Many people, especially teenagers, equate intimacy with sex. Intimacy, it must be stressed, and sex are not the same thing. Intimacy is usually first experienced within the context of same-sex friendships and then develops in romantic relationships. Friendships provide the first setting in which young people can practise their social skills with those who are their equals. It is with friends that adolescents learn how to begin, maintain and terminate relationships, practise social skills and become intimate.

Adolescence is the first time that young people are both physically mature enough to reproduce and cognitively advanced enough to think about it. The teenage years are therefore the prime time for the development of sexuality. Education about sexuality will largely determine whether or not they develop a healthy sexual identity. There is no doubt that the mixed messages teenagers receive about sexuality contribute to problems such as teenage pregnancy and sexually transmitted diseases.

REFLECTIVE ACTIVITY 8.3

First experiences

Discuss in groups of three the following issues.

- *When did you first go on a vacation or an overnight trip without your parents?*

- *If you drink, when did you first have an alcoholic drink and when did you first drink in front of your parents?*

- *Can you briefly describe an adolescent you have met who showed evidence of rapid or slow social development for a particular reason?*

Discuss what may account for the differences in your personal experiences, especially the speed of social development.

Social redefinition in adolescence

One extremely important concept that provides an appreciation of the changes imposed by society upon young people is, according to Muuss (1996), the process of *Social redefinition*. Adolescents will feel more mature and more self-governing, and therefore think differently about dating, marriage and sexuality. This process of social redefinition gives them the right to enter the workforce and could well bring changes in the kinds of relationships and behaviours that are permitted and expected.

Social redefinition is a long process involving many steps, and could well involve initiation ceremonies to signify the adolescent's transition into adulthood. These could be traditional and formal, such as the bar mitzvah or graduation ceremonies. They could, however, be more contemporary, such as college fraternity and sorority 'hazing' ceremonies, and in Europe the concept of the debutante.

In the United States, hazing is defined as harassment, abuse or humiliation by way of initiation. It is a process that may occur in many different contexts, such as schools, colleges, the armed forces and even the workplace (Davis, 1998). It is most 'celebrated' in the context of fraternities, as young people seek acceptance in schools and universities. Although hazing has been prevalent throughout the years, it is poorly understood, partly due to the secretive nature that often accompanies such situations.

In England and France, a debutante is a young lady from an upper-class family who has reached the age of maturity and, as a new adult, is introduced to society at a formal presentation known as her 'debut'. This tradition stemmed from the idea that a girl should be presented to society because she was of marriageable age and needed to find a husband of suitable and similar social standing.

The timing of initiation ceremonies varies across cultures. Within formal initiation, adolescents may be taught the 'hows and whys' of being an adult and this could involve the passing on of cultural, historical and practical conventions between generations. Initiation ceremonies are often performed separately for males and females and there could even be an emphasis upon physical and social differences between males and females. In some traditional Southern Pacific cultures, it could be so extreme as to encourage brother–sister avoidance whereby, after puberty, a brother and sister may have no contact until they are respectively married (Benguigui, 1989).

Social redefinition

A boy of 17 has left home because he wants to live with his girlfriend. He is still studying, receives some money from his parents and always asks for extras. Although he says his parents do not understand him, he still calls his mother every day. He would like to quit his studies like some of his friends have, but says he does not want to accept any job that is not socially rewarding.

Discuss the issues that have affected this young man, paying particular attention to the concept of social redefinition.

Adolescence as psychosocial process

According to Steinberg (1999) young people tend to go through puberty earlier now than 100 years ago, and because of the pressures of schooling the period of adolescence is prolonged. Young people find themselves marginalised, caught between childhood and adulthood, and according to Nightingale and Wolverton (1993) have just a vague sense of when, and how, they become adults. The *social passage of young people into adult roles is too long, too vague and too rocky* (Steinberg, 1999: 91).

As children grow and interact with their environment, the processes underlying their development become increasingly complex. By adolescence, the biological, cognitive, social and cultural have become so intertwined that untangling their separate influences becomes very difficult. Furthermore, the complexity of these processes produces much greater variability in adolescent development than will ever be seen during infancy and childhood.

The inventionist perspective

Inventionists such as Lapsley et al. (1985) argue that, beyond the impact of the cognitive and biological changes, adolescence as a separate developmental stage is primarily defined by society's official recognition of an individual's status as a child, adolescent or adult. The argument is that the social definition of adolescence contributes to many of the problems of contemporary adolescents (Bakan, 1972).

Adolescence has become a label attached by adults to young people, may be because of the boundaries and parameters that are created by society. A line is drawn between childhood and adolescence through the transfer of children from primary school to secondary school, and a further line is created between adolescence and adulthood with the point at which young people can take a job or leave school. The inventionist perspective considers that adolescence is considered explicit only because adults see it as such (Steinberg, 1999: 92).

Many of the behaviours and problems that are apparently characteristic of adolescence are more related to the way that young people are defined by society than biological or psychological influences. This contrasts radically with the traditional, *nativist* viewpoint where adolescence as a concept is driven by puberty, and therefore 'biological destiny'. Adolescence was considered a *turning point* in psychological growth, with childhood regarded as an extension of embryological development (Levinson, 1978).

According to Steinberg (1999) the term 'adolescence' as we now know it was 'invented' around 1900 in the midst of the Industrial Revolution. Prior to the Industrial Revolution, the prime industry was agriculture, and children were viewed as miniature adults. When a youth secured ownership of property, that person was then treated as an adult.

With industrialisation, it became more important for a young person to learn career skills and contribute to society in a way that couldn't be handed down from parents. Schooling took on greater significance and young people were more likely to spend their day with peers. Industrialisation also brought with it the replacement of workers with machines. Children and adolescents were cheap labour, but jobs were scarce and child labour laws were established to protect youth from harsh working conditions. One might also suggest that these laws protected jobs for adults.

REFLECTIVE ACTIVITY **8.5**

Adolescents preparing for adulthood

- *What do you consider to be the **primary roles** of adulthood? How do adolescents currently receive training for these roles?*

- *In an ideal world, how do you think they **should** receive training for these roles?*

- *Do you agree or disagree with the claim that adolescents in contemporary societies are not adequately prepared for the responsibilities they must take on as adults? Why?*

Emerging adulthood

The extension of the time before an individual becomes an adult has created a post- adolescent phase of *emerging adulthood*. Young people within this phase of emerging adulthood face a range of developmental issues. Havighurst (1952) suggested that these include work and relationships. Levinson (1978) focused on changing relationships and on exploration, while Erikson (1968) commented on intimacy and commitment to goals. Super (1980) suggests that exploring and crystallising vocational choice are important to older adolescents and young adults. What seems evident is that older adolescents and young adults enter transitions anticipating empowerment, as they strive to meet evolving personal and career related needs.

Dramatic changes in job opportunities and post-secondary educational opportunities mean that adolescents are often confronted with the challenge of meeting their personal and career needs when neither can guarantee certainty or a sense of personal control. Developmentally, young people encounter personal and career-related needs, involving considerable uncertainty. A lack of progress in one area could impact dramatically upon the other. If, for example, a young person is unable to gain admission to higher education or a job, their ability to move from being a dependent adolescent to an independent adult could be seriously compromised.

In modern society, many young people in their early twenties cannot afford to live on their own, and typically live with their parents or with financial assistance from parents. Many young people feel little motivation and eagerness to enter what they perceive to be a job market with little promise.

Pro-social and anti-social behaviour

Young children who have difficulty regulating emotions are likely to retain this trait through adolescence. The consequences could well be increased aggression, and impaired development of moral judgement. There are dramatic changes in children's understanding of moral obligations. With age, children develop an increasingly sophisticated understanding of rights and responsibilities to others. Sophisticated moral reasoning should lead to higher levels of pro-social behaviour and a lower likelihood of behaving in an anti-social fashion.

It is appropriate that in considering the concept of adolescence and its relationship with pro-social and anti-social behaviour, the work of Piaget (1932) and Kohlberg (1984) should be acknowledged, because their respective theories are seminal in the investigation of moral thinking.

Piaget's two stages of moral reasoning

Piaget (1932) was of the opinion that younger children's moral judgement was governed by unilateral respect for adults and adults' rules. This is called the *heteronomous stage* since children judge that moral rules are fixed and laid down by others, particularly by authority figures, and must be obeyed.

As a result of interaction with peers and through experience, children develop a morality of co-operation and social exchange. Children come to understand that intentions matter, that roles can be reversed. Moral conflicts must be resolved through discussion and compromise with peers. This latter form of reasoning Piaget termed the *autonomous stage* of moral reasoning since it is an internalised process, developing out of children's ability to empathise. Obligations, rights and rules are no longer felt to be one-way or unilateral, but reciprocal. This stage becomes more common in late childhood.

Kohlberg's six stages of moral judgement

Kohlberg (1984), building upon the work of Piaget, proposed a stage theory of moral thinking. Kohlberg identified six stages of judgement.

At the first of these stages, *punishment and obedience orientation*, in common with Piaget's *heteronomous* stage, children believe that 'right' and 'wrong' are determined by powerful adult figures. Morality is something that big people say they must adhere to.

At the second stage, *instrumental morality*, children become increasingly aware of the intentions and desires experienced by others. This appreciation impacts upon moral judgement only when the aspirations of others affect one's own desires and goals. At this stage children appreciate that there is not just one opinion and different people have different points of view.

The third stage, *interpersonal normative morality*, involves a greater level of empathy for the perspectives of others towards oneself. People should meet the expectations of the family and community and behave in 'good' ways. There is an apparent shift from unquestioning obedience to a relativistic outlook. In contrast to the previous stage in which the desires and intentions of others mattered only if they caused conflict with one's own desires, individuals are concerned with how the self is evaluated by others. Individuals seek to be viewed as 'good' and feel guilt when it is likely that others would condemn their behaviour.

Reasoning works best in two-person relationships, particularly with significant others. An appreciation of the perspectives of others is expanded at the next stage, *social system morality*. Individuals understand that all members of a society have intentions and aspirations. Moral judgement focuses on the congruence of one's actions with the rules necessary to preserve social harmony. Moral decisions come about from the perspective of society as a whole, and so thinking is from a 'full-fledged member-of-society perspective' (Colby et al., 1983: 27).

At stage five, *human rights and social welfare morality*, individuals make use of ethical principles to guide moral judgements. People begin to think about society in a very theoretical way, stepping back from their own personal situation to consider the values that society ought to uphold. Colby et al. (1983: 22) insist that social and moral reasoning needs to be respected, and that property has little meaning without life. Young people are trying to determine 'logically what a society ought to be like' (Kohlberg, 1984; Gibbs, 1977).

This stage is concerned largely with the conception of the good society. The suggestion is that certain individual rights are worthy of protection and disputes should be addressed through democratic processes. Democratic processes alone do not always result in outcomes that we intuitively sense are just. A majority, for example, may vote for a law that oppresses a minority. Kohlberg considers that there must be a higher stage, *universal principles*, which articulate the concept of justice. In actual practice, such decisions can be reached merely through empathy.

How moral development occurs

These stages are not the product of maturation. The sequences do not simply unfold according to a genetic blueprint or rite of passage. The stages are also not entirely the product of socialisation.

The stages emerge, instead, from experience. Social experiences promote development, by stimulation of cognitive processes. As we enter discourse and debate, our views may be questioned and challenged and we are therefore motivated to come up with new, more comprehensive points of view. As children interact, they learn how viewpoints differ and how to co-ordinate them in collaborating with others. This enables a tangible appreciation of what is fair and just. These interactions are most successful when they are open and democratic. If children feel pressured simply to conform to authority, they will find it far more difficult to formulate their own ideas.

The work of Kohlberg interrelates with the work of Erikson (1968) because each fundamentally deals with questions that relate to the inseparable topics of ego and character development.

According to Pritchard (1988: 473), character can be seen in the way that one conducts oneself. Character and values are not synonymous, because values are seen as one of the foundations for character, and could be considered orientations or dispositions. Character, in contrast, involves the application or the activation of this knowledge and these values (Walberg and Wynne, 1989).

SUMMARY OF KEY POINTS

The physical changes that signify adolescence occur alongside psychological and social changes that mark this period as a critical stage in becoming an adult. Several models or theories have placed adolescence in a period of human development from birth to death. Most of these are 'stage' models, with each stage completed before the individual moves on to the next.

Each model identifies a different set of 'tasks' as defining adolescence. Piaget simplistically focuses on cognitive development, seeing the development of abstract thinking abilities as making possible the transition to independent adult functioning. Kohlberg considers the moral dilemmas encountered during development. Erikson considers the tensions around the development of personal identity as central to the notion of adolescence.

Adolescence is usually described as a period in which independence is achieved. It is more accurate, however, to talk about a change in the balance of independence and dependence with other aspects of the young person's life, particularly in their interaction with significant others. As adolescents redefine themselves in relation to others, there is a subsequent move to a position where they define other people in relation to themselves. The timing of these changes depends on the different social and cultural expectations of the environment in which the young person lives.

ERENCES

Arnett, J. J. (1999) 'Adolescent storm and stress reconsidered', *American Psychologist*, 54: 17–326.

Bakan, D. (1972) 'Adolescence in America: from idea to social fact', in J. Kagan and R. Coles (eds), *Twelve to Sixteen: Early Adolescence*. New York: W. W. Norton.

Barone, C., Aguirre-Deandreis, A. I. and Trickett, E. J. (1991) 'Mean-ends problem-solving skills, life stress, and social support as mediators of adjustment in the normative transition to high school', *American Journal of Community Psychology*, 19 (2): 207–25.

Benguigui, G. (1989) 'The middle classes in Tonga', *Journal of the Polynesian Society*, 98 (4): 451–63.

Colby, A., Kohlberg, L., Gibbs, J. and Liberman, K. (1983) 'A longitudinal study of moral judgment', *Monographs of the Society for Research in Child Development*, 48 (1) (Serial No. 200).

Davis, P. (1998) 'The burgeoning of benchmarking in British local government – the value of learning by looking, in the public services', *Benchmarking for Quality Management and Technology*, 5: 260–70.

Elder, G. (1979) 'Historical change in life patterns and personality', in P. B. Baltes and O. G. Brim (eds), *Life-span Development and Behaviour*, Vol. 2. New York: Harcourt, Brace and Jovanovich: 118–57.

Erikson, E. H. (1968) *Identity: Youth and Crisis*. New York: Norton.

Gibbs, J. (1977) 'Kohlberg's stages of moral judgment. A constructive critique', *Harvard Educational Review*, 47: 43–61.

Havighurst, R. J. (1952) *Developmental Tasks and Education*. New York: David McKay.

Hayward, C., Killen, J., Wilson, D. and Hammer, L. (1997) 'Psychiatric risk associated with early puberty in adolescent girls', *Journal of the American Academy of Child and Adolescent Psychiatry*, 36 (2): 255–62.

Hertzog, C. J., Morgan, P. L., Diamond, P. A. and Walker, M. J. (1996) 'Transition to high school: a look at student perceptions', *BECOMING*, 7 (2): 6–8.

Hogan, D. and Astone, N. (1986) 'The transition to adulthood', *Annual Review of Sociology*, 12: 109–30.

Kohlberg, L. (1984) *Essays on Moral Development, Vol. II, The Psychology of Moral Development*. San Francisco: Harper & Row.

Lapsley, D., Enright, R. and Serlin, R. (1985) 'Toward a theoretical perspective on the legislation of adolescence', *Journal of Early Adolescence*, 5: 441–66.

Levinson, D. (1978) *The Seasons of a Man's Life*. New York: Ballantine.

Lewin, K. (1948) *Resolving Social Conflicts*. New York: Harper & Row,

Mizelle, N. B. (1995) *Transition from Middle School into High School: The Student Perspective*. Paper presented at the Annual Meeting of the American Educational Research Association, San Francisco.

Muuss, R. E. (1996) *Theories of Adolescence*. New York: McGraw-Hill.

Nightingale, E. O. and Wolverton, L. (1993) 'Adolescent rolelessness in modern society', *Teachers College Record*, 84 (3): 472–86.

Phelan, P., Yu, H. C. and Davidson, A. L. (1994) 'Navigating the psychosocial pressures of adolescence: the voices and experiences of high school youth', *American Educational Research Journal*, 31 (2): 415–47.

Piaget, J. (1932) *The Moral Judgement of the Child*. London: Routledge & Kegan Paul.

Pritchard, I. (1988) 'Character education: research prospects and problems', *American Journal of Education*, 96 (4): 469–95.

Rutter, M. and Smith, D. J. (1995) *Psychosocial Disorders in Young People: Time Trends and Their Causes*. Chichester: J. Wiley & Sons.

Steinberg, L. (1999) *Adolescence*. New York: McGraw-Hill.

Super, D. E. (1980) 'A life-span, life-space approach to career development', *Journal of Vocational Behavior*, 16: 282–98.

Walberg, H. and Wynne, E. (1989) 'Character education: toward a preliminary consensus', in L. Nucci (ed.), *Moral Development and Character Education: A Dialogue*. Berkley, CA: McCutchan.

Part 3

Difference, diversity and multidisciplinary perspectives

9 Children with Special Educational Needs

Martin Ward Fletcher

Learning objectives

By the end of this chapter you should be able to understand the:

- **relationship between theories of social construction and ways in which disabled children's lives are constructed for them;**
- **development of Special Educational Needs education in England;**
- **concept of normality in relation to the experience of disabled children;**
- **experience of children with specific disabilities and the basis upon which they receive additional support;**
- **relationship between the professional and the institution and the child.**

Introduction

This chapter uses the term 'disabled' to refer to all children who require additional support in whatever context, including within education. The terms 'disabled' and 'Special Educational Needs' (SEN) when used in relation to children have become increasingly interchangeable. There is a significant difference between the term 'disabled (SEN) children' and 'children with disabilities (SEN)'. A disabled child can be defined as one who, because of his or her physical or intellectual state, requires an appropriate response from the society in which he or she lives in order for her or him to have equivalent access to that society. This can be compared with the official definitions that have existed in various government documents since the 1981 Education Act. The 2001 Code of Practice (DfES, 2001) defines children with 'special educational needs' thus:

> *Children have special educational needs if they have a learning difficulty which calls for special educational provision to be made for them. Children have a learning difficulty if they:*
>
> *(a) have a significantly greater difficulty in learning than the majority of children of the same age; or*
>
> *(b) have a disability which prevents or hinders them from making use of educational facilities of a kind generally provided for children of the same age in schools within the area of the local education authority, or*
>
> *(c) are under compulsory school age and fall within the definition at (a) or (b) above or would so do if special educational provision was not made for them.*
>
> *Children must not be regarded as having a learning difficulty solely because the language or form of language of their home is different from the language in which they will be taught.*
>
> (DfEE, 1996)

In addition, Part 2 of the Special Educational Needs and Disability Act 2001 amends the Disability Discrimination Act 1995 to prohibit all schools from discriminating against disabled children in their admissions arrangements, in the education and associated services provided by the school for its pupils or in relation to exclusions from the school. The reasonable adjustments duty on schools does not require the provision of auxiliary aids and services or the removal or alteration of physical features. Decisions about the provision of educational aids and services for children with SEN will continue to be taken within the SEN framework.

Labelling

Labelling is an issue of considerable debate within the disabled community. Educationalists such as Child (2004) have been aware for several decades that applying a label to a child can have the effect of determining both individuals' (such as teachers') and institutions' interaction with the child in such a way that the effects of the label are reinforced in positive or negative ways; if a teacher identifies a child as stupid there is a good chance that their lives in the classroom will be constructed by the teacher and eventually by the children and the school in ways that ensure that they will perform in ways that conform to the construction of stupid. Disabled children are faced with the additional requirement by society that they meet the criteria that allow them to be regarded as 'normal'. Thus if the teacher and others think the child is going to be unable to function in ways that society determines to be normal then what is the point in educating them according to the curriculum experience offered to other children?

All of us have our lives constructed by the interactions that we have with all of the elements in our lives. This is a persistent process that places the emphasis on the interactive process. Thus the professional has an influence upon the construction of a child's life and the child's understanding of him or herself, particularly as such elements as self-esteem and behaviour form their personal narrative that is itself communicated to others. Therefore both parties to an interaction are responsible, in part, for the construction of the other's self. This process does not simply operate between individuals; it also works between the individual and groups as well as within groups of people and even between the individual and institutions. The school and its structures and regulations may not only have an effect upon the individual (and teacher) but the child will have an effect upon and create change in the institution. There are many factors such as empathy, position and power that mitigate the influence that the child can have upon a teacher or the institution that they are part of. In many cases the teachers' and schools' lack of understanding of this process, which results in their failure to listen to the messages that the child is giving, leads to the alienation of the child and the slow descent into failure, rejection of the school and non-standard and challenging behaviour, and in some cases the decision of the school to exclude the child or the child to exclude themselves from the school.

Segregation, integration and inclusion

The last 65 years of the education system's response to children with special educational needs has been characterised by significant change in the basic philosophy that underpins the provision of support for disabled children. Furthermore these changes can be seen to parallel the two models of disability that are discussed below. The 1944 Education Act (Dent, 1968) and the subsequent development of 11 categories of need represented a process where a small percentage of children (2–3 per cent) medically were diagnosed as having significant levels of need which meant that they were removed from mainstream education and segregated from their peer group (and often their families) in institutions that were 'designed' to cater for their particular need.

The Warnock Report (1978) represents the first flowering of the move away from segregation to integration and subsequently inclusion in mainstream school. In addition the report identified the fact that 'one in five' children will at some time require additional support while in school. Thus we see the first acknowledgement that special needs constitutes a broader category than the one that had previously applied. The Warnock Report led to the 1981 Education Act (Cox, 1985). The 1981 Act abolished the 11 categories, introduced the process of statementing (later formalised in the semi-legal Codes of Practice (DfES, 2001). In addition the 1981 Education Act gave a strong steer to local education authorities that they should be moving towards a structure that integrated children with special educational needs into mainstream schools. Weddell, writing at the end of 1980s, saw the 1981 Education Act as representing a significant shift from the view that the child's special educational needs were located solely in the individual child's pathology to a view that there is an interactive dimension to the child's needs (Weddell et al., 1988). The 1980s saw a focus upon the development of the ability of mainstream schools to accommodate children who had previously been educated in special schools. The response was, however, patchy with some authorities moving many of the children to mainstream and other authorities overseeing a growth in the numbers of children in their special schools. Furthermore the response to 'Warnock's 20%' of children with special needs was also patchy with some local authorities creating advisory teams but putting little in the form of direct resources into their schools while others increased the amount of resources for schools. Even today 28.4 per cent of disabled children still attend segregated special schools (Disability Awareness in Action, 1997).

The 1990s and the start of the twenty-first century are characterised by a move from integration to inclusion. Professionals working with disabled children found that the experience of disabled children in mainstream was actually one of exclusion and segregation and that in many cases the curriculum experience of the disabled child was not centred on the same objectives as the rest of the class. Thus it provided an experience which was unnecessarily different and fell outside the normal boundaries of curriculum planning described by the proper process of differentiation in classroom planning, practice and delivery. The first Code of Practice (DfEE, 1994) with its emphasis in the early stages of identification and support went some way towards resolving the issue but the attachment of Individual Education Plans to the child in many cases failed to solve the issue of separate provision and different objectives and agendas. The move towards a process of full inclusion and away from an integration policy was supported by the Labour government in its 1997 Green Paper (DfEE, 1997) and further emphasised by the 2001 Disability and Special Educational Needs Education Act and the subsequent publication of the second Code of Practice (DfES, 2001). Inclusion demands that schools and teachers provide all the support required to enable all children to participate in all aspects of the curriculum. The disabled child in the corner of the classroom with a learning support assistant velcroed to him or her and pursuing a largely separate curriculum is not being included; indeed this model of 'support' represents only the poorest form of integration.

Inside the social construction paradigm reside the dominant models that have influenced and arguably controlled thinking in the area of disability studies for the last 30-plus years. Barnes (1991), Barnes and Mercer, (1996), Barton and Oliver (1997) and Oliver (1990, 1996a, 1996b) were among those who pulled together the thinking that was present in the previous 15 years to form the persistent analysis of the position of disabled people and, by extension, children with special educational needs into the form of two models.

The medical model (also known as the individual model and often, in North America, as the social pathology model) has been, and probably remains, the dominant model of disability. This is a deficit model. The model states that the social, educational and economic restrictions that disabled people experience reside in the diagnosed medical concerns of the individual disabled person and from that diagnosis must be determined the appropriate response or prescription. The use of the word 'medical' highlights the centrality of the medical profession and associated 'experts' in their diagnostic role. This has significant implications for the disabled person, for the issuing of a prescription to the disabled person enables the professionals, including teachers, to persuade themselves that they have done all that they can for the individual and it is now the individual's responsibility to respond to that prescription and 'improve' or 'get better'. For many teachers this means that they can reassure themselves that they are not responsible for a child's failure and allows them to blame the child for their lack of achievement in school, including in this blame category any factors the child experiences outside the school. The parallels with the pre-1978 philosophy of segregation for the severely disabled child and the passive acceptance of their failure, together with the education system's persistently ignoring the needs of the balance of Warnock's 20 per cent of children and the medical model, are clear.

The development of a social model that evolved from the work of symbolic interactionists sees the individual as in receipt of a set of discourses from other people that enable the individual to develop an awareness of the view of themselves that others have (Berger and Luckman, 1967). The social interactions between the individual and their environment socially construct each individual's life just as he or she contributes to the construction of other lives. The social model of disability holds that the medical or other concerns of the individual are not the sole locus of the disability. It is the response of society, its institutions and individuals and their inability to understand, support and enable the disabled person that emphasises, constructs and creates the disabled person's disability (Oliver, 1990). Oliver usefully divides the social model into two elements. He sees the, now dominant, model of social construction as being one which is concerned primarily with the interaction of individuals or groups with the disabled person whereas he seeks to make a distinction between the interactions of individuals and the theory that *the problem is located within the institutionalised practices of society* (Oliver, 1900: 83).

The social creation model recognises that aspects of society are disablist as a result not only of the response to disabled people by individuals and social processes but also the institutions of society. This is based upon a sociology of institutions that argues that institutions are identifiable, separate elements in people's lives. This is particularly apparent when we explore the institution of the school and its associated structures such as classroom or school grouping by ability and the processes of withdrawal or restriction of curriculum access based upon decisions (widely variable between individual schools) about the child's level of achievement. Other regulations and rules (formal and informal) may also create and construct the disabled child's life while in school in ways that are negative and depressing. Would a school be prepared to place a child with learning difficulties at the head of the annual production just before the mid-winter break? We can extend this thinking to include all of the bureaucratic and regulatory paraphernalia that is part of the modern education system.

REFLECTIVE ACTIVITY 9.1

Factors that influence the experience of the disabled child in mainstream school

Research and analyse the relationship between parental choice, Ofsted, the publication of school results and the experience of the disabled child in mainstream school.

This chapter has, so far, provided a summary of the central historical elements that have constructed the lives of the disabled child together with the framework of social construction that is central to an understanding of the life of the disabled child. The chapter will now explore the experience of disabled children in three areas: attention deficit hyperactivity disorder, autism and dyslexia. These three groups of disabled children have been selected because they enable the reader to understand the common elements within these children's lives as well as the elements that distinguish one group from another. The terms 'special educational needs' and 'disabled' embrace a very broad category and while all children with special needs may have their lives constructed according to certain common narratives, for example, being seen as an object of pity and a subject for well meaning but ultimately dysfunctional charitable concerns, nevertheless each category of disability needs to be explored by the professional involved with the child while at the same time being aware that it is only pathologies that can be seen as common, each individual within a category must necessarily be thought of and considered as an individual.

Attention deficit hyperactivity disorder

From: http://www.adhdalliance.org.uk/What_is_ADHD.asp

Attention-Deficit/Hyperactivity Disorder (ADHD) is a common condition affecting several per cent of school age children. It is more common in boys but girls may currently be under-diagnosed. There are three subtypes: ADHD mainly inattentive, ADHD mainly hyperactive-impulsive, and ADHD combined. The first of these is sometimes referred to as ADD (Attention Deficit Disorder). When ADHD is combined with motor-perceptual problems (also referred to as Developmental Coordination Disorder or dyspraxia) some clinicians refer to DAMP (Deficits in Attention, Motor control and Perception). When problems are very severe and all the diagnostic features listed below are present the criteria for Hyperkinetic Disorder may be met. Thus, ADD, DAMP, and Hyperkinetic Disorder are all subtypes of ADHD.

The diagnostic features are:

- *Inattentiveness – very short attention span, over-frequent changes of activity, extreme distractibility.*

- *Overactivity – excessive movements, especially in situations expecting calm such as classroom or mealtimes.*

- *Impulsiveness – affected person will not wait their turn, acts without thinking, thoughtless rule-breaking.*

The problems are disabling, start at an early age and they are present in more than one situation, for example home and school. Sometimes affected children show underachievement at school, poor sleep, social interaction difficulties, autistic-type features, speech-languages difficulties, discipline problems, temper tantrums, unpopularity, and accident-proneness. However, all these can have other causes too. IQ can be high, normal, low normal or in the learning disability range.

Various genetic and environmental risk factors for ADHD have been identified. Hereditary aspects, neuroimaging data and responses to pharmacotherapeutic agents support the suggestion that ADHD has a biological component. However, there is a continuing debate over the causes of ADHD.

ADHD, in common with the other two disabilities considered in this chapter, is characterised by the individuality of the disability so that no two people experience the disability in the same way. The potential effects of the disability can be very severe, both for those close to the person and the person him/herself. Assessment of the number of people who have the disability is between one and two per cent in the United Kingdom but clearly many more people are affected by the lives of these disabled children. Even though many of the young people who are affected by the disability find that it disappears in early adulthood nevertheless the effects of disrupted education and disrupted social development can be severe and last for many decades in the person's life.

Estimates of the prevalence of ADHD vary widely within and between countries. It is estimated to affect 3–9% of school-aged children and young people in the UK, and about 2% of adults worldwide would meet the DSM-IV diagnostic criteria for ADHD. Prevalence estimates for hyperkinetic disorder are around 1–2% in the UK.

f) *Diagnosis of ADHD is about three to four times more common in males than in females, although this gender imbalance may be inflated to some extent by referral biases (that is, more boys are sent for clinical assessment of ADHD than girls).*

g) *The prescribing of stimulant drugs for ADHD reflects the increased frequency of diagnosis of this condition. In 1998 there were about 220,000 prescriptions in England for stimulant drugs (methylphenidate and dexamfetamine) at a net ingredient cost of about £5 million; in 2004 this number had almost doubled to 418,300 at a cost of almost £13 million.*

(NICE [National Institute for Clinical Excellence], 2006)

There is a number of views concerning the 'causes' of ADHD but there is clearly no sole pathology that is clear and identifiable. What we can observe is the fact that ADHD operates in many people's minds as a subset of a larger group of children with emotional and behavioural disturbance (EBD). The central issue behind the failure of many schools and teachers to develop appropriate strategies for the ADHD child to enable them to learn effectively is the fact that there is a shared construction of what is normal in school and what constitutes behaviour that is not normal and therefore justifies the school giving up on the child and, in many cases, excluding the child from the school. Teachers and schools in most cases see nothing wrong in this process. Their view of the child is that it is the child's fault that they are not deemed to be normal enough to be accepted by the school and there is frequently a failure on the part of the teacher and the schools to accept that the problems that the child is experiencing in school are located in the teacher's, the school's and the education system's failure to provide a learning environment that is appropriate to the child's needs.

It is important to note that in all these debates we have to be careful about the issue of resources. People within the education system will often argue that they cannot 'deal' with particular children – especially the 'disruptive' child – when they actually mean that they do not have the resources to support the child, the teachers and the school as a whole. It may be that many teachers are content with the status quo preferring to be relieved of the problem rather than have to work within an appropriately funded resource envelope to provide the support that the disabled child needs. Teachers who are properly supported should not have to put in extra hours of preparation and thought in order to support a particular child: the resources should be there to enable them to do this.

Thus the ADHD child is constructed as an outsider with all the consequences that that has from a failure to engage with most of the aspects of the school curriculum to the lack of a positive social group of peers. The negative relationship between schools and children with ADHD is only one example of the way in which people with ADHD have their lives constructed in ways that lead to negative outcomes. For example, it is probable that many people inside prisons and young offenders institutions have a form of ADHD:

> *How strong is the link between ADHD and crime? Figures from the US suggest that between 18 and 76 per cent of prisoners have ADHD. UK figures on ADHD are harder to come by, but in 2001 the HM Inspectorate of Prisons said 50 per cent of young people on remand had a mental health problem, 10 times the level in the population as a whole.*

(Haymarket Publishing, 2006)

Similarly, statistics for other vulnerable groups find ADHD present in significant numbers. For example, a Scottish Health Department survey of young homeless people identified ADHD as a significant factor in young homeless people, especially those who were hard to contact and who were inclined to spurn offers of support (Watt, 2006).

REFLECTIVE ACTIVITY **9.2**

Supporting children with ADHD

1. *Explore the debate about the management of ADHD through a course of drug therapy. While some accept that this is an appropriate process for these children, others oppose it.*

2. *Explore the issues that professionals working with children with ADHD will encounter and potential strategies for supporting the children.*

Autism and Asperger's syndrome

The adoption by the professionals who work with children with autism and Asperger's Syndrome of the term 'Autistic Spectrum Disorder' (ASD) which is a term devised by Wing (1996). The term is used in order that children whose previous labels (which may or may not continue to be used) embrace a wide field. Jones identifies a number of other labels that fall into the realm of ASD: *Asperger Syndrome, High functioning Autism, semantic pragmatic disorder (SPD), atypical autism,* and *pervasive developmental disorder – not otherwise specified (PDD-NOS)* (Jones, 2006: 3).

Possible causes of autism

There is no known and definitive cause of autism. The Environmental Illness Resource (EIR, 2006) list the leading theories for the cause(s) of Autistic Spectrum Disorders as:

- **genetic;**
- **vaccinations;**
- **yeast/candida;**
- **heavy metal toxicity;**
- **chemical exposure;**
- **low glutathione and oxidative stress;**
- **gluten and casein.**

The issue of incidence is a contentious one. Readers will readily find studies that suggest the incidence of ASD has risen significantly in the last 20 years. It is clear from other studies, however, that this is not a growth in incidence but a growth in the boundaries that define ASD. This debate when reflected in the media has a profound affect upon the public (BBC, 2001a; BBC, 2001b). Jones discusses the difficulties of establishing data concerning prevalence and, in addition, notes the difficulties involved in diagnosing the child with ASD (Jones, 2002).

Certainly once a child has obtained a 'label' then we can speculate that his or her life will be constructed in a way that emphasises the differences between the child and the 'normal' child. While it is clear that labels in English society are a critical factor in accessing resources to support a child, nevertheless the public's (and many professionals'?) understanding of many disabilities including ASD is poor, and poor and inaccurate information can only lead to ineffective and possibly damaging interactions with the ASD child.

The nature of ASD is such that it is very challenging for any professional who works with these children and adults. The failure by them to understand our world and the near impossibility of understanding their world means that we can interpret the person with ASD's interactions with their environment only in our terms. It is possible that with practice and experience we will come to an understanding of how to interact with ASD people but having identified strategies and behaviours that appear to work according to our analysis we still have no way of knowing why our interactions and strategies do so.

The concept of normality is a particularly critical one in the life of the child or adult with ASD. Clearly many ASD people face reaction by many if not all of the people who they meet on the grounds that they are not able to develop the knowledge, understanding, values and behaviours that will enable them to join in with the 'normal' club. For many people with ASD who are within the top end of moderate to severe category this may not be something that concerns them but many people in the bottom end of moderate and the mild categories (including those who are diagnosed with Asperger's syndrome) have an awareness of their disability. Professionals will become aware of this and, once again, must make sure that there are appropriate strategies in place to enable this group to feel included while at the same time ensuring that they are not required to deny their disability. It is hard for any disabled person to be asked to deny their disability in order to be able to join in the normals' club and many of those who do find themselves experiencing negative social and emotional reactions as a product of their denial.

Dyslexia

This has been and continues to be a disability that is subject to considerable debate and, in some professionals' minds, significant questions about the nature and extent of dyslexia within the population still exist. The label persists although the, arguably no more useful, term 'specific learning difficulties (dyslexia)' (Payne and Turner, 1998) is preferred by some groups of professionals. The word 'dyslexia' is used to describe *Children who have difficulties in reading, writing, spelling or manipulating number which are not typical of the general level of performance* (Payne and Turner, 1998: 3). For example, the British Dyslexia Society on its web page (**http://www.bdadyslexia.org.uk/ whatisdyslexia.html**) offers a significantly different response to its question 'What is dyslexia?' Thus anyone seeking to find an absolute and definitive explanation of the meaning of the term dyslexia is likely to encounter a host of variations. This inevitably leads to confusion especially when it is linked to the position that there are levels of dyslexia: mild, moderate and severe. The professional is therefore faced with many variations on the central theme and a category of disability that is lacking in precision; in short it is not much more useful as a 'diagnosis' that the term 'disability'.

The incidence of dyslexia in the population is said by Dyslexia Action (formerly the British Dyslexia Institute) to *vary greatly – from 4–10% of the population. It is believed to be four times more prevalent in males than females* (**http://www.dyslexia-inst.org.uk/articles/adult_dyslexia.htm**) and a knowledge and understanding of the raft of individual learning issues subsumed under the word dyslexia must be part of any teachers' professional toolbox. In addition there is increasing evidence of the effects that many people, who fail to have appropriate support provided for them at school because their learning difficulties fall within the dyslexia boundaries, will experience additional difficulties in adult life. The National Literacy Trust on its website (**http://www.dyslexia-inst. org.uk/articles/adult_dyslexia.htm**) quotes a figure of 50 per cent as the number of young offenders who have dyslexia. The Literacy Trust also notes that a similar study at Polmont prison in Scotland produced similar results.

Clearly there are many people, both children and adults, who have learning difficulties that can correctly be placed within the boundaries described by dyslexia. It appears, however, that each person has their own individual set of learning difficulties that need to be addressed and supported with a programme that is particular to the individual. In the real world, of course, this is not always possible given the limitations of resources and, presently, expertise. People with dyslexia, however, will benefit from one or more of a number of established strategies which address their particular form of disability. Therefore professional diagnosis and support from trained professionals who understand dyslexia and its subsets are essential for the generalised professional. All professionals who are working with people who are using their literacy skills need to be aware of some more general principles of support which should inform their work with people with dyslexia. For example, strategies for lecturers in further and higher education recommended by the British Dyslexia Association (**http://www.bdadyslexia.org.uk/extra330.html**) are for the most part simply examples of good practice that it would be sensible for all lecturers to adopt if they do not already do so.

Dyslexia also illustrates many of the issues that are contained in the experience of the disabled person. The model of social construction seeks to counter the view that the disability is a matter of individual pathology and that the prime responsibility is for the disabled individual to 'get better' as a result of the 'prescription' that he or she is offered. In the case of the dyslexic person and particularly the dyslexic child, this is a particularly inappropriate model. In the first instance many dyslexic children (and their parents) have to struggle to have their disability recognised and then to have the correct and appropriate resources allocated to them in order to support their learning. Teachers who worked with children before the disability of dyslexia became generally recognised and accepted are aware that many children obviously went through their entire school career labelled as 'lazy' or 'stupid' or 'disorganised' or any one of a number of related labels. In many cases these children received little or no effective education and were condemned to a life of restricted opportunity and frustration as a result. There was a view that such 'diagnoses' meant that the learning disability of the child was fixed and immutable and that teachers were not required to provide any additional support for these children.

Furthermore the application of any label to an individual such as dyslexic immediately constructs in the minds of individuals such as teachers and institutions such as schools a model of the 'dyslexic child' which then influences their interactions with the child. Often this model will be a negative one. Certain teachers may welcome a diagnosis which confirms the reason for the child's failure to learn effectively and which sanctions, in the mind of the teacher, their reaction to that child. This reaction can be a positive or a negative one. The reaction to the child with dyslexia being a negative one and children failing to prosper in the school environment meant that in some cases these children were caught in a spiral of failure and associated responses such as deviant behaviour, truancy and other behaviours viewed by society as the behaviour of people for whom the 'system' need have little or no regard.

REFLECTIVE ACTIVITY **9.3**

How the lives of children with other disabilities are constructed

Explore two other disabilities commonly found in children and young people and the ways in which their lives are constructed.

The experience of disabled children has changed quite dramatically in the time since the publication of the Warnock Report (1978). Many disabilities have been identified correctly in children through a significant increase in the quality of screening and diagnosis. Disabled children are living in a world that does not exclude them to the extent that they were once segregated and made to feel rejected and useless. Inclusion has gained much ground as the preferred structure for all children and there has been a clear recognition that 'normal' is a very broad term which, as a result, is now arguably redundant as society accepts that all children should be thought of as normal and included.

REFLECTIVE ACTIVITY **9.4**

Exploring the concept of inclusion

Explore the final paragraph through your reading and research and consider the ideas within it. To what extent are all children included in society and the educational process?

SUMMARY OF KEY POINTS

This chapter has explored the relationship between theories of social construction and considered ways in which the lives of disabled children are constructed for them. The development of special educational needs education in England has been traced and the concepts of segregation, integration and inclusion introduced. How the concept of normality relates to the experience of disabled children has been expounded along with the relationship between the professional and the institution and the child. Three areas of disability – attention deficit hyperactivity disorder (ADHD), autism and Asperger's syndrome, and dyslexia – have been explored to better understand the experience of children diagnosed with these disabilities and the basis upon which they can receive additional support.

REFERENCES

Barnes, C. (1991) *Disabled People in Britain: A case for Anti-discrimination Legislation*. London: Hurst.

Barnes, C. and Mercer, G. (eds) (1996) *Exploring the Divide*. Leeds: Disability Press.

Barton, L. and Oliver, M. (1997) *Disability Studies: Past Present and Future*. Leeds: Disability Press.

BBC (2001a) *Autism rates 'not rising'*, 15 February at:
http://news.bbc.co.uk/1/hi/health/1170424.stm

BBC (2001b) *Autism levels are '10 times higher'*, 27 February at:
http://news.bbc.co.uk/1/hi/health/1193046.stm

Berger, P. and Luckmann, T. (1967) *The Social Construction of Reality*. London: Allen Lane.

Child, D. (2004) *Psychology and the Teacher*. London: Continuum.

Cox, B. (1985) *The Law of Special Educational Needs: A Guide to the Education Act 1981*. London: Croom Helm.

Dent, H. C. (1968) *The Education Act, 1944*. London: University of London Press.

DfEE (1994) *Special Educational Needs: Code of Practice 1994*. London: Stationary Office.

DfEE (1997) *Excellence for All: Meeting Special Educational Needs*, Green Paper. London: DfEE.

DfES (2001) *Special Educational Needs: Code of Practice 2001*. London: HMSO (also at: http://www.teachernet.gov.uk/_doc/3724/SENCodeOfPractice.pdf)

Disability Awareness in Action (1997) *Disabled Women*. London: Disability Awareness in Action.

Environmental Illness Resource (EIR) (2006) *Autism Spectrum Disorders*. See:
http://www.ei-resource.org/default.asp

Haymarket Publishing (2006) *Young People Now*, 10 November 2006 at:
http://www.ypnmagazine.com/news/index.cfm?fuseaction=full_news&ID=7463

Jones, G., (2002) *Educational Provision for Children with Autism and Asperger Syndrome*. Trowbridge: Cromwell Press.

NICE (National Institute for Clinical Excellence) (2006) *Attention Deficit Hyperactivity Disorder (ADHD) (draft scope)*. NICE, at:
http://www.nice.org.uk/page.aspx?o=290259

Oliver, M. (1990) *The Politics of Disablement*. Basingstoke: Macmillan.

Oliver, M. (1996a) 'Defining impairment and disability: issues at stake', in C. Barnes and G. Mercer (eds), *Exploring the Divide*. Leeds: Disability Press.

Oliver, M. (1996b) *Understanding Disability: From Theory to Practice*. Basingstoke: Macmillan.

Payne, T. and Turner, E. (1998) *Dyslexia: A Parents' and Teachers' Guide*, Parents' and Teachers' Guides No. 3. Clevedon: Multilingual Matters.

Warnock, M. (chair), Committee of Enquiry into the Education of Handicapped and Young People (1978) *Special Educational Needs: Report of the Committee of Enquiry into the Education of Handicapped Children and Young People*. London: HMSO.

Watt, G. (2006) *Young, Single Homeless People*. Edinburgh: NHS, Scotland.

Wedell, K., Goacher, B., Evans, J. and Welton, J. (1988) *Policy and Provision for Special Educational Needs*. London: Cassell.

Wing, L. (1996) *The Austistic Spectrum*. London: Constable.

10 Entitlement and potential – overcoming barriers to achievement

David Stewart and Tina Harris

Learning objectives

By the end of this chapter you should be able to:

- **understand what is meant by potential;**
- **recognise how to unlock potential across a range of children with differing abilities and needs in a busy classroom;**
- **ensure that all pupils are able to access the learning they are entitled to in order to reach their potential.**

Introduction

In entering into any analysis around barriers to achieving potential, regardless of setting or vocation, it is critical to note and understand the entitlement of each individual and the responsibilities placed upon organisations. Schools in particular must take account of the general teaching requirements of the Revised National Curriculum, published in 2002, to provide an inclusive curriculum as detailed in the statutory inclusion statement:

> Schools have a responsibility to provide a broad and balanced curriculum for all pupils. The National Curriculum is the starting point for planning a school curriculum that meets the specific needs of individuals and groups of pupils. This statutory inclusion statement on providing effective learning opportunities for all pupils outlines how teachers can modify, as necessary, the National Curriculum programmes of study to provide all pupils with relevant and appropriately challenging work at each key stage. It sets out three principles that are essential to developing a more inclusive curriculum.
>
> 1. Setting suitable learning challenges.
>
> 2. Responding to pupils' diverse learning needs.
>
> 3. Overcoming potential barriers to learning and assessment for individuals and groups of pupils.

This is the challenge faced every day by the many teachers in our schools. This chapter discusses that challenge and offers some practical advice and strategies to overcome the barriers to achievement. Statutory engagement in the meeting of each individual's entitlement to education belies the complexity of how to complete the journey to where he/she can independently realise his/her own potential and overcome his/her own challenges. What follows in this chapter are the views of two practitioners: Tina Harris, Leader of the County Inclusive Resource, and David Stewart, Executive Headteacher, based at Beacon Hill School in Suffolk. The school caters for pupils with moderate learning difficulties and provides a countywide outreach service for all mainstream schools in Suffolk that engage in a holistic approach alongside other agencies and, of course, parents. Experiences within our day-to-day roles have convinced us that the views and strategies expounded in this chapter will have a relevance and resonance with all professionals who are engaged in child development, study and learning, and of the barriers to achievement and how they can be surmounted.

Ensuring access to learning

Being able to access learning is dependent on many factors that include the following.

- Understanding the expectations.
- Feeling the work is at the right level.
- Accessing the medium the work is presented in.
- Being motivated to undertake the task.

All of these factors are important in order for the pupil to be in a position to access the learning. The teacher should consider these points in a personal checklist to make sure that the pupil is on track and actively engaged with learning. In considering these factors the area of motivation is complicated by being so interlinked with other factors, hence its length in this chapter.

Understanding the expectations

Understanding what is expected is so important. Some pupils will need more guidance than others in this area. Some pupils may need differentiated worksheets that give guidance on where and how much to write, whereas for other pupils an empty page is appropriate. Checklists can be helpful for pupils who find it hard to keep in mind the complete task. If pupils see only each small step in the task and need to be continually prompted to complete each part, they are likely to become very prompt-reliant and are less likely to ever independently manage or take responsibility for their learning in any meaningful way.

Feeling the work is at the right level

For the pupil to feel the work is at the right level the teacher needs to have pitched it correctly: too hard and the pupil may switch off, too easy and it won't provide enough of a challenge. However, the messages that our expectations give to a pupil are complex and need further consideration. If the teacher has low expectations of the pupil, the pupil will learn to have low expectations of him/herself. If the parent has low expectations of the child, this will both initiate the child's acceptance of that assessment and reinforce the low expectations of the teacher. 'I can't' almost always means 'I am unwilling to make the effort', and 'he/she can't' is very often an unconscious signal from the adult that the prospect of trying to elicit a sufficient effort from the child is too wearisome to undertake for long. Faint-heartedness, or even sheer lassitude, on the part of adults, expressed in the forms of low expectation of what a child may be able to achieve or a reluctance to allow the child to take responsibility for his/her actions, frequently constitute the most formidable barriers to a successful educative process. Peter Mittler (2000: viii) has summarised this admirably: *I have come to believe that the main obstacles to change lie in ourselves, in our attitudes and fear, in our tendency to underestimate people and to exaggerate the difficulties and disappointments they might encounter if they 'failed'.*

Expectations should be kept high but realistic. If pupils are led to believe that their abilities are better than they really are, then the adults who have allowed this to happen are guilty of setting these pupils up for, at best, disappointment but more likely failure and rejection. A just realism is more ethical and more fair than false encouragement.

Accessing the medium the work is presented in

Considering the learning style of the pupil is vitally important. Shaw and Hawes (1998) discuss visually-orientated learners, auditorily-orientated learners and kinaesthetically-orientated learners and reinforce how important it is to use different presentation styles and provide access to different learning materials and activities to ensure that children have opportunities to learn through their preferred representational system.

For some pupils even when work is presented in their preferred learning style, tasks can still appear too 'busy', with too many areas to deal with at once. Stripping work down to the most important concept is sometimes necessary in order for pupils to engage.

Sometimes it is necessary to help pupils to reframe their thinking around what they see as work. A classic response from a visual/kinaesthetic learner to the teacher is to say 'hurry up and finish talking so that I can get on with the work'. This learner needs support in how to access information given orally. Pupils are often expected to sit and listen during this part of the lesson, whereas if they were given paper to take notes or make diagrams from the oral information suddenly there is a point to listening and a focus for the visual learner.

Being motivated to learn

This area is so interlinked with the other factors it is almost impossible to distinguish it as a separate factor. Pupils will feel more motivated to work if they understand the expectations, can connect with the way work is presented and are free from distractions. However, even with all these factors in place, pupils can still lack motivation, so it is important to consider in more depth where our motivation stems from and how it is possible to encourage intrinsic motivation in order to develop a deep-rooted positive attitude to learning.

Motivating pupils to learn involves our taking for granted that they have certain skills and it is therefore wise to make sure that these skills are actually in place and in a state to be developed. A pupil's motivation, for example, depends heavily on his/her understanding of cause and effect, and it is important to consider this, as the responses from and interaction with adults which a child gets from a very young age will shape his/her motivation by making him/her respond to situations in specific ways.

We are all motivated by different things and at different times. Why we choose to do something will be affected by:

● materialistic motivation;
● social motivation;
● intrinsic motivation.

Often we do something because of all three. Working adults may be doing a job for money but enjoy their work and put in over and above what is required to get intrinsic satisfaction from doing a good job. They may receive positive feedback from colleagues for doing this, which also makes them feel good. Children gain intrinsic satisfaction from getting *their* work completed, presenting it neatly, keeping their book looking nice and so forth, and they are likely to get positive feedback from their teacher which encourages them to continue to work hard. Receiving a merit adds materialistic motivation into the mix. Judging children's level of engagement with an activity will show how intrinsically motivated they are. It is really important to foster this intrinsic motivation, as children will truly learn only if they are engaged with the task.

Intrinsic learners are problem-solvers who take real responsibility for their actions and learning. It is this that builds self-esteem and an ability to evaluate ourselves and make greater progress at improving our skills. Looking for affirmation and reassurance from others is a good thing up to a point, but without intrinsic motivation we are not able to take full responsibility for our work or actions or know if we have done a good job unless we have had it confirmed as such by others. Children who have not developed this intrinsic motivation are usually not very good at problem-solving. They are reliant on firm adult boundaries, and if these are not present we often see a regression in their behaviour. Eventually these are the pupils who respond negatively to a range of teaching styles at secondary school (especially when a supply teacher is covering a lesson), because these children have not acquired the internal mechanisms to self-evaluate and monitor themselves and their learning. Often, too, these pupils lack self-esteem and do not have a good image of themselves.

What we do also depends on short- and long-term gratification. These two are often in direct conflict with each other. In order to avoid getting into trouble, for example, a pupil must avoid the short-term gratification of thumping a peer who has called him/her a name. Often resisting a short-term motivator is very hard and it is only really having strong intrinsic motivation at that point that will make the difference and allow long-term gratification to be reached. As children begin to make their own choices as toddlers it is the immediate short-term gratification that motivates them. As they get older they begin to develop the skills to put off something immediately desirable in order to get an even better reward, for example saving up pocket money for something big. But some children often seem to find it hard to focus on longer-term motivators. However much you talk through what will happen later as a longer-term consequence, in the heat of the moment it is the short-term motivator that drives the action. It is really important to consider what that short-term motivator is for the child at that particular moment. If we can realise this then we can steer the action. For example, if the motivating factor is the actual adult interaction, by not interacting at that point we remove the motivator and the child's actions are not reinforced. Let us put this in the context of a child running off. Why is he/she responding to a situation in that way? It could be that he/she is confused and anxious and running away from a situation. It could be to get a reaction and see what will happen. If it is the latter, the child is likely to look back while running to see what is happening, which may well mean that the child is highly socially motivated and has learnt that one gets plenty of adult attention by running off. The motivating factor is the adult reaction and the intrinsic feeling of being in control. If the adult does not follow the child, the motivating factor (i.e. the adult) thereupon becomes the reason for the child to return and not run off. Patterns of behaviour can be turned around in this way, but the child needs to experience consistent consequences in order not to revert to previous responses.

The language of choices works exceptionally well with children, but it needs to be communicated and followed through with conviction. By putting the responsibility upon the child, we are getting him/her to be accountable for his/her actions. We are also absolving ourselves from being the extrinsic punishment or motivation. 'It's your choice' is the message the child is getting. If we do not do this, then secondary responses can become directed at the adult, which can then often turn into a more serious incident than the initial trigger. Only by putting the responsibility upon the child and allowing him/her to see the consequences of his/her choices does real intrinsic learning take place. An alternative to talking is writing and diagrams. Consequences can be made explicit. Drawings, stick people, key words and arrows can be used to show how the choices made are linked to what happens next. It can be talked through with the child and the adult can engage him/her in the final tick on each consequence diagram to show if that course of action was a good choice or not. Some children, as we have discussed, are visual learners, and therefore putting something on paper will make the learning process more concrete and permanent.

REFLECTIVE ACTIVITY **10.1**

Duties not to discriminate

Search the Disability Discrimination Act 1995, Part 4, Code of Practice for Schools online at **http://www.drc-gb.org/Docs/2008_220_schoolscop2.doc** *that stipulates new duties (from 2002) not to discriminate. Read section 5.2 and define the duties within the code that relate to 'The duty not to discriminate'.*

Dealing with disengagement and conflict

Being able to deal with disengagement and conflict effectively is vital to ensure that pupils are able to get back on track as quickly as possible.

Disengagement is relatively easy to spot in pupils, but often harder to unpack and turn round. The two main causes of disengagement are problems associated with work and problems associated with peer disagreements. It is vitally important to ascertain what the problem is before making any assumptions. If we presume the problem stems from finding the work hard and step in and give support with the work, it is likely that the pupil will remain disengaged and the help is either rejected rudely or the adult ends up doing the work for the pupil, with perhaps the odd disengaged grunt in response, as the pupil continues to lay back in his/her chair, very clearly off task.

It is important to find out the reasons for disengagement in order to know how best to support the pupil. If the reasons for disengagement are not work-related then the pupil needs to understand that they should do one of the following things.

- Communicate what the problem is.
- Cope with the problem and get on with his/her work.
- Take a break (if this is part of an agreed strategy).

Giving pupils choices in this way to deal with 'shutdown' and disengagement is a really positive strategy that puts responsibility clearly with the pupil for how to manage their difficulty. We should not assume that the pupil will want to communicate the problem at that time to that adult, but if choices are given around how to deal with it, the pupil can really start to take ownership of their feelings and how to deal with them.

In dealing with conflict and disengagement the effective adult needs to be able to do the following:

- Stay in control.
- Be firm, but fair.
- Listen and rationalise back to pupils.
- Be decisive and know their own expectations and boundaries.

The message that the pupil receives around how effective the adult is at managing any difficulty is so crucial in shaping and managing future potential conflict. Very often this is not so much about being effective at managing the situation but being effective at not getting into a situation where you are being perceived as ineffective. For example, if the adult says 'Pick that up now' and the pupil refuses, the adult just isn't able to enforce the pupil to do it 'now' so therefore appears ineffective in carrying out the command. However, if the initial interaction starts with a statement of reality, for example 'There is a book on the floor', and there is then some opposition to this, the adult has time to adjust the next response. For example: 'You don't sound in a good place right now, but it does need to be picked up by the end of the lesson. By the way, if there is a problem that is bothering you that you want to talk about I can come and have a word with you once I've got the class started.' Considering how an invitation to talk was also worded in that interaction is important. If the adult had said 'If there is a problem that is bothering you that you want to talk about then come and see me once I've got the lesson started' the pupil may not have felt able to get up and initiate the contact. However, the way it has now been left with the pupil, the teacher can go over to the pupil and initiate a conversation, checking out whether the pupil wants to share anything that is on his/her mind.

Getting to the root of the problem as quickly as possible is the key to successful intervention and therefore the key to getting pupils back on track as quickly as possible.

Positive adult interaction during disengagement and conflict will support pupils to learn how to:

- cope with distractions in order to maintain concentration and engagement with the task;
- cope with disagreements;
- communicate and manage emotions.

Coping with distractions

In order to support pupils in dealing with distractions it is necessary to consider how the brain thinks and learns. Information is taken in through the senses and then links are made in the brain to previous knowledge and experience. For some pupils, particularly monotropic thinkers, it is harder to make these connections as open, lateral thinking relies on polytropic skills of being able to multi-channel information, ideas and concepts. Some pupils will need more support to help them make these connections in order to really learn from their experiences.

Monotropic attention implies *having few interests highly aroused* which leads to *tending to perform the task well and tending to lose awareness of information relevant to other tasks* (Murray et al., 2005). Monotropic thinking suggests a switching of attention rather than an ability to multi-channel attention which polytropic thinkers are able to do effectively and at times effortlessly and sometimes at a subconscious level. For example, a polytropic thinker will be able to sit and listen to a lecture, take in the hardness of the chair they are sitting on, be vaguely conscious of a buzzing fly that is in the room, feel that they should have put on another jumper because it's a bit chilly and still be able to focus on the main essence of the lecture. For the monotropic thinker however, any of the sensory distractions in the room could become the sole focus of attention and draw attention away from the content of the lecture at that time. Regaining focus for monotropic thinkers can sometimes be quite a challenge and teachers need to be aware of allowing time and opportunity to encourage and support pupils to switch attention in order to refocus on the work task. Pupils may need time to get a distraction out of their head in order to get back on track with work. A genuine sensory distraction needs addressing for some pupils in order for them to be able to think about work. If the distraction is a peer-related issue it is sometimes advantageous to take time to deal with this, there and then, in order for pupils to move on effectively. In some cases where it isn't possible to resolve situations at the time, giving a time for dealing with it later can allow monotropic thinkers to switch their attention back to the work task. Pupils can be given alternatives in order to distinguish if this is a genuine monotropic issue rather than a 'cop out' of work. Listening and rationalising back to pupils around this issue will almost always distinguish the genuine problem from the attempt to get out of work.

Coping with disagreements

Social interaction difficulties can be one of the most challenging areas for teachers to have to deal with. Unpacking situations from two or more perspectives and supporting pupils to find a resolution is challenging but rewarding. Pupils need to be aware of the following points.

- It's alright to feel angry/annoyed etc.
- It's alright to deal with it in a positive way, but not alright to deal with those feelings by hitting/throwing/swearing, etc.

Often by acknowledging the feelings of the pupil and identifying where the disagreement started is sufficient to then separate out 'it was alright to do this' but 'not alright to do that'. If the initial feeling is acknowledged and recognised, pupils are much more likely to take responsibility for having made the wrong choice in how they dealt with that feeling.

Communicate and manage emotions

Developing pupils' emotional intelligence is an area to develop and promote through personal, social, health and emotional (PSHE) education as well as other curriculum areas. Pupils may need support in order to recognise their own range of feelings as well as the feelings of others and there are many commercial packages to support this, for example *Mind Reading* (Baron-Cohen, 2003). In times of stress and anxiety pupils can become non-communicative and may need symbols to support them in communicating their feelings appropriately. Having the feeling acknowledged can often diffuse a situation considerably.

Opening up a channel of communication with pupils who have become quite non-communicative around any kind of problem is essential to move pupils on. For some pupils this may be in written form to begin with if verbal interaction is too demanding at that point. Some pupils may benefit from a notepad to write down problems in this way to either show to an adult at the time or at a later prearranged 'chat time'. A positive intervention strategy designed to help pupils learn to manage their emotions and levels of stress is that of implementing a break system, as detailed below.

Breaks: a strategy for self-management of stress and anxiety

A break system is designed to be a positive intervention strategy that aims to enable pupils to manage their emotions and their learning independently and reduce the likelihood of a situation escalating.

It is necessary to consider the reasons why a pupil is experiencing difficulties. It may not be a 'break system' that is needed but rather consideration of the following:

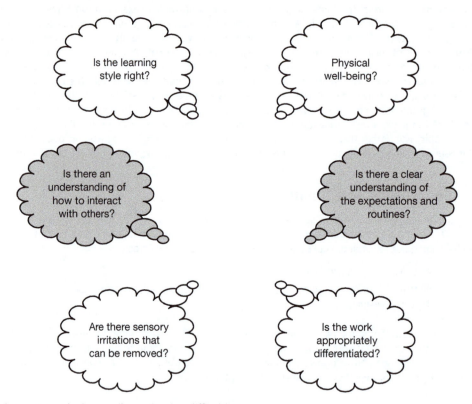

Figure 10.1 Why is a pupil experiencing difficulties?

Therefore, a break system should be needed only for pupils who have significant difficulty managing their emotions appropriately.

Prior to introducing a break system to a pupil, the adults should discuss how many breaks the pupil is going to be allowed to take daily and how long each break is going to be. This will vary for individuals. Whatever is decided (e.g. 4 breaks of up to 10 minutes per break) needs to be made explicit to the pupil. It may help to have the rules stated on a laminated sheet with spaces for the break cards (see 'What is needed' and 'How it works' on p.118). The actual break area also needs to be discussed. Where is it going to be? How accessible is this to the pupil? Will other children need to use this area? If it is going to be within an area such as a library then can a small area be identified, within the library and sectioned off in some way? It is a good idea to separate work areas from break areas so that pupils do not get confused about what is expected in the different areas. If pupils are moving around to different areas of the school and a formal break area is not available (or necessary) then this can be as easy to organise as a chair outside the classroom or a walk down the corridor.

All school staff will need to be made aware of this strategy as the pupil can indicate to any adult that they need a break. When discussing the break system with staff it is important to make explicit the differences between this and the concept of 'time out', which can be seen as more of a crisis management strategy dictated by the adults. A break system gives the responsibility to the pupil to take a break at any time that they feel they need to. Staff also need to be aware of the rules for the break area to prevent any preconceptions about what is going on and ensure consistency. The rules enable the pupil to get back on task after the break; the break is controlled by the adults at the onset by deciding the boundaries for the break system for that pupil. The pupil manages their breaks within the boundaries of the rules that have been set by the adults.

The break is seen as positive and therefore the break area is comfortable and inviting, with favourite items, books, magazines, etc.

The system is often introduced alongside an 'angry line' or 'feelings line' continuum. The pupil is shown that they need to take a break around number 2 or 3 on their line, long before getting to complete melt down at number 10. When explaining this to pupils it is important to explain that it is alright to feel strong emotions, but it is what we do as a consequence of these emotions that can cause problems.

What is needed?

- Break cards or an agreed alternative system, e.g. logging sheet in the back of a planner.
- Rules for the break area.
- A designated break area that contains items that will engage the pupil e.g. favourite books, items, magazines, etc.
- A timer (a digital timer is recommended – it is easy to set and can be heard at the end of the designated time).

Initially pupils may need help in recognising when a break is needed. They may not recognise what their emotions are at number 2 on an angry line. Quite often pupils will quickly escalate to number 10 without being aware of any feelings along the way. We want pupils to recognise these early signs so that they can use strategies lower down on their line to prevent getting to number 10. This is quite hard and pupils will need help at first. There may be some resistance to taking a break – pupils, after all, on the whole want to be included – so it is vital that the break area is inviting and seen positively by all involved. As the pupil becomes more used to the system, discussions can be held about whether they want to have any interaction with the adult during their break. It is their time so respect it if they prefer no contact with the adult during the break. It may be necessary, however, to set the guidelines initially that the adult needs to wait in the same area, depending on the needs of the pupil.

How it works

- Pupil communicates they want a break.
- Pupil is instantly allowed to go to the break area. No further verbal explanation is required of the pupil.

- If the pupil has a support assistant then this person would accompany the pupil to the break area and may be the one to set the timer; for some pupils it may need the structure of the rule that only the adult touches the timer. It may have been agreed that the pupil is able to go to the break area independently and set the timer for the agreed amount of time, but initially it is likely to need adult support.

- When the time is nearly up it might be necessary to draw the pupil's attention to this and start to prepare them for the next step.

- After the set amount of time the pupil needs to go back on task. This may be the same activity or piece of work or if the activity has now finished, e.g. a singing or physical education lesson, then the pupil would be expected to move onto the next lesson or activity on the timetable.

If they have enough cards left another break card can be used consecutively if more time is needed. It is possible for a pupil to use all their break cards in one go like this. It is their system – let them explore it. Eventually pupils may save a card for the 'just in case' scenario.

REFLECTIVE ACTIVITY 10.2

Further strategies to promote children's potential

Visit the website for Beacon Hill School at http://www.beaconhillschool.co.uk and search the County Inclusive Resource (CIR) pages. Identify key texts, contacts, resources and strategies that are being used to provide high-quality learning experiences and environments to enable pupils with autistic spectrum disorder (ASD) to complete their education in mainstream provision.

What strategies can you take from this search to promote the learning experiences of children with whom you work and care for?

SUMMARY OF KEY POINTS

This chapter has illustrated that understanding school dynamics is more important than acquiring a detailed grasp of recent educational legislation. It has reviewed entitlement and potential, and shown that these are complex concepts not only in themselves but also in their relationship with each other. It has provided strategies for addressing a wide variety of barriers to learning which are fruitful for everyone concerned, whether adult or pupil. One of the most important lessons from this chapter is that the way adults communicate with children is crucial to the successful implementation of any school strategy, and indeed is of fundamental importance to a child's development both in school and in the wider environment/community.

REFERENCES

Baron-Cohen, S. (2003) *Mind Reading: An Interactive Guide to Emotions*, DVD. London: Jessica Kingsley.

Beacon Hill School online at: **http://www.beaconhillschool.co.uk** (accessed 24 January 2007).

Department for Education and Skills (DfES) (2004) *National Curriculum for England*. Online at: **http://www.nc.uk.net/index.html** (accessed 24 January 2007).

Disability Discrimination Act (1995) *Part 4, Code of Practice for Schools*. Online at: **http://www.drc-gb.org/Docs/2008_220_schoolscop2.doc** (accessed 24 January 2007).

Mittler, P. (2000) *Working Towards Inclusive Education: Social Contexts*. London: David Fulton.

Murray, D., Lesser, R. and Lawson, W. (2005) 'Attention, monotropism and the diagnostic criteria for autism', *International Journal of Research and Practice: Autism*, 9 (2): 139–56.

Rogers, B. (2006) *Cracking the Hard Class*. London: Paul Chapman.

Shaw, S. and Hawes, T. (1998) *Effective Teaching and Learning in the Primary Classroom*. Available from: Equip, PO Box 12, Oadby, Leicester LE2 5AE.

11 Policy into practice – working with children in need of protection

Geoff Tookey and Amanda Wawryn

Learning objectives

By the end of this chapter you should be able to:

- **recognise the roles and responsibilities of professionals involved with child protection;**
- **understand the importance of information-sharing and collaborative working between agencies;**
- **identify government legislation on child protection issues;**
- **debate how to translate policy into effective practice;**
- **distinguish between different levels of intervention.**

Introduction

This chapter begins by focusing on the inquiry into the death of Ainlee Labonte and examines the roles, responsibilities and expectations of professionals directly involved with this case. Accountability is brought to the fore and positioned within government legislation that aims to reconfigure agencies involved with the protection of children into collaborative partnerships. How Ainlee Labonte 'slipped through the net' is scrutinised to better understand that collaboration requires agencies to work closely together, communicate, share information and co-operate fully in the child protection planning process.

There have been many advances in multi-agency co-operation in childcare and child protection over the past 20 years. However, the effects of stereotyping and what seems to be poorly researched popular television programmes can sometimes detract from the important tasks of working together with families and other agencies. It is therefore necessary to focus on roles and responsibilities and to achieve greater understanding in order to prioritise the needs of children. The latter part of this chapter focuses on strategies for enabling multi-agency debate to produce good practice from policy.

Case study

Ainlee Labonte was born on 24 December 1999 and at the time of her birth, Ainlee's family was an open case to Newham Social Services. There was involvement with the family from various agencies including health, housing, police and social services, but despite this level of involvement, Ainlee died on 7 January 2002. A post mortem revealed over 60 injuries to Ainlee's body including cigarette burns and a body weight well below that expected for a child of her age. The cause of Ainlee's death was chronic abuse and neglect (Kenward, 2002).

The Chapter 8 Review (ibid.) highlighted failings on the part of all agencies involved. Ainlee's parents, Leanne and Dennis, were intimidating, abusive and manipulative which had eventually led to all agencies refusing to visit the family home. Fear of the family led to 'paralysis in terms of action' where those who should have protected Ainlee were more concerned about protecting themselves. There was also criticism regarding the level of information-sharing and collaborative working between the agencies involved and the recommendations of the inquiry were that all agencies must address these issues in order to protect children more effectively (Kenward, 2002).

Health visitors

The health visitors who would have been involved with Ainlee during her life would at that time have been qualified registered nurses who had gained at least two years' practice and had undertaken further training in order to work as a health visitor (**http://www.nhscareers.nhs.uk,** (2006)). At the time of Ainlee's death, health visitors were registered to the UK Central Council for Nursing, Midwifery and Health Visiting (UKCC), although in June 2002 they were registered to the Nursing and Midwifery Council (NMC) and covered by the Code of Professional Conduct (**http://www.nmc.uk.org,** (2004)). Health visitors would have been professionally accountable to the UKCC, but were personally accountable for their practice, making them answerable for their actions. They were also required to work in the best interests of Ainlee and her family (**http://www.nmc.uk.org,** (2004)).

Health visitors provide a universal service based primarily on health promotion, and spend the majority of their time visiting clients in their homes, especially new mothers and children under the age of five. Health visitors should be skilled at getting on with people of all backgrounds and ages; they should also have excellent communication and management skills and the emotional maturity to deal with distressing issues (**http://www.learndirect-advice.co.uk,** (2006)).

When looking at the health visitor's role in Ainlee's case and comparing it with the role of the social worker, it is necessary to look at them as a profession and how they identify with their profession, as this has implications for how they work. Health visitors operate within the values laid down by their professional code of conduct. They must respect their client as an individual and obtain their consent before giving treatment or care, protect confidential information and co-operate with members of their own team, maintain professional knowledge and competence, be trustworthy and act to identify and minimise risks to clients (**http://www.nmc.or.uk,** (2004)). When these values are compared with those in social work laid down by the General Social Care Council (GSCC) they reveal an emphasis on professional conduct rather than how they engage with the client to promote independence, respect diversity or how they collaborate with other agencies in order to ensure that their client's needs are appropriately met (**http://www.gscc.org.uk,** (2002)).

Professional culture

In addition to differences in the value base, there is the matter of professional culture. Each professional group has its own understanding of presenting problems and the possible solutions. Social workers involved with Ainlee held the belief that the cause of her family's problems were social and supported them with housing and rehabilitation, whereas health visitors held the belief that the problem was medical and focused on developmental checks, refusal by the mother to have Ainlee immunised and weight loss (Barrett et al., 2005).

Research has shown that professionals can be encouraged to view problems from an alternative perspective but if professionals cannot acknowledge this, the tension and conflict between agencies will continue (Irvine et al., 2002). Joseph Luft and Harry Ingham, during research into human personality at the University of California in the 1950s, developed a communication model they termed the 'Johari window' (**http://www.mindtools.com/CommSkll/JohariWindow.htm**) that can be used to improve understanding between individuals within a team or group setting. The four quadrants within the Johari window illustrate how the process of disclosure and feedback contributes to an understanding of our own self and that of others. As we get to know people we reveal more of ourselves which results in us receiving constructive feedback. A professional who feels safe and develops trust within their team will feel less threatened, behave less defensively and will feel more confident in their role which enables them to work more effectively with other agencies (Coulshed and Orme, 1998).

Health visitors had the responsibility of visiting Ainlee from 14 days to the age of five, which put them in a unique position of being able to identify the risk factors to Ainlee as laid down in their value base. Their responsibilities in relation to protecting her were clearly laid down in the form of the Children Act 1989, *Working Together to Safeguard Children* (DoH, 1999a) and the *Framework for the Assessment of Children in Need and their Families* (DoH, 2000a). Health visitors were aware that Ainlee's family was experiencing difficulties and should have expressed their concern that Ainlee was a child in need of support and safeguarding. The health visitors should have had discussions with their manager and a referral should have been made to Newham Social Services. When social services received the referral a social worker should have completed an initial assessment that would have required close collaborative working with the health visitor requiring them to provide vital information about the family (DoH, 1999a).

The Framework for the Assessment of Children in Need and their Families

The Framework for the Assessment of Children in Need and their Families gives specific guidance on assessing black children in need and their families. If Ainlee had been assessed as a child at risk of significant harm rather than a child in need, a core assessment should have been completed and a child protection conference should have been held (DoH, 2000a). At the time of this case, conferences were overseen by the Area Child Protection Committee (ACPC). A senior nurse with a health visitor qualification (designated senior professional) would have sat on the ACPC and the health visitor should have participated in the child protection conference, played a part in the child protection plan by monitoring Ainlee and attended subsequent reviews of that plan (DoH, 1999a).

A child protection conference did not take place for Ainlee, despite the fact that the professionals involved were fearful of her family owing to domestic violence. Feminists argue that physical, sexual and emotional abuse is used by men to exercise power and control over women and because it usually goes on behind closed doors it has never been perceived by professionals as being the remit of the statutory services (Mullender, 2002). Ainlee's family echoed the findings from research at that time which showed that 23 per cent of women suffered violence from a partner, the family was in a lower socio-economic group and in poor health (Leanne suffered from a skin complaint), 50 per cent of women lived with children under the age of 16 and 29 per cent of those advised that the children had witnessed the violence (Mirrlees-Black, 1999). Research also showed *a strong overlap between physical, sexual and emotional abuse of children and domestic violence, and high proportions of those experiencing abuse from parents also experience frequent violence between carers.* Domestic violence features in 88 per cent of cases of neglect, 75 per cent of cases of physical abuse and 71 per cent of cases of emotional abuse (Cawson, 2002).

Institutional racism has also been identified in response to domestic violence from statutory agencies (Mullender, 2002). Research indicates that black and minority ethnic groups have a higher representation as users of the criminal justice system (**http://www.homeoffice.gov.uk**, (2005)) therefore domestic violence in black families could be perceived by professionals as being more of a threat than in white families. Ainlee and her family were discriminated against because the professionals involved viewed them as an aggressive black family (Thompson, 2001). During that time the national press noted that the police had made 53 visits to Ainlee's home, 32 of which involved incidents of domestic violence. The Protection from Harassment Act 1997 could have been used by the police to take action when called out to incidents between Leanne and Dennis but, with regard to child protection, the police should have enquired with social services if any children in the house were on the Child Protection Register (CPR). There should have been a high level of concern and they should have made a referral to social services or utilised the power of a Police Protection Order to remove the children to a place of safety (DoH, 1999a).

Social workers in this case were afraid for their own safety when visiting the family but they ignored the violence because to their knowledge the children had not been harmed. They minimised the effect of children witnessing the domestic violence, they did not recognise the link between the domestic violence and possible child abuse and paid little attention to specific issues of Leanne being a black woman needing support (Humphreys, 2002). In addition, they paid little heed to concerns expressed by health visitors or the fact that they would agree to see the family only at the clinic. This was not a satisfactory way of monitoring the children and due to Leanne's historical reluctance to engage with professionals of any kind, the case was at one stage closed by Newham Social Services (Kenward, 2002).

From the health perspective, there was much upheaval in community health care delivery. The NHS Plan 2000 had introduced Primary Care Trusts that had put responsibility onto GPs to become managers (DoH, 2000b). As a result of GPs experiencing extra responsibilities they became adept at delegating to health visitors with regard to child protection cases. The only real protection for the professionals came under the remit of the 1974 Health and Safety at Work Act so the health visitors should have discussed this case through supervision with their line manager in order to find strategies to protect Ainlee and themselves (Humphreys, 2000). *Making a Difference* (1999b) states explicitly that nurses, midwives and health visitors were expected to engage in inter-professional practices, so they should have requested to do joint visits with the social workers (DoH, 1999b). However, over the Christmas period 2001/2002 Ainlee was not visited for six weeks and as a result she died on 7 January 2002 (Kenward, 2002).

Recommendations

Recommendation 1.3 of the inquiry states that cognisance must be given to the importance of information held within all agencies. The action suggested was to review current ways of sharing information and consider additional ways of ensuring that information is fully shared (Kenward, 2002). As a result of the Laming Inquiry (2003), the Children Act 1989 was updated in the Children Act 2004, *Every Child Matters*, which focused greatly on information-sharing and working collaboratively (DoH, 2004). Local authorities are now responsible through Children's Trusts for developing integrated services and working co-operatively with the police, primary care trusts, schools and youth offending teams which will focus on early identification and intervention in cases such as Ainlee's. ACPCs have been replaced with Local Safeguarding Children Boards (LSCB) responsible for the overall well-being of children, focusing particularly on the outcome 'staying safe'. Under section 12 of the Children Act 2004, a national information-sharing index has been proposed and all agencies will use the same assessment tool, the common assessment framework (CAF), for making referrals (Quinney, 2006). *Working Together to Safeguard Children: A Guide to Inter-agency Working to Safeguard and Protect the Welfare of Children* (DoH, 2006), focuses on how agencies can collaboratively achieve the five outcomes for children.

The death of Ainlee is not an isolated case. The Commission for Social Care Inspection (CSCI) reports that over 26,000 children in England would have a better life if parents were given more help and support and thus avoid tragedies and the need for intervention in the form of child protection (**http://www.csci.org.uk**, (2006)). If all agencies work together as advocated in the Children Act 2004, vulnerable children should not slip through the net. Early intervention through Child in Need and very robust Child in Need plans can be as effective and protective as child protection plans if collaboration and information sharing takes place effectively (DoH, 2004).

Learning to work in multidisciplinary groups

Important points to bear in mind are the following.

- All children have needs – a very good update of Maslow's hierarchy is available at: **http://www.businessballs.com**
- The government's five priority outcomes (detailed in Appendix 1) include:
  - Be healthy
  - Stay safe
  - Enjoy and achieve
  - Make a positive contribution
  - Achieve economic well-being.
- Learning to work in multidisciplinary teams is different from learning to work in a single-agency environment.

Ground rules

Different professional backgrounds have different unwritten rules about participation and diversity issues, e.g. some agencies work in an openly hierarchical manner whereas others follow a more democratic model. Some agencies find it acceptable to use the term 'handicapped' and others would feel it more appropriate to talk about the 'individual needs of a child'. Some agencies recognise that anti-discriminatory practice has been dealt with using only blatant scenarios whereas others will naturally explore all aspects of oppression. It is advisable to have some set of ground rules when working in multidisciplinary groups in order to self-regulate. However this is carried out, ground rules normally break down into the following six broad areas.

- Respect for others/working with difference.
- Keep yourself safe.
- (Limited) confidentiality.
- Sensible cousins/no such thing as a daft question.
- Time keeping.
- Phones off/thinking caps on.

Some of these are self-explanatory. Respect for others includes not speaking over others, allowing people to form their views but developing towards a shared language. Working with difference includes all areas of anti-oppressive and anti-discriminatory practice. However, this is never static and there is probably greater importance in everyone being prepared to be part of the journey than expecting all learners to be at exactly the same point.

The next two points are also very important. According to the National Society for the Prevention of Cruelty to Children (NSPCC) and popular magazine surveys, about one quarter of adults will have suffered from abusive childhoods. There will also be a large percentage of adults experiencing family violence. It could be argued that within a class of 40 students, 10 or 12 may fall into either of those categories. In order for you to feel safe to participate it is useful to understand these figures and realise that as survivors, people have different mechanisms for dealing with their present or past and it is alright for them to contribute or not, or seek out the tutor after any part of the session.

Confidentiality frequently comes up as a ground rule. This normally means that what is said in the room stays in the room. However, we need to consider that post the Laming Inquiry (2003) the government made it clear that child protection is everyone's responsibility (DoH, 2004). It is therefore useful to translate this rule into limited confidentiality. This means that if any dangerous practice is identified, you and your tutor have a responsibility to ensure this is addressed outside the session.

Every professional background will have its own way of explaining the world. Within every professional grouping individuals will be at a different developmental point. Experience has shown that it is useful to be able to translate throw-away or humorous/tension-relieving remarks into their sensible cousins.

Shelf issues

Teaching cannot resolve all issues. In the multidisciplinary arena there may be opportunities for you to take issues away and explore them more fully with practitioners in your workplace ready for subsequent sessions. A shelf is a means of acknowledging ideas and clarifying how they can be taken forward and by whom. Four bookshelves will usually suffice and can be divided into items for:

- an individual to take away;
- the group to take away;
- exploration on a single-agency basis;
- future teaching sessions.

Scenarios

There is a need to avoid over-reliance on social services cases. Inevitably there will be a need to discuss child-in-need issues and children-in-need of protection. Sometimes, case scenarios are generated by a chance discussion: for example, one of my students was delayed for a meeting at her placement and through discussion with the manager the following scenario arose.

The setting:	Day nursery
Age ranges:	6 months to 5 years
Specifics:	Child of 2 years who bites other children and leaves visible marks
Who is complaining:	Parents of other children
Issues:	Who do you go to for advice? What are the legal parameters? What is your plan of intervention?

REFLECTIVE ACTIVITY **11.1**

Examining the above scenario

Discuss whose role it is to do which aspects, e.g. the law, policy and guidance.

What level of intervention is needed?

If we concentrate on the needs of the one (i.e. the child who is biting) what happens to the needs of the many?

If we concentrate on the needs of the many (i.e. the rest of the group) how do we help the one integrate into society?

If we ignore the problem what is the likely outcome for the one and the many?

*REFLECTIVE ACTIVITY **11.1** continued*

Is it better to intervene and do the 'wrong' thing or better to sometimes do nothing?

Are we safer doing only what our professional group would sanction than coming up with an imaginative answer?

If we do not have the answers where can we find them?

The random scenario generator

Often you will not believe the scenarios as they give every possible complication or do not relate to ethnicity and disability. The tools needed are very simple. A number of wooden blocks is required. One is for the gender of the child or children; another for age, ethnicity, disability, etc. Each block has six surfaces. Each surface needs a symbol to depict the information as follows:

Block 1	Child or children
Surface 1	Square to represent boy
Surface 2	Circle to represent girl
Surface 3	Two squares to represent twin boys
Surface 4	Two circles to represent twin girls
Surface 5	Blank for group to decide
Surface 6	Triangle to represent stillbirth

Four levels of prevention model

When undergoing qualifying training I understood this to be a model devised by one of my tutors. However, subsequent research has shown it is a model already well used in health-care, e.g. when looking at stages of prevention for HIV/AIDS. The somewhat unusual language does not emanate from agencies but descriptions for various stages in the Ice Age. The importance for practice is not who *invented* this model but that social care and health both use it. The step for a multidisciplinary approach is to adapt the model to aid under-standing of each other's roles and search for any gaps in provision. The start point is a simple model that you can add to as you progress through the exercises.

Simple model	
Primary level	Services based in the community with universal access
Secondary level	By referral services (including self-referral)
Tertiary level	Need for the state to intervene
Quarternary level	Irreversible change needed

If we apply the model to heart care, the right-hand column might include some of the following issues:

HEART CARE	
Primary level	Leaflets, healthy eating, five-a-day campaign
Secondary level	Referral for eating clinic
Tertiary level	Intrusive intervention – open heart surgery
Quarternary level	Intensive care to prevent further deterioration

Broadly speaking there are four types of agency. Education and schools is a large grouping. Health can be split into community health and hospital based health. Social control agencies include the police, probation, prisons and statutory aspects of social services work. Social care includes other aspects and work of the voluntary agencies (conducted in their own right and not as a result of a service level agreement). Once you have thoughts on four agencies, move on to who does what at each level. Avoid the temptation to confuse 'status' or years of training with the level at which certain professionals operate.

The next step is to place this information within one grid:

	Health	Social care	Education	Police
Primary	Health visitors, GPs	The community	Nurseries, schools	
Secondary		Duty/intake/ assessment team	Education welfare	
Tertiary				
Quarternary				

From the completed grid it should be possible to see not only who does what, but also where there are gaps, e.g. it is unusual these days for social services to provide universal services at a primary level.

Child protection

In the triangle below the perpetrator will strive to create opportunities to groom the child and abuse him/her. It is not appropriate to put the responsibility for protection onto the child. There is the need for at least one protective adult to ensure the opportunities are not there or are reduced as far as possible.

REFLECTIVE ACTIVITY **11.2**

Questions associated with child abuse

If parents and carers are to be fully protective how can they do this if they are not informed about potential risk from known paedophiles in their area?

Is the debate correctly focused when approximately one-third of risk comes from adult males who are known to the victim, one-third from adolescent males known to the victim and a third from strangers?

Do the statistics matter or should we concentrate on the effects on victims instead?

Do perpetrators surrender their human rights the day they abuse a child?

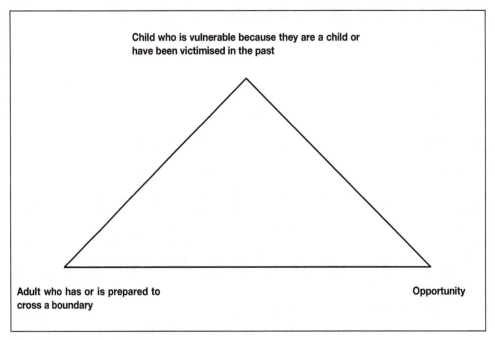

Child who is vulnerable because they are a child or have been victimised in the past

Adult who has or is prepared to cross a boundary

Opportunity

Figure 11.1 Child abuse triangle

The child protection (safeguarding) process

There is some essential pre-reading for you to do in order to complete the following exercise. You should visit the government websites for the legislative area in which you are learning. Although the laws are fairly similar, the four countries in the UK can and do have slightly different laws and/or bodies overseeing child welfare. It is also essential to search for *Every Child Matters* (DoH, 2004), and other guidance on what to do if you suspect that a child is being abused. Also, visit websites for your local Children's Safeguarding Board. In some areas this will be via a local authority site giving information for parents and other service users. In most areas there are slight variations in the procedures. There are useful single-agency websites, e.g. **http://www.teachernet.gov.uk** and those introduced above. However, a useful shortcut is to register onto **http://www.info4local.gov.uk** and select topics relevant to childcare to receive regular updates.

It is important to remember that this is third-level intervention and the aim should always be to return to a primary level of intervention when it is safe to do so. There is also no reason why the whole process should be followed to the conference and core group stage if it is discovered at any point that there are protective adults in control and/or there is minimal future risk.

REFLECTIVE ACTIVITY **11.3**

The child protection process

From the pre-reading re-arrange the following into steps of the process.

- *Child/ren's name(s) removed from CPR and lower level supports put into place*

- *Core group*

- *Strategy meeting of police, social worker and professionals who understand the child*

- *Sufficient future risk to warrant inclusion of child/ren's name(s) on CPR*

- *Family group conference system used*

- *Referral for family support*

- *Section 17 children in need investigation*

- *No further action*

- *Review conference*

- *Child/ren interviewed by social worker (and police)*

- *Initial conference*

- *Discussion between social worker and referring agency*

- *Social worker causes inquiries to be made*

- *Incident, concern, disclosure of abuse or neglect referred to childcare/duty team*

Draw up a list of all the family/supportive networks and professionals who might have something to contribute to a child protection conference. Rank this from those at the top who know the child best and write this order down. Repeat the process but this time put those at the top whose views are likely to be given the most weight at a conference. Write this down. Turn the second list upside down and compare.

Why do some people who know the child least well get listened to more at official meetings?

Where is the child's voice?

Are primary level interventions about democracy and empowerment whereas tertiary level interventions about necessary state intervention?

What if a child wants to tell you something?

The report into alleged incidents of child abuse in Cleveland came up with an important concept. It moved away from the issue of sorting out what was 'true'. After all, given the nature of some abuse, only the perpetrator and the victim really know the full extent of what has happened. The Cleveland concept was that we should take what children say seriously.

The false memory syndrome debate has somewhat skewed the argument. There are two important concepts that counter this. The first is that children cannot make up something that is beyond their age and understanding. The second is that any child who wants to use official mechanisms to seek to have someone removed from their life still needs to be listened to. Most, if not all, children who tell want the abuse to stop.

It is not known why children seek out a particular adult to tell what has been happening to them. Sometimes they use a situation where eye contact cannot be made, i.e. when you have your back to them while doing washing up or at a work surface or when your concentration needs to be on a task like driving. The child will not distinguish between your role at the primary level and child protection at the tertiary level. Also, remember the government has stated that child protection is everybody's business. If the child does choose you then you need to be ready. If you tell them this is not the right time the message may be they are wrong to tell. If your face expresses shock this may also convey a negative message.

The local Child Safeguarding Board may issue some useful advice including the phone number for the duty/intake social worker. The general advice is stay calm, listen, do not ask questions, although you can repeat the child's words back to them to make sure you have understood properly, do not make any promises, and tell them that because you take what they have said seriously you have to let a limited number of people know. If you know the next steps then let the child know. If you do not know it is alright to say so. Write your notes up as soon afterwards as possible and keep them on a confidential section of your agency's recording.

If you do slip up and ask the child a question make sure your recording details this. Remember that perpetrators operate by distorting matters and we do not want to cause confusion in a police or social services case by having less than accurate records. Appendix 2 provides guidance for dealing with disclosures.

The child protection conference

Some situations cannot be kept at the primary or secondary level of intervention despite the best efforts of the professionals and the family. Other situations can suddenly come into the child protection arena when there had been no previous concerns. For example, when working in a large shire county, three out of the six tragic deaths of babies were in families where there had been no social work involvement. The important functions of the conference are to share concerns and build up a consensus about the level of future risk. Only those cases where there is a high likelihood of future risk should come to conference in the first place.

REFLECTIVE ACTIVITY **11.4**

Child protection plan

Return to the case study of Ainlee Labonte at the beginning of this chapter and extract all the relevant issues associated with this case from the involved agencies – document these accurately and progressively and consider what level of intervention should have been realised, when, for whom and by whom, to provide the much needed support

In multi-agency working groups devise a child protection plan that could be used in a similar case to protect and safeguard the welfare of a child.

SUMMARY OF KEY POINTS

This chapter has highlighted the importance of information-sharing and collaborative working between agencies if children in need of protection are to be both identified and safeguarded. The case study of Ainlee Labonte and the inquiry report on Victoria Climbié demonstrate how some children have 'slipped through the net' when government policy has not been translated into practice. A range of strategies for learning to work in multidisciplinary groups has been introduced and there are four levels of prevention/intervention covering all children, from children in need to those in need of protection/safeguarding. Appendix 3 provides a succinct summary of the challenges professionals must overcome to ensure that they work collaboratively in the interests of all children.

FERENCES

Allan, H., Bryan, K., Clawson, L. and Smith, P. (2005) 'Developing an interprofessional learning culture in primary care', *Journal of Interprofessional Care*, 19 (5): 452–64.

Barrett, G., Sellman, D. and Thomas, J. (2005) *Interprofessional Working in Health and Social Care*. Basingstoke: Palgrave MacMillan.

Cawson, P. (2002) *Child Maltreatment in the Family: The Experience of a National Sample of Young People*. London: NSPCC, pp. 37–8.

Coulshed, V. and Orme, J. (1998) *Social Work Practice*. Basingstoke: Macmillan.

Department of Health (1999a) *Working Together to Safeguard Children: A Guide to Inter-Agency Working to Safeguard Children and Promote the Welfare of Children*. London: Stationery Office.

Department of Health (1999b) *Making a Difference*. London: DoH.

Department of Health (2000a) *Framework for the Assessment of Children in Need and Their Families*. London: DoH.

Department of Health (2000b) *The NHS Plan: A Plan for Investment a Plan for Reform*. London: DoH.

Department of Health (2004) *Children Act 2004 'Every Child Matters'*. London: DoH.

Department of Health (2006) *Working Together to Safeguard Children: A Guide to Inter-Agency Working to Safeguard and Protect the Welfare of Children*. London: DoH.

Humphreys, C. (2000) *Social Work, Domestic Violence and Child Protection. Challenging Practice*. Bristol: Policy Press.

Humphreys, C. (2002) 'Domestic violence', in M. Davies (ed.), *The Blackwell Companion to Social Work*, 2nd edn. Oxford: Blackwell.

Irvine, R., Kerridge, I., McPhee, J. and Freeman, S. (2002) 'Interprofessionalisation and ethics: consensus or clash of cultures?', *Journal of Interprofessional Care*, 16: 199–210.

Kenward, H. (2002) *The Ainlee Labonte Inquiry*. Newham: HMSO.

Laming, Lord (2003) *The Victoria Climbié Inquiry*. Norwich: HMSO.

Mirrlees-Black, C. (1999) *Domestic Violence: Findings from a New British Crime Survey Self-Completion Questionnaire*, Home Office Research Study 191. London: HMSO.

Mullender, A. (2002) 'Persistant oppressions: the example of domestic violence', in R. Adams, L. Dominelli and M. Payne (eds), *Critical Practice in Social Work*. Basingstoke: Palgrave.

Quinney, A. (2006) *Collaborative Social Work*. Exeter: Learning Matters.

Robinson, M. and Cottrell, D. (2005) 'Health professionals in multi-disciplinary and multi-agency teams: challenging professional practice', *Journal of Interprofessional Care*, 19 (6): 547–60.

Thompson, N. (2001) *Anti-Discriminatory Practice*, 3rd edn. Basingstoke: Palgrave.

WEBSITES

http://www.amicustheunion.org (2006) 'Health visitors in demand at government bid to help most deprived families'

http://www.businessballs.com

http://www.crimereduction.gov.uk (2005) 'Responding to domestic violence'

http://www.csci.org.uk (2006) *Supporting Parents, Safeguarding Children: Meeting the Needs of Parents with Children on the Child Protection Register*

http://www.gscc.org.uk

http://www.homeoffice.gov.uk (2005) Statistics on race and the criminal justice system

http://www.info4local.gov.uk

http://www.learndirect-advice.co.uk (2006) Health visitors

http://www.mindtools.com/CommSkll/JohariWindow.htm (2007) *The Johari Window: Creating Better Understanding Between Individuals and Groups*

http://www.nhscareers.nhs.uk (2006) Health visitors

http://www.nmc-uk.org (2004) Accountability and codes of conduct

http://www.teachernet.gov.uk

Part 4

Researching childhood and youth

12 Approaches to research

Paula Zwozdiak-Myers

Learning objectives

By the end of this chapter you should be able to:

- **distinguish between two major research traditions;**
- **recognise the central characteristics of a range of approaches to research, specifically, scientific, survey, action research, case study, and ethnography;**
- **identify ethical issues in relation to human research.**

Introduction

Research into aspects of childhood and youth development is both fascinating and challenging. It is fascinating, because although your research study might, for example, aim to focus on cognitive development, the results of your investigation will need to take into account other factors that influence this development, such as personal, social and emotional experiences. By adopting this wide perspective, a more holistic understanding of each individual's uniqueness or 'blueprint', one that is shaped by his/her personal biography, can be realised. Hence the challenge! How do we unravel or demystify such uniqueness in coming to understand why individuals think, learn, behave or interact as they do, and where does one begin?

REFLECTIVE ACTIVITY **12.1**

Descriptive or interpretive narrative?

In the following scenario

1. *search for clues in relation to cognitive, social, personal and emotional development that could explain changes to the patterns of behaviour demonstrated by Rosanna;*

2. *identify whether these clues are descriptions based upon factual evidence or interpretations of possible causes that have led to behavioural change.*

Scenario

Rosanna is 12 years of age, and can be characterised as a 'high flier', easily passing examinations and tests with seemingly little preparation, research or effort. A straight 'A' grade, multi-talented student who as yet has to be truly challenged, she excels in all aspects of the school curriculum, is an accomplished athlete and is fully at home when performing lead roles on the stage. Her bedroom, however, is more like a war zone! It receives attention only when all parental strategies have been exhausted and when fears of being 'grounded' become a reality! Lately, Rosanna's demeanour has become markedly polarised – she used to be exceedingly positive about herself, her aspirations and the world at large but her recent behaviour conveys quite a different message. Where open channels of communication and joint planning were once the norm, Rosanna now has an almost guarded, secretive and less accessible side to her nature. She can completely close down and withdraw from the outside world. Since the onset of puberty her body has undergone a major physiological transformation and she does have a well-proportioned feminine physique. Thus self-image ought not to be the problem. An exploration of possible causes that have given rise to such changes in her patterns of behaviour reveal that Rosanna has, on the one hand, become a victim of 'gang' bullying possibly triggered by jealousy from her peers and, on the other, she has recently learned that her father, with whom she has a good and close relationship, has a terminal illness.

From this scenario we can begin to build a picture of Rosanna and recognise that to enhance our understanding of how circumstances might have influenced changes in her behavioural patterns, further investigation of the many complex and interrelated components of cognitive, social, personal and emotional development is required. In this sense, research can be likened to work undertaken by the detective whose strategic plan might take the following line of inquiry: evidence is gathered from all relevant sources and placed under the microscope; possible leads or explanations are pursued; relationships between each fragment of evidence are considered and analysed; elements of the complex matrix or jigsaw puzzle are re-examined and then woven together so that conclusions can be drawn from a well-informed platform and strong evidence base. In the social sciences, in order to resolve problems, to follow a line of inquiry and/or to expand upon existing knowledge, we must engage with research as a systematic method of inquiry and way of asking questions in much the same fashion.

Major traditions

Approaches to research fall within two main traditions that can be distinguished, on the one hand, by differing viewpoints about the role and placement of theory, and on the other, by the relationship to and sequence of events and activities that are involved. For example, one tradition proposes that all relevant data must be collected before the analysis begins whereas the other interweaves data collection with ongoing analysis. The former tradition includes approaches that have been variously termed 'experimental', 'positivist', 'quantitative' and 'scientific' and those of the latter as 'action research', 'case study', 'ethnography', 'interpretive', 'naturalist' or 'qualitative'. Although some topics and situations can effectively be researched using a positivist or an interpretive approach, Bryman (1988: 173) suggests there are others that can be *better served by a marriage of the two traditions*.

Each tradition uses different methods of data collection: *quantitative* research, for example, is concerned with gathering facts and figures for the purpose of statistical analysis whereas *qualitative* research seeks to gain an understanding and insight into individuals' experiences or perceptions. Once you have identified an area to research you might find that a *mixed method* or *hybrid* approach is more relevant to your particular study. The approach you adopt and the methods of data collection you select will depend upon the nature of your inquiry and the kind of information you require (discussed further in Chapter 13).

Within the space of this chapter it is not possible to provide in-depth analysis of the many well-established approaches to research. The following accounts introduce you to central characteristics of a range of approaches that span the positivist–interpretive continuum. This serves to act as a springboard and catalyst for further reading and to furnish you with ideas about strategies and approaches that you might use for your own research investigation.

Scientific approach

Also referred to as experimental design, this approach is concerned with trying out new ideas or techniques both to observe what happens and to gauge what effect the impact might have on something else. Topical exemplars might include the emergence and subsequent application of advanced technology and new knowledge to the fields of acquired immune deficiency syndrome

(AIDS), cancer and stem cell research. Although all research strategies may share the common goal of providing evidence about causal relationships the scientific approach is frequently cited as being the most appropriate for establishing *causal* relationships. Robson (2002: 78) describes experimental research as:

- the assignment of subjects to different conditions;
- manipulation of one or more variables (called 'independent variables') by the experimenter;
- the measurement of the effects of this manipulation on one or more other variables (called 'dependent variables');
- the control of all other variables.

A central feature of this highly focused approach is the need to know what you are doing before you begin. The importance of accuracy and precision in the handling of independent and dependent variables is paramount. Fisher (1935) devised a procedure that has been developed for use in experimental psychology to find out whether a new technique or fertiliser (the treatment or independent variable) would have an impact on the yield of crops (effect of the treatment or dependent variable) in agricultural research. He introduced the notion of *random sampling* by assigning plots of land to a range of different treatments so that the possible effect or outcome of each treatment could be measured more accurately, rather than be biased by such external factors as the amount of rainfall, sunshine or type of soil. The ability to rule out the impact of external factors or bias is crucial for getting to the heart of cause-effect relationships and vitally important when interpreting your results – this relates directly to issues associated with *validity* and *reliability* (Robson (2002: 66–72) provides a comprehensive discussion of validity and reliability issues.

In the social sciences, Bryant and Bradley (1985) used a large-scale correlation study combined with a small-scale experimental study to establish whether a child's experience of categorising sounds, as in rhyming and alliteration, had an effect on learning to read and spell. In the large-scale study, 118 four-year-olds and 285 five-year-olds who could not yet read were tested on: their ability to categorise sounds by detecting the odd word out; verbal intelligence (the English Picture Vocabulary Test); and a memory test. To provide evidence for causal relationships 65 children (divided into four groups) were selected from the large-scale sample to engage in an experimental training programme that spanned two years. Using standardised tests for reading, spelling, IQ and mathematical ability, Bryant and Bradley retested the children four years later, when they were either eight or nine years old. They concluded that training in sound categorisation does have an influence on reading and spelling but, moreover, when combined with alphabetic teaching, it was found to be even more effective. Results from these combined studies provide strong evidence for a causal relationship along the lines they had hypothesised.

Any approach to research needs to consider and be able to justify decisions made that relate to sampling. Where a *population* refers to all cases or units, a *sample* refers to a selection of cases or units derived from that population. Types of sampling are commonly based on *probability* samples and *non-probability* samples. The former type is often referred to as representative sampling and allows for statistical inferences about the population to be drawn from responses derived from the sample. For example, from the total population of 403 children in Bryant and Bradley's (1985) study, the 65 selected for the experiment were considered to be representative of the population as a whole and subsequent findings could be *generalised* across the whole population from which they had been drawn. Conversely, in the case of the latter type of sampling, where the probability of the selection of each participant is not known, statistical inferences are not appropriate. It might be possible to present some reasonable conclusions about the outcomes of your study but these will not be based on statistical grounds.

The extent to which this type of scientific approach is appropriate to the study of people, however, does need careful consideration. The key assumption in experimental design is that factors operating under the 'closed system' of the study also operate in the 'open system' of nature (Bhaskar, 1978). Although Locke (1986) supports this view and suggests that the generalisability of findings from laboratory to real-world settings is considerable, Wilson (1979: 22) challenges this view and suggests that social causes do not operate singly but rather the outcome (with reference to an examination of high IQ or low school achievement) is the product of multiple causes:

> *To isolate each cause requires a new experimental group each time and the length and diffi-culty of the experiment increases rapidly. It is possible to run an experiment in which several treatments are put into practice simultaneously but many groups must be available rather than just two ... causes of social phenomena are usually multiple ones and an experiment to study them requires large numbers of people often for lengthy periods.*

This leads one to question whether 'how people behave in experimental situations is *relatable* to what they actually do in other situations'. You might pursue this question further by referring to the effects of 'demand characteristics' and 'experimenter expectancy' on bias, highlighted by Barber (1976) in an analysis of some pitfalls that can arise in the experimental context with humans.

Survey

Bryman (1988: 104) describes survey research as:

> *the collection of data on a number of units and usually at a single juncture in time, with a view to collecting systematically a body of quantifiable data in respect of a number of vari-ables which are then examined to discern patterns of association.*

This approach is commonly used to gather information that can be analysed and compared to estab-lish emergent patterns or trends, such as the rise in levels of obesity, teenage pregnancy, binge drinking or anti-social behaviour in children and adolescents. A *census* is one example of a survey – information can be gathered by means of self-completed questionnaires (postal survey), telephone survey or by means of questionnaires, schedules or checklists that are administered by an inter-viewer. The objective is to gather responses to the same standardised questions (worded carefully after piloting to ensure that the questions mean the same thing to different participants) from a large number of individuals in order to compare and relate one characteristic to another and ascer-tain whether certain features are predominant in particular categories.

Surveys are frequently used for *descriptive purposes* to provide information about the distribution of a wide range of 'people characteristics', and of relationships between such characteristics (Robson, 2002). In relation to the onset of puberty Tanner (1989) used this approach to provide an extensive and systematic account of the nature and timing of physical changes during childhood and adolescence. The physical characteristics of large samples of children of different ages were recorded to establish the normal or average progress of development, to chart variations in age between the onset and comple-tion of different developments and to compare the growth patterns of girls and boys.

Surveys can also be used for *interpretive purposes* in that causal relationships can be suggested by providing possible explanations to clarify what has been described. Coleman (cited in Coleman and Hendry, 1990) developed his 'focal' theory from a UK study in which girls and boys aged 11, 13, 15 and 17 completed tests that were designed to investigate their attitudes to a range of relationships, specifically those with parents, peers and the opposite sex. In contrast to the 'storm and stress' model which advocates that disruption (during adolescence) occurs simultaneously in all areas, Coleman concluded that concerns about difficult issues reached a peak at different points during adolescence. Such diverse viewpoints highlight some of the complexities associated with interpretation.

Surveys can provide you with answers to questions that search for reasons to do with the what, how, where and when of situations and phenomena, yet it is very difficult to determine causal rela-tionships – in other words, to establish the why. Surveys can also be associated with the deliberate manipulation of one or more variables (Robson, 2002) such as carrying out a series of surveys before, during and after an intervention or initiative to determine the effectiveness of its impact.

The emphasis on quantifiable data, variables and sampling from known populations is a similar approach to research as that adopted by those who engage in scientific inquiry and experimental design. Clarity of those variables you seek information on needs to be transparent from the outset of your study. Not only will this determine your sample size and sample selection but also the number of categories that you will use to subdivide your data. How you plan to collate and analyse data also needs careful consideration in the design stage of your study. Hakim (1987) provides a useful reference guide and resource for the design of small-scale surveys.

Action research

Action research, as defined by Carr and Kemmis (1986: 162), is:

> *A form of self-reflective enquiry undertaken by participants in social situations in order to improve the rationality and justice of their own practices, their understanding of these practices, and the situations in which the practices are carried out.*

This approach to research is one that is firmly embedded within the realm of the practitioner who aims to develop an understanding, to solve a problem and/or to investigate an issue. *The ultimate aim of inquiry is understanding; and understanding is the basis of action for improvement* (McKernan, 1996: 3). This interpretation focuses on self-appraisal as a way of working and is closely linked to Schön's (1991) concept of reflective practice as exemplified through the rigorous and systematic process of *reflection on action* (discussed further in Chapter 14).

In seeking to improve practice and personal understanding McKernan (1996) suggests that an inquiry must be carried out by the practitioner, in the first instance, to clarify and define the problem, and secondly, to specify a plan of action that includes the testing of hypotheses by action to the problem (in other words, how your proposed intervention(s) have been designed to resolve the problem). This is followed by evaluation to monitor and establish the effectiveness of the action taken. In the final stage, *participants reflect upon, explain developments and communicate results to the community of action researchers* (McKernan, 1996: 5).

An important feature of action research is the cyclical nature of the ongoing process to improve the quality and effectiveness of practice. Cohen and Manion (1994: 192) explain that *ideally, the step-by-step process is constantly monitored over varying periods of time and by a variety of mechanisms (e.g. questionnaires, diaries, interviews and case studies) so that the ensuing feedback may be translated into modifications, adjustments, directional changes, redefinitions, as necessary*. Elliot (1991: 69) clarifies that the purpose behind this cyclical process is that it aims:

> *to feed practical judgement in concrete situations, and the validity of the 'theories' or hypotheses it generates depends not so much on 'scientific' tests of truth, as on their useful-ness in helping people to act more intelligently and skilfully. In action research 'theories' are not validated independently and then applied to practice. They are validated through practice.*

The critical and analytical study of relevant literature is a vitally important aspect of action research and one that should be undertaken both to guide the formulation of a research question and the subsequent plan of action. Macintyre (2000: 16–17) has developed a series of questions that can be asked for the purpose of comparing, contrasting and evaluating literature that might be relevant to your study.

Through undertaking an action research investigation you can begin to appreciate different aspects of your personal professional development and progress. In relation to the teaching-learning context, Hargreaves et al. (2001) consider that 'professional discretion' is demonstrated when teachers ask searching questions of educational practice that arise from their own professional circumstances, interests and commitments, for example: how to develop pupils' observational skills through reciprocal/peer teaching approaches; how to enhance pupil self-esteem by using different forms of feedback; how to develop the use and range of questioning techniques to challenge the most able pupils; and how to improve the effectiveness of classroom management techniques or non-verbal communication skills. Such teachers exemplify a commitment to continuous learning by seeking new ideas, evaluating and reflecting on their impact and trying out new practices and ways of working to improve their own effectiveness in the teaching-learning environment.

This particular approach is of relevance to many aspects of work within the social sciences. It is appropriate in any context when *specific knowledge is required for a specific problem in a specific situation, or when a new approach is to be grafted onto an existing system* (Cohen and Manion, 1994: 194).

Case study

Characterised by an in-depth empirical investigation of a particular 'case', in a particular timeframe and within a particular context, this approach to research uses multiples sources of evidence. The case that readily springs to mind is of an individual person and one that provides a detailed account of that person by focusing on cultural, social and contextual factors to explore possible causes, factors or experiences that might contribute to a particular outcome. The expansive 400-page report by Lord Laming (2003) of the inquiry into the death of Victoria Climbié is a poignant exemplar of one case that examined evidence from people across four London boroughs, three health trusts, one health authority, the Metropolitan Police, the NSPCC, eight police officers, one social worker and 20 witnesses. Parton (2004) compares and contrasts this report with that on Maria Colwell and argues that differences between the two cases in terms of the inquiries themselves, globalisation and identity, expert knowledge, systematic care, responsibility and accountability, managerialisation, trust and uncertainty and the legislative contexts exemplify the changing contexts of child protection in England over the past 30 years.

Case studies are not limited solely to the study of individuals. This approach can be, and is, used much more widely to study particular groups, organisations and programmes, and the roles, responsibilities, events and relationships within a particular service, such as education, health or social work. This approach enables you to concentrate on a specific situation or instance in its natural context to identify the various interactive processes in operation.

The effectiveness of a case study is highly dependent upon the trustworthiness of the *human* instrument (you as the researcher). Miles and Huberman (1994: 46) suggest that one needs: *some familiarity with the phenomenon and the setting under study; strong conceptual interests; a multi-disciplinary approach ...; good investigative skills, including doggedness, the ability to draw people out, and the ability to ward off premature closure*. This particular view, however, is controversial as lack of familiarity with the setting and the importance of a strong disciplinary stance are more commonly advocated (Robson, 2002).

The design of a particular case study will be influenced by the questions you seek to answer and by how you decide to select data so that conclusions can be drawn. You can pre-structure the design from the outset of an inquiry but will need to be aware of some problems associated with a strong conceptual framework at this stage, such as missing vital clues or key features of the case because your focus is predetermined. On the other hand, your case study design might be 'emergent' and evolve during the study itself. A potential concern here, however, is that a lack of focus might result in gathering data from any and everything that you consider 'might' be important; as Miles and Huberman (1994: 27) caution, *a loose highly inductive design, is a waste of time. Months of field-work and voluminous case studies will yield a few banalities*. One might perhaps aim to strike a balance between these two extremes. It is important to view case study design as a flexible and continuous process, so that you can respond to the opportunity of modifying or changing your focus, as and when appropriate. It is also important to make some preliminary decisions in relation to the design of your case study around such factors as: a conceptual framework, a set of research questions, a sampling strategy and methods and techniques to be used for data collection.

The conceptual framework aims to *encourage you to be explicit about what you think you are doing. It also helps you to be selective, to decide which are the important features; which relationships are likely to be of importance or meaning; and hence, what data you are going to collect and analyse* (Robson, 2002: 150–1). The research questions you formulate during the initial stages of your study can be general if your approach is relatively unstructured or more specific if your approach is quite structured. These questions can be refined or revised as your study progresses. Devising a sampling strategy entails decision-making about who you will observe or interview, where this will take place and when, and what particular activities, events, situations or processes you plan to observe. Based upon the nature and needs of your study you might consider *purposive sampling*; this relates to your judgement as to the typicality or interest of individuals, events, settings, situations and processes most appropriate for providing answers to your research question/s. Denscombe (1998: 36–7), for example, in relation to the case study of a small primary school, states that:

> The extent to which findings from a case study can be generalised to other examples in a class depends on how far the case study example is similar to others of its type … The researcher must obtain data on the significant features (catchment area, the ethnic origins of the pupils and the amount of staff turnover) for primary schools in general, and then demonstrate where the case study example fits in relation to the overall picture.

Bassey (1981: 85) suggests that *relatability* rather than *generalisability* is more important when analysing and reporting on the outcomes of a case study as *an important criterion for judging the merit of a case study is the extent to which the details are sufficient and appropriate for a teacher working in a similar situation to relate his decision making to that described in the case study.*

Ethnography

Originally developed by anthropologists to study a society or a particular characteristic of that society, ethnography focuses on the interpretation and meaning of social phenomena that, in simplified terms, involves the study of people as they go about their daily lives (Emerson et al., 1995). According to Geertz (1973) human actions signal a world of multiple social meanings that must be understood through the recognition of various contextual clues. An ethnographer, through direct involvement with a group, tries to work out these meanings and provide a rich description that interprets the experiences of those people within the group. This *naturalist* approach to fieldwork research in the hermeneutics is one that explores social phenomena, as they exist, unaltered in the world.

Ethnography can be used for several different purposes, including the elicitation of cultural knowledge, the holistic analysis of societies and the understanding of social interactions and meaning-making (Hammersley and Atkinson, 1983). The latter is perhaps the most relevant to the study of childhood and youth development and was used by Dunn (1988) to observe how and why sibling–child and parent–child relationships differ, how they influence one another and how they develop over time. In order to understand children's emotional and social development and their experiences (not just the causes of unhappiness and insecurity, but rather what excites, arouses and interests children) she believed that it was important to study them in situations of emotional significance to them, notably with their family and friends. From her initial goal of studying newborn children with their mothers, a keen interest to focus on the relationship between the baby and his/her older sibling evolved. Dunn noted that interactions between the two children were very different from those between each child and parent, in relation to social repertoire and style of communication, and she highlights the importance of describing such social processes as affective expression and conversational exchanges at different levels.

Ethnography involves the intensive, continuous and often microscopic observation of small samples (Corsaro, 1996). Traditionally, this has focused on a group or a single setting. Different methods of data collection are employed to draw together information from a range of sources that Agar (1996) refers to as 'encyclopedic anthropology', involving a synthesis of historical, political and economic aspects of the cultural context that impinge on daily experience. The principle method or hallmark of ethnography is *participant observation*. In research literature you will often find that the terms 'participant observation' and 'ethnography' are used interchangeably which can obscure both the relationship and distinction between them.

Participant observation, by means of partial or complete integration within the group being studied, is based upon the premise that to understand human action, we must use a methodological approach that gives access to the rich, social meanings that guide behaviour, and that our innate capacities as social actors can provide us with such access (Buchbinder et al., 2006). Integration within the group enables the researcher to share the same experiences as those being studied and better understand why they act and behave as they do and *to see things as those involved see things* (Denscombe, 1998: 69).

Ethnography is complementary to childhood and youth research for several reasons. First, an intimate rapport between the researcher and individual participants can be established that allows the researcher access to the long-removed world of childhood from an insider's perspective (Corsaro and Molinari, 2000). Second, the longitudinal nature of ethnography is appropriate to the study of children over a given time frame, and is well positioned to capture critical periods of transition that shape processes of human development (Corsaro, 1996). Third, Weisner (2002) suggests that developmental pathways are shaped by the cultural underpinnings of daily life; for example, daily routines are important units of cultural analysis because they form the cultural pathways that shape human experience. Fourth, given the emphasis that research studies place on the social and emotional development of children as a contributory factor in their readiness and disposition to learn (Wesley and Busse, 2003), ethnography can help researchers to articulate and understand the various daily practices, relationships and cultural forces that contribute toward social and emotional development.

Ethical issues in relation to human research

Ethical issues arise in human research when the conduct of the researcher involves the interests and rights of others. By their very nature, social (cultural) and educational research involves studying people's activities in one way or another. Research involving interviews or observation, particularly where veridical records are kept on audio or video tape for example, may impinge on the confidentiality, privacy, convenience, comfort or safety of others and constitute ethical problems.

The use of children as participants necessarily raises ethical issues in that the researcher cannot assume their capacity to comprehend the nature of the research and therefore to freely volunteer as a participant or to freely opt out without prejudice. Parents and guardians cannot consent to the possibility of their child being harmed but they can give permission for their child to participate in a study in which they have full confidence that their child's rights will not be infringed and that they do not face the possibility of harm or injury. Your susceptibility as researcher to possible charges of negligence are necessarily great.

Many professions that undertake research with human participants have devised an ethical code of practice or set of principles, for example the Revised Ethical Guidelines for Educational Research (British Educational Research Association, 2004) and the Code of Conduct, Ethical Principles and Guidelines (British Psychological Society, 1997). These provide important benchmarks and reference sources in coming to recognise your responsibilities to protect the well-being of research participants. For example, the former (available at **http://www.bera.ac.uk**) provides guidance in relation to Voluntary Informed Consent, Deception, Right to Withdraw, Children, Vulnerable Young People and

Vulnerable Adults, Incentives, Detriment Arising from Participation in Research, Privacy and Disclosure. In support of these guidelines your higher education institution will have ethical principles and procedures in place for undertaking research with human participants, which you should consult and respond to appropriately.

REFLECTIVE ACTIVITY **12.2**

Selecting an approach to research

From the scenario in the introduction to this chapter identify:

- *what information you would need to gather to provide possible reasons for the change in behaviour;*

- *how you could go about gathering this data;*

- *which of the approaches to research you consider to be the most appropriate and why;*

- *what ethical procedures you would need to observe.*

SUMMARY OF KEY POINTS

This chapter has provided you with the basis for distinguishing between two major research traditions, recognising the central characteristics of a range of approaches to research and identifying ethical issues in relation to human research. To help you further, Chapter 13 guides you through key stages of the research process and introduces data collection techniques. This should enable you to undertake a research study to further enhance your knowledge and understanding of factors that influence childhood and youth development.

FERENCES

Agar, M. (1996) *The Professional Stranger: An Informal Introduction to Ethnography.* San Diego, CA: Academic Press.

Barber, T. (1976) *Pitfalls in Human Research: Ten Pivotal Points.* Oxford: Pergamon.

Bassey, M. (1981) 'Pedagogic research: on the relative merits of the search for generalization and study of a single event', *Oxford Review of Education,* 7 (1): 73–93.

Bhaskar, R. (1978) *A Realist Theory of Science,* 2nd edn. Brighton: Harvester.

British Educational Research Association (2004) *Revised Ethical Guidelines for Educational Research.* Southwell: BERA (available at: **http://www.bera.ac.uk**).

British Psychological Society (1997) *Code of Conduct, Ethical Principles and Guidelines.* Leicester: BPS.

Bryant, P. and Bradley, L. (1985) *Children's Reading Problems.* Oxford: Basil Blackwell.

Bryman, A. (1988) *Quality and Quantity in Social Research.* London: Unwin Hyman.

Buchbinder, M., Longhofer, J., Barrett, T., Lawson, P. and Floersch, J. (2006) 'Ethnographic approaches to child care research', *Early Childhood Research,* 4 (1): 45–63.

Carr, W. and Kemmis, S. (1986) *Becoming Critical. Education, Knowledge and Action Research*. Lewes: Falmer.

Cohen, L. and Manion, L. (1994) *Research Methods in Education*, 4th edn. London: Routledge.

Coleman, J. and Hendry, L. (1990) *The Nature of Adolescence*, 2nd edn. London: Routledge.

Corsaro, W. (1996) 'Transitions in early childhood: the promise of comparative, longitudinal ethnography', in A. Colby, R. Jessor and R. Shweder (eds), *Ethnography and Human Development: Context and Meaning in Social Inquiry*. Chicago: University of Chicago Press.

Corsaro, W. and Molinari, L. (2000) 'Entering and observing in children's worlds', in P. Christensen and A. James (eds), *Research with Children: Perspectives and Practices*. London: Falmer Press.

Denscombe, M. (1998) *The Good Research Guide*. Buckingham: Open University Press.

Dunn, J. (1988) *The Beginnings of Social Understanding*. Oxford: Blackwell.

Elliott, J. (1991) *Action Research for Educational Change*. Buckingham: Open University Press.

Emerson, R., Fretz, R. and Shaw, L. (1995) *Writing Ethnographic Fieldnotes*. Chicago: University of Chicago Press.

Fisher, R. (1935) *The Design of Experiments*. Edinburgh: Oliver & Boyd.

Geertz, C. (1973) *The Interpretation of Cultures*. New York: Basic Books.

Hakim, C. (1987) *Research Design: Strategies and Choices in the Design of Social Research*. London: Allen & Unwin.

Hammersley, M. and Atkinson, P. (1983) *Ethnography: Principles in Practice*. London: Tavistock.

Hargreaves, A., Earl, L., Moore, S. and Manning, S. (2001) *Learning to Change: Teaching Beyond Subjects and Standards*. San Francisco: Jossey-Bass.

Locke, E. (1986) *Generalizing from Laboratory to Field Settings*. Lexington, MA: Lexington Books.

Lord Laming (2003) The Victoria Climbié Inquiry: Report of an Inquiry by Lord Laming. London: Stationery Office (available at: *http://www.everychildmatters.com*).

Macintyre, C. (2000) *The Art of Action Research in the Classroom*. London: David Fulton.

McKernan, J. (1996) *Curriculum Action Research*, 2nd edn. London: Kogan Page.

Miles, M. and Huberman, A. (1994) *Qualitative Data Analysis: A Sourcebook of New Methods*, 2nd edn. London: Sage.

Parton, N. (2004) 'From Maria Colwell to Victoria Climbié: reflections on public inquiries into child abuse a generation apart', *Child Abuse Review*, 13: 80–94 (available at: **http://www.interscience.wiley.com**).

Robson, C. (2002) *Real World Research*, 2nd edn. Oxford: Blackwell.

Schön, D. (1991) *The Reflective Practitioner*. New York: Basic Books.

Tanner, J. (1989) *Foetus into Man*, 2nd edn. Ware: Castlemead Publications.

Weisner, T. (2002) 'Ecocultural understanding of children's developmental pathways', *Human Development*, 45 (4): 275–81.

Wesley, P. and Busse, V. (2003) 'Making meaning of school readiness in schools and communities', *Early Childhood Research Quarterly*, 18 (3): 351–75.

Wilson, N. (1979) *Research Methods in Education and the Social Sciences*, Course DE304. Buckingham: Open University Press.

13 The research process

Neil Burton

Learning objectives

By the end of this chapter you should be able to:

- **understand the key structures of a written report on empirical research;**
- **recognise the importance of clarifying the focus for a research activity;**
- **justify the approach adopted for the gathering of evidence;**
- **identify how to present and analyse research findings effectively.**

Introduction

The analytical nature of an empirical research assignment in synthesising theory and practice cannot be overemphasised. It should offer you the opportunity to review critically a body of knowledge or set of skills and allow you to demonstrate your own understanding within a particular context through comparison, application or exemplification. In an ideal situation it should enable you to analyse objectively an issue in a given professional context and identify potential for improvement, for both the context and your own practice. By developing the skills which enable you to make research-informed decisions, you will become much more objective, rational and 'professional' in your outlook, enabling you to progress with confidence. There is a structure that can be applied to research activity that both clarifies and simplifies the process for the practitioner-researcher (a professional who uses research to inform their decision-making) as opposed to a practising researcher (someone who performs research for purely academic interest).

A structural overview

By taking a structured approach to research, you can identify elements that constitute good and effective practice. It is important to adopt a methodical and systematic approach rather than jumping to 'intuitive' conclusions. The five sections indicated below provide a means for synthesising theory and practice, and are interdependent.

1. *Starting point* – examination of the national and/or local context to refine the research question and justify its purpose.
2. *Theoretical perspective* – critical examination of relevant conceptual and empirical literature in order to provide a wider understanding of themes connected to the research question.
3. *Research methodology* – use of theoretical literature to clarify *what* to ask; reference to the context, such as identifying key stakeholders, to determine *who* to ask; and acknowledgement of research limitations, such as resource availability, to clarify *how* to ask. The development of research tools, consideration of ethical issues and justification of your approach should also be clarified.
4. *Presentation and analysis of findings* – comparative analysis of different sources of information with respect to the research question and reflection on the findings and suggested expectations of previous published research.
5. *Conclusions and recommendations* – identification of key findings and a suggested course of action following analysis.

Starting point

You should begin by choosing a potential focus, since you cannot progress until you have established your research area. You may find it helpful to discuss your ideas with colleagues or practitioners within the field before conferring with your tutor.

REFLECTIVE ACTIVITY **13.1**

Selecting an area to research

Ask yourself: 'In this area of study, what are the key issues for me and my host institution within the broader research context?' Focusing on an issue that has the potential to realise 'practical outcomes' (Bell, 2005: 28) may give your research greater meaning. You may identify two or three potential areas of interest this way. Your next step would be to evaluate the viability and potential impact of each area by determining whether:

- *it has a clear theoretical/conceptual base;*

- *the study is manageable – be realistic and consider the probable scope and timescale of your proposed study in relation to research constraints;*

- *you will have access to key sources of information, e.g. confidential management documents within the host organisation;*

- *the study will benefit you and/or your host institution, e.g. does the study support your career aspirations?*

Once you have satisfied yourself that the study will be worthwhile and manageable, you can move to the starting point.

Once you have established a viable research area, draft a title that identifies the intended focus and scope of the study, for example:

Early diagnosis of Attention Deficit and Hyperactivity Disorder (ADHD) in preschool children: an examination of the role of parents in the identification process

The title offers a conceptual focus (ADHD), a context (preschool children) and a core research population (parents). By narrowing the focus, the research activity immediately becomes more manageable, such as:

Social inclusion of English as an Additional Language (EAL) for teenagers: an evaluation of community-based support strategies offered by one urban local authority

Again this title offers direction and focus. EAL is the main issue, but social inclusion for teenagers is brought to the fore. However, the phrasing of the title implies that the respondent base is not limited to teenagers but could include such stakeholders as parents, schools, social workers, local politicians and community workers.

Once you have formulated the focus of your research, you will need to justify your decision by explaining your rationale. Firstly, you should contextualise your focus in order to demonstrate why your study matters. Within the realm of the social sciences, this can usually be achieved at both a national and local level. At the national level, there is likely to be a large body of documentation for you to draw upon. Your sources may be in the form of government policy directives, empirical research or newspaper articles highlighting key issues gleaned from original texts. Up-to-date debate surrounding national policies and problems will help you verify the wider significance of your research. At the local level, the context for your research will narrow. It will become more person-alised and manageable; furthermore, it should enable you to identify a core research population. This contextual positioning of your study then leads to an explanation of the purpose – 'what are you actually trying to find out?' – which can be achieved by breaking the direction given by the title down into more easily achieved research questions. In the examples given above these might be as follows.

- What is meant by 'ADHD'?
- What diagnostic processes/strategies are available/applicable?
- How can/are parents involved in the process?

And secondly:

- Is language a barrier to social inclusion?
- What strategies can be applied to overcome these barriers?
- How can the effectiveness of strategies be judged?

You should address these questions throughout the study to guide and structure both the research and the reporting of that research in order to maintain coherence and continuity.

Theoretical perspective

Although your research question should have a streamlined focus, your study as a whole should incorporate a wider theoretical perspective. If you neglect to explore previous published research within the field or fail to base your study within a larger theoretical framework, your research will risk being overly insular. Furthermore, you are likely to miss key insights for potential solutions or improvement areas.

Periodically consult the key questions that you established at the starting point for guidance as you review relevant literature. There are various ways of approaching this task. If the focus of the study is relatively unfamiliar, you might begin by scanning general texts to obtain an overview of major ideas and key authors. Alternatively, if you already have knowledge of your focus area, you could begin with a list of key ideas to provide an initial structure. Often the initial structure will incorporate the following.

- Defining – identify key terms and ideas.
- Refining – focus on the ideas as they relate to the context of the study.
- Applying – explore previous research that focuses on your research area or a similar context. (You may also pick up some very useful ideas for research methods and tools from these sources.).

Searching for sources

We currently live in an information-rich environment. At the press of a button, the internet can provide access to millions of thematic links. These links, however, have various degrees of reliability and many sites provide neither a source of accountability nor verification of the information's accuracy. University-hosted web pages and electronic and paper-based journals and textbooks offer appropriate and reliable sources of information, both theoretical and empirical (e.g. published findings from previous research).

Access to sources may depend on several factors. Firstly, successful online research requires that the search terms be both clear and appropriate. If you select terms that are too general in your search, such as 'ADHD', there may be too many 'hits' to be manageable. Conversely, if you are too precise with your terms, such as 'ADHD and preschool children *and* parental involvement *and* diagnosis', your search may return too few links. You may, also, run the risk of missing important sources that could be helpful, since they would be beyond the scope of the search parameters.

A second significant factor is the nature of the search engine used. Specialist databases (e.g. **http://www.inclusion.ngfl.gov.uk**) usually provide more relevant lists than general databases (e.g. Google®) and can accelerate your research. Thus by selecting the most appropriate search engine you should be able to expedite the research process.

Thirdly, a lack of financial resources can affect a researcher's access to sources. University or college libraries may not always have the books or journals you require, although it may be possible to arrange 'visitor' access to other academic libraries that do have the sources available. You should be able to arrange an inter-library loan, but there is usually a fee for this service. With this in mind, it is worth closely reviewing the source's abstract to ensure its relevance before ordering it. Similarly, you should ascertain whether your academic library subscribes to an electronic journal before paying for personal access.

It is likely that books, either single or joint-authored, and edited collections of chapters will help outline the theoretical framework for your study's focus. Internet sources, newspapers and professional journals will provide a wider contextual setting and some general applications. Academic journals and some of the more prestigious websites will provide examples of current research in the field. An appropriate combination of these sources should provide a suitable conceptual framework on which to base a small-scale study by 'redeveloping' rather than 'reinventing' the wheel. Other texts, such as Denscombe (2003) and Bell (2005), address these issues in greater detail.

Constructing a review of the literature

Some of the more general texts within the field will help to define the parameters and scope of the study and clarify the terminology. The more specific texts (often edited collections of chapters) should help to refine some of the key ideas the research will be based upon. Journal articles (often the authors of the books will be engaged in more current research) will provide examples of research findings and, quite often, research methodology and tools that could be adapted for use in a small-scale research project.

A frequent mistake in literature reviews is that they are presented as an annotated bibliography or a report of the content of the literature, jumping from source to source or quote to quote, rather than an analysis of the content and meaning of sources and comparison of them to identify possible similarities and differences. Some of the best reviews will combine the best elements of theories and research findings to construct a more powerful model that can then be used as a benchmark against which to compare the reality as reflected in the research activity. Overall, it is important to demonstrate that ideas and current thinking have been considered and that elements from the reading will be taken forward as a basis for the research activity. This shows that the research will be based upon something more tangible and meaningful than speculation and unsubstantiated instinct.

REFLECTIVE ACTIVITY **13.2**

Preparing for the review of relevant literature

Plan to perform a review of relevant literature.

- *List key conceptual terms that your study will address (these will be your key search terms).*
- *List the contextual factors that you can use to restrict the scope of your search (age range, location, conceptual aspect, etc.).*
- *Identify journals that might publish articles in the field of study.*

Research methodology

You should choose your method of gathering evidence by determining the most appropriate and practical options. Your decision should follow consideration of proposed outcomes, contextual constraints and potential obstacles. In order to assess various research methods objectively, you might ask: what would be the most effective way to collect the evidence I need?

In essence, the research methodology should consider three key questions.

- *What* needs to be asked?
- *Who* needs to be asked?
- *How* can they be asked?

These questions are not mutually exclusive and the outcomes of one may influence those of another. Therefore you should maintain an inclusive overview of the questions throughout the research process.

What needs to be asked?

The purpose of reviewing literature before embarking on your own research is to help to identify and clarify the key issues you wish to explore. Both conceptual and empirical literature should help you construct your own study. Many elements of previous work may be transferable to your research, such as choosing research tools, populations and methodology. You may choose to perform a comparative study by using the same tools and methodology but in a different context or, perhaps, adapting them to your context as you can learn from weaknesses within the previous study. Be sure to recognise and acknowledge where influences on your research came from, however, since you will analyse your findings in relation to them.

Who needs to be asked?

Consider the two example titles given earlier:

> *Early diagnosis of ADHD in preschool children: an examination of the role of parents in the identification process*

and

> *Social inclusion of EAL teenagers: an evaluation of community-based support strategies offered by one urban local authority.*

The key research populations are already explicitly stated in the titles – parents of ADHD preschool children and urban EAL teenagers – although to get a full picture of the situation, it may be necessary to go beyond the initial focus groups. For the EAL teenagers, it may be important to compare the perspectives of those participating in the strategies and those who do not, other members of the communities themselves, professionals providing support/structure for the strategies and possibly the schools which the teenagers attend. Extending the focus of the study should develop a more rounded perspective but by increasing the range of respondents it may also cause problems with access, differentiation of research tools and, potentially, the scale of the research study. Consequently, rather than assessing an entire population, it may be necessary to *sample*, or to obtain the views of a subset of the population to represent the views of the population as a whole. The construction of this 'representative sample' must be handled with great care and there is a number of well-defined ways of achieving this.

The example of EAL teenagers is already a sample from a much larger population – it is, as the constructed title suggests, a case study of one urban local authority among many, a case study being a 'bounded system' (Nisbet and Watt, 1984: 79) in that it is a well-defined group such as the participants on a particular course or those working in a specific office. However, a case study may offer a population which is too large to manage as part of a small-scale research activity, so further action must be taken to systematically reduce the potential number of respondents. The main choices are between *probability* (random) and *non-probability* (purposive) sampling.

A probability sample *draws randomly from a wider population* (Cohen et al., 2000: 99). If the whole population is known – all EAL teenagers who have attended a support group in the past year, for example – it might be possible to perform a systematic sample of every twentieth person on a list of 400. But how representative is a random sample? It may be necessary to subdivide the population into smaller, well-defined subsets to ensure a full representation of the population within the sample (*stratified* sampling). In the ADHD example it may be necessary to subdivide the population of parents into 'cohabiting birth parents' and 'single parents', and perhaps still further by gender or ethnic group and then randomly sample from each of those subsets to get a truly representative sample. Where there are very large numbers that need to be reduced to a more manageable figure, this could be achieved by multi-level sampling. A random selection is made from a sample that has already been randomly selected, e.g. from a random selection of ADHD assessment centres, ADHD assessors are selected and from their caseloads parents are randomly selected for the research (*stage* sampling). Where the selection criteria change at each stage it is known as *multi-phase* sampling.

Non-probability sampling is often more convenient and less difficult to arrange although it is unlikely that it will be rigorously representative of the population as a whole. The most straightforward is convenience sampling where those who are in close proximity to the researcher become the sample, e.g. the parents of ADHD children who attend a 'self-help' group that the researcher has access to, or the teenagers attending the Thursday evening community group which the researcher helps to run. *Quota* sampling is the non-probability version of a stratified sample where the proportions in the sample (e.g. male/female; age distribution) are the same as in the population as a whole. It may be possible to individually select a sample to represent the population (*purposive* sampling). With the guidance of professionals who work with the parents, a representative group may be selected to provide a range of perspectives of the ADHD diagnosis procedures. A final approach is known as *snowballing* where an initial small group of respondents is asked to recommend other potential respondents.

How can they be asked?

Once you have established *what* and *who* to ask, you can progress to determining the most effective means of gathering your evidence. To a large extent the key determining factors are access and time, which will affect the breadth and depth of your study. Given the constraints of your research, you may have to compromise between what is ideal and what is possible. Thus you will need to determine an appropriate balance of approaches to provide the most meaningful responses possible. The data gathered is likely to be a combination of first- and second-hand information – first-hand being that information which is directly collected either through observation of events or by explicit questioning of participants; second-hand being that information which is to be found in documents or by questioning the perceptions of the participants. In all cases the methodology employed should maintain a strict focus on the key research questions (as discussed above).

The most common research methods are the following.

● *Surveys* – a standard set of questions employed to elicit specific facts, attitudes or opinions from respondents within a given population. Surveys usually take the form of either questionnaires or interviews and can be conducted directly by the researcher (interviews) or indirectly by self-completion by respondents (questionnaires).

- *Observations* – the researcher obtains a consistent perspective on an observable phenomenon. If the conduct of ADHD diagnostic meetings were to be the focus of the research, then relying on the responses of the individuals concerned would be subject to their individual perceptions and biases. An independent observer would be able to offer a degree of objectivity to the research – or at least the degree of bias and subjectivity should be consistent!

- *Documentary analysis* – where documents can provide a perspective for your study. Documents are most often used as a means of triangulating information from other sources: participants may provide a perspective on what *is* happening, managers on what they *think* is happening but a document might provide information on what *should* be happening (the policy) in specific circumstances (such as ADHD diagnostic processes). In this way, the document acts as a 'base line' against which other perceptions can be compared.

- *Action research* – where there is interaction between the researcher and the phenomenon being studied. The researcher is actively engaged in attempting to influence the outcomes by taking direct action to bring about improvement. This is very similar in approach to reflective practitioners who evaluate their performance in order to inform subsequent planning, with a view to improving performance. The intervention and the resulting changes can be recorded by the researcher through the use of a participant diary, triangulated by the use of external observers or a survey of other participants in the process. (Refer to Chapters 12 and 14 for further discussion of action research and reflective practice, respectively.)

Surveys

Surveys can be conducted either directly by the researcher through *interviews* or indirectly through *questionnaires*. Interviews offer a degree of interaction between the researcher and the respondent that is not possible through a questionnaire. However, interviews are much more time-consuming than questionnaires and must be more carefully negotiated with potential respondents. Questionnaires allow the researcher to control the focus and format of responses but may lack the subject flexibility of interviews. In either case, conceptual frameworks developed from the literature can be used as a basis for the questions, allowing you to make direct comparisons between responses and the theoretical perspectives.

There are three main types of interviews: structured, semi-structured and unstructured. In *structured interviews*, the interviewer works through an interview schedule that is usually composed of closed questions (discussed later in this chapter) that limit the response options of the respondent. The interviewing process ensures the full completion of responses and allows the interviewer to work through a large schedule on a 'critical path' basis. One drawback of this approach is that, with such limited flexibility, your data may lack evidence that is pivotal to your research and your questions may not offer a sufficient range of responses to gain a fully nuanced overview of the topic.

Semi-structured interviews offer a more flexible style that can be used to collect information equivalent to that of the structured interviews. The researcher usually begins by identifying a number of key questions that not only elicit specific types of response, but also act as prompts. Furthermore, probing can be used to ensure that the respondent understands the questions. Then, depending on the responses received, the interviewer can choose to either ask further questions to explore a specific area in greater detail or move onto the next key question.

Unstructured interviews are the most flexible and may allow you to gather complementary evidence. This approach is generally used to explore an area in preliminary research, for people with access to specialised information or for those able to provide you with a unique perspective on an issue (such as a principal community support worker). Since the success of such interviews depends heavily on the dexterity of the interviewer, you should enter the interview with extensive knowledge of the subject area, demonstrated by posing informed questions, and be able to adapt to the situation by reacting perceptively to new leads.

Interviews can be conducted face-to-face or by some form of communication technology (such as a telephone, web 'chat room' or video conference). Since interviews are time-consuming, be sure to identify and approach the individuals whose responses will be the most beneficial to your study.

Regardless of the interview approach you select, before starting your interview, you should:

● clarify your status;
● explain the background of the study and clarify its relevance;
● ensure that the respondent understands why they were chosen for interview;
● ensure agreement and consent over how to record and report the interview;
● observe the respondent's right to withdrawal, anonymity and confidentiality;
● establish a time limit.

The other survey option is to use questionnaires. If you choose to employ questionnaires, the way in which you construct your questions will be of vital importance, since no interviewer will be on hand to demystify problem areas. To be most effective, keep the format as simple as possible. Be careful to construct questions that minimise confusion and subsequent frustration. Questionnaires that are quick and easy to complete are more likely to be answered fully and returned.

When formulating questions, make sure they are:

● *clear* – construct questions simply and avoid combining questions;
● *concise* – minimise ambiguity and avoid 'information overload';
● *accessible* – use appropriate language and avoid complicated grammar such as double negatives;
● *unbiased* – structure your questions impartially and avoid 'leading questions' that may bias responses. Where possible, choose denotative over connotative language.

There are several question types you can incorporate into your questionnaire that will provide varying degrees of information. *Closed questions* give the respondent definitive choices and limit the responses to a 'yes' and 'no' format. Although these are very quick to answer and collate, they may not provide the range of response required. For example, the question 'Have you been to the community centre in the last six months?' will not provide information that may be important to your study, such as the frequency of visits or length of each attendance.

Multiple-choice questions offer a range of possible responses and are relatively quick to complete, since the respondent can tick an option rather than spend time writing. This method allows for a coherent collation of responses and can serve as a means for gauging respondents' *level* of agreement with a certain statement, e.g. 'the meeting with the ADHD specialist helped me to understand my child's needs – strongly agree, agree, disagree, strongly disagree'. Multiple-choice questions, however, may not offer essential nuances since the questions may not provide adequately comprehensive responses and may not address reasons *why* respondents select a given option.

Ranking questions require respondents to place a list of alternatives in order of importance or preference. As with multiple-choice questions, these are relatively quick to answer and allow the researcher to gauge degrees by providing a frame of reference. However, the answers may prove misleading since many choices may not apply to the respondent but will be included due to the ranking nature. One variation may be to include a 'check all that apply in order of importance/preference ...' clause to minimise misleading data.

Open questions allow the greatest degree of flexibility with responses since questions are phrased in such a way as to allow respondents to answer in their own words. Of all the question types, open questions will allow the greatest depth of response and may allow you to select quotations to emphasise points within your analysis and provide 'colour' for the presentation of your findings. It should be noted, however, that open questions might be too time-consuming to be realistically manageable and too unstructured to gather coherent and consistent data.

When constructing your questionnaire and choosing question types, be sure to consider the following points.

- Ease/speed of completion.
- Depth of response desired.
- Nature and number of respondents.
- Nature of desired information (factual – perceptions).
- Ease of analysis (comparability and categorisation of the different responses).

In some cases your questionnaire might not elicit all the information that the respondent is able to provide, because it does not ask the right questions. Therefore it may be useful to ask the respondent at the end for any other information they might offer on the subject that has not been requested elsewhere.

Observations

Observations provide the researcher with first-hand data, since the researcher is working in the field and able to personally interpret evidence. This approach allows the researcher to manipulate variables and construct personalised studies. There are, however, drawbacks to this method of research. First, it is difficult to ensure objectivity when dealing with individual perceptions, which may jeopardise the credibility of the research as a whole. Another problem may be consistency, since the researcher's subjectivity may lead to variance when gathering the data.

It may be possible to counter these pitfalls by creating a schedule that specifically outlines what should be observed and how it should be categorised and recorded. By producing a *proforma* the researcher may be able to simplify the recording of the observations. For example, for an observation of an EAL community meeting the researcher may want to focus on who is speaking and the language being used. The researcher might also choose to analyse the nature of the communication and code it according to a predetermined set of categories, such as determining whether questions are open or closed and whether they elicit information, perceptions or attitudes. The observation *proforma* may be used to further determine whether statements are factual or opinion-based and if they are encouraging, neutral or discouraging, etc.

Another concern with observations is that the process can potentially influence the behaviour of the subject. Thus the chosen nature of observation may be significant. *Overt observations*, whereby the observer is revealed and the purposes of the observations are made explicit, are likely to affect the behaviour of the subject. The way in which the participant reacts may be of interest to the observer, but it does mean that the behaviour may not be accurately representative. Although overt observation may affect behaviour, this can be acknowledged and allowed for in the analysis of the findings. Over time it is possible that the effect on behaviour of the observation will be lessened and a more 'realistic' set of observations will be possible. Alternatively, the changed behaviours may become normalised.

Another approach is to use *covert observations*, whereby the observer is concealed and the purposes of the observations are hidden. Observing covertly may reduce the extent to which the observation process impacts the situation and alters behaviour, thus providing more accurate representation. However, the value of the discoveries made in such observations needs to be balanced against the ethical considerations of performing an observation without the knowledge of the subject. For example, attendance at a meeting as a non-participating, covert observer could lead to future repercussions for the observer if the observation is revealed. Clearly, protection of confidentiality and anonymity is essential in such circumstances, although such measures may not negate the ethical implications of covert observation.

Documentary analysis

Previously published documents should provide a foundational basis for your study. You may use them as a preliminary means of exploring the issues you wish to address in your study, as the literature may identify potential areas for inquiry and highlight patterns. However, reliance on preceding studies can be problematic since, unlike questionnaires and interviews specifically designed for your study, the documents you find may not have been written with the same intended focus. Thus critical analysis will be necessary to evaluate the relevance of previous research and to interpret their findings in light of your own research questions.

Both general and specialised texts may be useful to your study. *General texts* within the field may help you define the parameters and scope of your study and clarify terminology. *Specialised texts*, such as edited collections of chapters, should help you refine the foundational ideas of your research. Journal articles not only report research findings but also exemplify research methodology and tools that can be adapted for your own use.

All documents offer two types of information: witting and unwitting. *Witting evidence* is information that the author intended to convey. By way of contrast, *unwitting evidence* is information that can be gleaned from the document due to style, language or omission that the author had not necessarily intended to convey.

While reviewing literature, avoid the mistake of regurgitating information rather than analysing it. Your research should not resemble an annotated bibliography or a literature report devoid of scrutiny. Instead of merely source-hopping, be sure to compare and contrast the content of each source. A convincing review would combine theoretical elements with research findings to construct a more developed model. This model could then serve as the benchmark for interpreting results from your own study. Essentially, you should demonstrate that preceding ideas have been both considered and advanced in order to establish the framework of your research. Since research requires more than speculation and unsubstantiated instinct, thorough analysis will make your argument more cogent and your research more credible.

REFLECTIVE ACTIVITY **13.3**

Selecting an appropriate research methodology

For each of the key research questions.

- *Identify who (the respondent groups) will be able to provide appropriate and useful information.*

- *Identify what information each group might be able to provide.*

For each respondent group.

- *Identify both the strengths and weaknesses of using different data-collection techniques and decide upon the most appropriate research methodology to use for gathering the necessary evidence.*

Presentation and analysis

Once you have gathered your data, the next step will be to present and analyse your findings. To ensure that your study is focused, consult your initial research questions for guidance with structure. For each of the initial questions, you should compare and contrast data from the different sources with your own findings, and interpret and explain both similarities and differences.

Your presentation might include a combination of quantitative and qualitative data. *Quantitative data* provides your study with empirical evidence. It can also provide impact, since numerical data often seems more convincing than theoretical interpretation. For example, '85% of parents (n = 38) claimed that …' indicates that the claim, whatever it may be, has significant backing and is, perhaps, more certain. (Note that when a percentage is used, it should be accompanied by the population size.)

The impact of numerical data can often be further enhanced and simplified through the use of tables and graphs. When presenting your findings graphically, it is important to ensure that the correct format is employed for the chosen data.

If you use mutually *exclusive* categorical data sets such as:

The meeting with the ADHD specialist helped me to understand my child's needs:

strongly agree (20)   *agree (12)*   *disagree (7)*   *strongly disagree (2)*

it is possible to use a pie chart to clearly present your data. Pie charts are frequently presented using percentage data as exemplified in Figure 13.1.

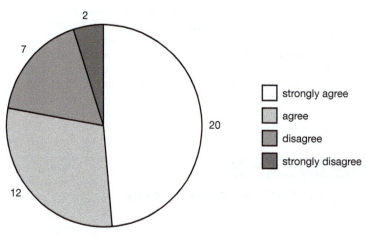

Figure 13.1   Pie chart

If the comparison is between mutually *inclusive* categorical data sets such as:

Which languages do you speak?

English ☐   *Polish* ☐   *German* ☐   *Arabic* ☐   *Urdu* ☐   *Other* ☐

which could result in participants providing more than one response, a block chart should be used as in Figure 13.2. The categories should be organised in some meaningful way, e.g. by size or alphabetical order.

If both data sets are numerical and a potential relationship between them is being sought, for example the number of teenagers speaking a particular language and the average number of sessions attended, you may choose to use a line graph to present your findings.

You should strike a balance between data included within the text and data presented within an appendix. Too much information presented in the text of a study may disrupt the 'flow' of the argument being presented. On the other hand, if you provide too little information, the reader will be forced to search for data to support your claims, which can result in a less convincing argument.

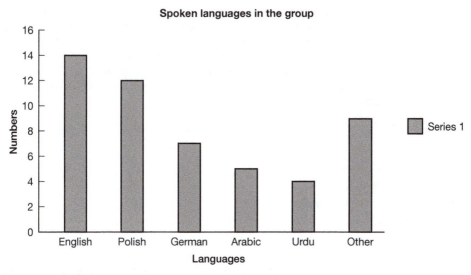

Figure 13.2 Block chart

Thus, if you are unable to fully elaborate due to space constraints or you feel that including certain data may jeopardise continuity, you can transfer data to an appendix and reference it within your study. The information placed within your appendix should generally be regarded as incidental rather than core.

Beyond simple presentation of quantitative data, *statistical tests* can be applied to further confirm the validity and reliability of your findings. This may be to gauge the extent to which data from different populations, e.g. the parents and counsellors of ADHD children, differ in their responses or perceptions. As there is insufficient space here to explain the workings and applications of statistical tests only a brief description of the purpose of the main tools can be offered. (Refer to Robson (2002: 309–69) for further details on the statistical analysis of quantitative data.)

Averages can be used in three different ways.

● *Median* – reduces the impact of outlining points of data that may skew the results.
● *Mode* – highlights the most popular response.
● *Mean* – incorporates all the data.

Standard deviations can be calculated to provide an indication of the spread of the data.

Spearman's rank is used to compare the extent to which two populations rank the same list of criteria differently, or the correlation between the rankings of two separate lists by the same population (Cohen et al., 2000: 81). The *chi-squared test* compares the extent to which two populations (e.g. male and female) respond differently to the same questions (e.g. attendance at support group sessions – if there are twice as many males as females eligible to attend the session, the expectation would be for there to be twice as many males actually attending if gender is *not* a factor).

Qualitative data, by its very nature, is more open to ambiguity and requires interpretation in order for it to be organised and collated. Responses may be unique to each respondent, so the researcher needs to be alert to potential patterns and opportunities for categorisation. Qualitative data has a benefit over quantitative data in that it can offer greater depth and exemplification. Although qualitative data can provide numerical responses, its real strength lies in the insight and humanity provided by direct quotations that enrich the analysis. Since data of this nature is concerned with *meanings and the way people understand things* (Denscombe, 2003: 267), when presented in narrative, it provides nuances and helps the reader to 'connect' with the research in a way that pure numerical data is unable to convey. By using quotations from interviews, observations, diaries or questionnaires, greater meaning can be added to quantitative data. However, qualitative data should be employed judiciously to avoid being perceived as too 'anecdotal' thus referencing to the respondent(s) is important.

An effective analysis involves:

- clear exposition of complex arguments and issues;
- identifying causal relationships;
- elucidating and explaining;
- presenting a sustained logical argument;
- comparing and contrasting;
- identifying and challenging assumptions.

In this section you should synthesise your findings and readings (practice and theory) and clearly and critically you should link theory and practice to derive valid conclusions.

Conclusions and recommendations

Your conclusions should be linked to the title and purpose of the study. They should emanate from the evidence that was presented earlier. Recommendations, where appropriate, should be feasible. In this section you should demonstrate the importance of your research and present your conclusions, which should be:

- explicitly derived from your analysis;
- cross-referenced to your literature review and findings;
- related to your title and original purpose.

SUMMARY OF KEY POINTS

This chapter has introduced a structured overview of the research process that enables you to:

> clarify the purpose of your study by examining its context and identifying key influential factors;

> identify key concepts for your study and use these to direct your reading of related literature;

> design methods for gathering evidence by establishing *what* to ask, *who* to ask and determining *how* best to collect the information;

> analyse findings to address your key research questions.

REFERENCES

Bell, J. (2005) *Doing Your Research Project*, 4th edn. Maidenhead: Open University Press.

Cohen, L., Manion, L. and Morrison, K. (2000) *Research Methods in Education*, 5th edn. London: RoutledgeFalmer.

Denscombe, M. (2003) *The Good Research Guide for Small-Scale Social Research Projects*, 2nd edn. Maidenhead: Open University Press.

Nisbet, J. and Watt, J. (1984) 'Case study', in J. Bell, T. Bush, A. Fox, J. Goodley and S. Golding (eds), *Conducting Small-Scale Investigations in Educational Management*. London: Harper & Row.

Robson, C. (2002) *Real World Research*, 2nd edn. Oxford: Blackwell.

14 The reflective practitioner

Paula Zwozdiak-Myers

Learning objectives

By the end of this chapter you should be able to:

- **identify key concepts and theories associated with reflection;**
- **apply key principles of reflection to aspects of your own practice in order to become a more effective practitioner;**
- **recognise why reflecting on practice is important to your professional development.**

Introduction

When the interests of children and young people are at the heart of your professional work, you will need to ensure that the knowledge, skills and understanding you bring to each situation is guided by good practice within your professional field. As you begin your career pathway and gain experience you will start to build your own repertoire of techniques that should guide your practice.

We are always learning and, as such, must be adaptable. Due to the nature of working in the social sciences, no one solution to a given problem will necessarily be effective in all cases where that problem might arise. You will find that some of your approaches work effectively in certain situations, yet may be less effective in others. Many factors contribute to this variation. Consider, for example, social, emotional and cognitive development along with cultural, racial and ethnic beliefs, values and sensitivities. There may also be issues related to gender or learning difficulties, such as attention deficit hyperactivity disorder (ADHD), emotional behaviour disorder (EBD), autism and dyslexia. Thus it should be clear that with the plethora of variables within any given situation, your approach should be both specialised and adaptable.

For this reason, it is vitally important that you adopt an approach to your work that challenges and questions 'why' you respond to particular situations as you do. Ask yourself whether your actions and reactions within a situation were the best strategies given the interests of all parties. Were there any alternative approaches that you could have tried? The process of thinking about how you do what you do and, more importantly, *why* forms the bedrock of theories associated with the reflective practitioner.

Reflection

The term 'reflection' has been interpreted by theorists and practitioners in a number of different ways and has been used for a range of purposes. Dewey (1933), for example, associates the term with the process of problem-solving, while Kolb (1984) identifies reflection within a cycle of experiential learning. Daudelin (1996) provides a definition that is appropriate for examining the nature of reflective practice within the social sciences. According to Daudelin (1996: 39), *reflection is the process of stepping back from an experience to ponder, carefully and persistently, its meaning to the self through the development of inferences: learning is the creation of meaning from past or current events that serves as a guide for future behaviour.* Several themes emerge from this definition, notably that reflection.

- can be a deliberate, thoughtful activity;
- has a particular focus;
- is used to promote understanding;
- draws upon personal biography;
- is integral to learning;
- can be used to inform future practice.

During the 1980s, Schön (1983, 1987) distinguished between two forms of reflection: reflection *on* action and reflection *in* action. The former describes the type of reflection explained above, which happens some time after an experience and involves retrospectively examining meanings embedded within the outcome. Reflection *in* action, however, describes the type of reflection that happens *during* an experience, as the situation unfolds. This distinction has implications for learning – for gaining knowledge, skills and understanding.

To explain this distinction, consider how you come to learn a new skill, such as playing the piano. Initially, you need to gain knowledge of each individual note, where it appears on the staff, what it sounds like ... this builds into scales, chords and melodies. Along with learning to read the musical score, you need to develop the dexterity and motor skills to play the music – perhaps the right hand initially and then graduate to using both hands simultaneously. If you are a vocalist, add to this a further dimension ... singing. At the outset, you will need to think through each manoeuvre, each new action before you do it. As you practise and gain experience, the learnt skills will be 'assimilated and accommodated' (refer here to Piaget's theory of cognitive development in Chapter 7) into your memory ... there is less need to think through every manoeuvre before you do it.

When you respond to situations by consciously evaluating what you do as you do it, you are reflecting in action. Metaphorically speaking, you are 'thinking on your feet' which involves simultaneously 'reflecting and acting'. This implies that the professional has reached a stage of competence that enables him to assess what is taking place and to modify actions accordingly. The process of interpreting, analysing and providing solutions to complex and situational problems happens during an action, *the period of time in which we remain in the same situation* (Schön, 1983: 278). In the example above, when a pianist becomes an accomplished player, he will be able to play without considering chords, rhythms and musical scores or what his fingers are doing.

At this point in your professional development, however, a measure of caution should be exercised. As indicated earlier, there will not necessarily be a 'correct' approach or solution effective in all scenarios. For this reason, perpetually assessing actions and their consequences is crucial to maximising effectiveness within your professional role.

Attitudes within reflective practice

Dewey (1933: 16) describes *reflective action* as the *willingness to sustain and protract that state of doubt which is the stimulus to thorough inquiry, so as not to accept an idea or make a positive assertion of a belief until justifying reasons have been found.* He contrasts this with routine action that is characterised by an individual's disposition to accept the most commonly held view for resolving a problem, rather than seeking to examine alternative viewpoints or strategies.

Dewey asserts that three attitudes are important prerequisites within reflective practice: *open-mindedness*, *responsibility* and *wholeheartedness*. Open-mindedness relates to a willingness to consider more than one side of an argument and attend to alternative possibilities. This requires an active desire to both listen and accept the strengths and limitations of your own and other people's viewpoints. In some instances, this may lead to the recognition that your former beliefs were misconceived. You may find that you made judgements about an issue and 'jumped to conclusions' without listening to others.

Responsibility relates to the disposition to carefully consider the consequences of your actions and to accept those consequences. When individuals *profess certain beliefs (yet) are unwilling to commit themselves to the consequences that flow from them* (Dewey, 1933: 32) confusion and misconceptions often arise. By reflecting on your practice and questioning whether your actions were appropriate and effective in a given context, you will demonstrate responsibility within your work.

Wholeheartedness relates to the way in which the attitudes of open-mindedness and responsibility are brought together through your interest and enthusiasm. Wholehearted practitioners are dedicated, and regularly examine their beliefs and assumptions along with the consequences of their actions. In this way, they adopt an approach to their work that is open and receptive to learning something new. The following activity provides a series of questions for you to engage with so as to better understand what is involved in the process of reflecting on your experience.

REFLECTIVE ACTIVITY **14.1**

Reflecting on experience

Think back to a recent experience you encountered in a working environment with children and young people. Identify the following:

- *The purpose or goal of the interaction.*

- *What approaches you used to achieve this goal.*

- *How children and young people responded to your approach.*

- *Whether you successfully achieved your goal.*

- *If yes, why? If no, why not?*

This process of self-appraisal involves a series of systematic stages that Boud et al. (1985: 19) refer to as returning to experience, attending to (or connecting with) feelings and evaluating experience. They use the following 'elements' to re-evaluate any given experience.

- ***Association*** – relating new data to that which is already known.
- ***Integration*** – seeking relationships among the data.
- ***Validation*** – determining the authenticity of the ideas and feelings which have resulted.
- ***Appropriation*** – making knowledge one's own.

By reflecting on your experience in this way and gauging the effectiveness of approaches, you will gain an insight into how you are developing within your profession. You must then use this knowledge to move forward. For example, you should place the approaches that were successful in your repertoire of skills and draw upon them in the future. The unsuccessful approaches should either be discarded or modified. In order to modify and improve aspects of your professional practice, you can work through the guidelines presented in the following activity.

This type of engagement with your professional work models action research, introduced in Chapter 12, that places reflection at the heart of the learning process. Action research is an ongoing cyclical process that uses new knowledge and insights gained to inform future planning and practice. In large measure, it is an important characteristic of reflective practice.

Improving your professional practice

Discuss your practice with peers, tutors or colleagues.

- *Identify aspects that need further development.*

- *Consider alternative strategies and approaches you could try.*

- *Set yourself precise goals and targets.*

- *Devise a plan of action that identifies when, where, how and with whom you can test these strategies.*

- *Implement your plan of action.*

- *Evaluate whether your plan of action was successful by looking back and responding to the questions raised in Activity 14.1.*

Levels of reflection

All experiences and events happen within particular contexts that are situated culturally, historically and socially. When you reflect on your own experience, the focus of your reflection(s) can operate on many levels. Van Manen (1977) identifies three levels that can be applied across the range of professions within the social sciences.

- *Technical reflection* – refers to acting efficiently on an everyday basis and is characterised by the application of existing knowledge to reach a given end that is not open to criticism or modification.

- *Practical reflection* – involves the process of analysing and clarifying assumptions, experiences, goals, meanings and perceptions that underpin practical actions. Reflection focuses on *an interpretive understanding both of the nature and quality of educational experience, and of making practical choices* (Van Manen, 1977: 222–7);

- *Critical reflection* – refers to the development of understanding that comes from reflecting and interpreting both personal experience and that of others. This level requires making judgements as to whether professional activity is just, equitable and respectful of others; this requires analysing the cultural and social context and challenging the assumptions that underpin behaviour and performance. Critical reflection takes such judgements further by placing any analysis of personal action within wider cultural, historical, political and social contexts. As Van Manen (1977: 227) explains, *universal consensus, free from delusions or distortions, is the ideal of a deliberative rationality that pursues worthwhile educational ends in self-determination, community, and on the basis of justice, equality, and freedom.*

While different contexts within the social sciences lend themselves more to one kind or level of reflection than another, it is important not to view the levels as an increasingly desirable hierarchy (Calderhead, 1989). All levels of reflection should be encouraged and are considered to be essential aspects of your development. For example, technical reflection is vitally important for your professional development and a precursor to other forms of reflection.

The content of reflection

Korthagen and Vasalos (2005) suggest that the most frequent aspects of reflection content include issues concerned with the *environment, behaviour, competencies* and *beliefs* and more specialised aspects of reflection content include issues concerned with *identity* and *mission*. Although their model (see Figure 14.1) was designed for use in teacher education, its principles and underlying concepts can be applied across all professions within the social sciences that involve learning to work with, and in the interests of, children and young people.

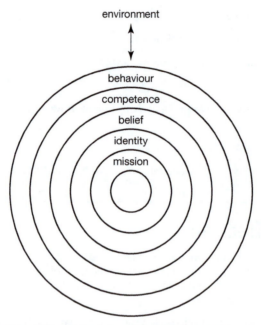

Figure 14.1 Model describing different levels in which reflection can take place
Source: Korthagen and Vasalos (2005: 54).

Korthagen and Vasalos (2005: 53) suggest that the *inner levels determine the way an individual functions on the outer levels, but there is also a reverse influence (from outside to inside)*. They equate the level of mission to what inspires us, what gives significance and meaning to our lives and work. The identity level relates to how we experience ourselves and how our concept of self develops. They further suggest that these deeper levels can only be reached through *core reflection*, in which the 'core of one's personality' provides the content for reflection. The focus of core reflection can be realised when you analyse an experience or event within a particular context and ask yourself:

● What is the ideal situation? What do you want to achieve?
● What are the limiting factors that prevent this from being achieved?

(Korthagen and Vasalos, 2005: 54)

By envisioning an ideal situation and recognising inhibiting factors, you may become aware of inner tension or discrepancies. It is at this point that you must step back to consider whether or not you will allow the limiting factor(s) to influence your behaviour. The purpose of core reflection is to heighten awareness of your inherent core qualities, such as courage, empathy, decisiveness, flexibility, sensitivity and spontaneity (ibid.). Ofman (2000) suggests that, although a core quality is always potentially present, the distinction between competencies and qualities lies primarily in the notion that competencies are acquired from the outside whereas qualities come from the inside. Within Korthagen and Vasalos' theoretical framework, the ability to 'reflect systematically' can be found at the competency level whereas core qualities or 'character strengths' (Peterson and Seligman, 2003) are embedded within the deeper levels.

Your reflections will be influenced by your personal theories and belief system. These theories and beliefs will originate from many sources, such as established practice, experience of what worked best, research- and educationally-based principles and procedures in addition to factors that can be attributed to your own personality. In relation to teacher education, Richards and Lockhart (1996: 30) suggest that teachers' belief systems are founded on *the goals, values, and beliefs teachers hold in relation to the content and process of teaching, and their understanding of the systems in which they work and their roles within it*. These same factors underpin the practical theories and belief systems that you hold about the different professions within the social sciences.

It is important to note that your reflections will be constrained, to some extent, by your perceptions. Your analysis of an experience will be guided by how you perceive the particular situation. This, however, provides only one of several 'lenses' through which to examine a situation. Brookfield (1995) uses the metaphor 'hunting assumptions' to describe an important step toward becoming *critically reflective* that can be used to systematically examine aspects of your practice from a range of 'lenses', or perspectives, rather than relying exclusively on your own interpretations. Brookfield advocates that, in addition to your personal interpretations, three lenses should be considered to further inform your practice: the children and young people directly involved, colleagues with whom you work and theoretical literature. Your willingness to consider these alternative views and perspectives clearly has resonance with Dewey's attitude of open-mindedness.

REFLECTIVE ACTIVITY **14.3**

Interpretations of the same situation

Ask three peers or colleagues to observe you or a video excerpt of you interacting with a small group of children or young people. To guide their observations ask them to focus on how information is conveyed between you and the individual members within your group through the following communication channels: verbal – spoken language, questions, answers and explanations; and non-verbal – gestures, eye gaze, listening, body language, spatial orientation and facial expressions

After the activity, ask each observer to provide feedback about their observations in addition to their interpretations of the meanings behind their observations.

- *Identify similarities and differences in feedback between the three observers.*

- *How can you explain the similarities and differences?*

- *Do their interpretations match with your own perceptions?*

- *If yes, explain how and why. If no, explain how and why not.*

The reflective practitioner

Schön's conceptualisation of the reflective practitioner emerged from the distinction between two theoretical forms of practice or action: *espoused theory* and *theory-in-use* (Argyris and Schön, 1974). Espoused theories refer to those that are formally seen by a profession to both guide action and encompass the formal philosophy of the profession. Theories-in-use refer to those patterns of behaviour that are learned and developed in the day-to-day work of the professional and it is these, Schön (1983) suggests, that characterise the real behaviour of professionals. The distinction arose from his concern that there was a significant gap between the prepositional (espoused) knowledge and theory that purports to underpin professional activity and the reality of how a professional behaves in practice.

Within such professions as social work and education, Schön (1983: 68) argues that there is no body of secure knowledge that can be used prescriptively to guide practice which can lead to a state of confusion as *real-world problems do not come well formed. They tend to present themselves, on the contrary, as messy, indeterminate, problematic situations*. The ability to cope with ill-structured, problematic situations with uncertain knowledge is considered a more advanced stage of the development of reflective thinking than one associated with problem-solving.

Schön (1983) distinguishes between 'scientific' and 'caring' professional work. The 'high, hard ground' of the former is exemplified in laboratory research that is supported by quantitative and objective evidence. The 'swampy lowlands' of the latter is exemplified by the social sciences, which are more concerned with interpersonal and qualitative issues that draw upon a particular kind of *knowing-in-action*. He argues that this knowledge is inherent, intangible, intuitive, spontaneous and tacit, yet it 'works' in practice. Schön (1983: 68) further recognised reflection-in-action that describes when someone:

> ... becomes a researcher in the practice context. He is not dependent on the categories of established theory or technique, but constructs a new theory of the unique case. He does not keep means and ends separate, but defines them interactively as he frames a problematic situation. He does not separate thinking from action ... His experimenting is a kind of action, implementation is built into his enquiry.

Thus a distinction is drawn (Morrison, 1996; Schön, 1987) between reflection *in* action, a process that is immediate, short-term and concerned with adapting strategies or approaches, and reflection *on* action, a process that takes place sometime after the event and is *an ordered, systematically structured, deliberate and deliberative, logical analysis of events and situations* (Morrison, 1996: 319). It could be argued that the latter encourages greater questioning of the principles and theories that underpin what we do and is more likely to create professional autonomy through the conscious exercise of judgement.

Cowan (1998) distinguishes between analytical and evaluative reflection, the former addressing the question 'How do I do it?' and the latter 'How well do I do it?' It is the second of these that is critical for judging and discerning. Without such critical evaluation, it would be difficult to complete the reflection process and for the learning from reflection to result in action and improvement.

Schön's framework can be used to embrace all forms and levels of reflection. His reflection in action and reflection on action incorporate an epistemology of professional practice based upon *knowing in action* and *knowledge in action* (Altricher and Posch, 1989; Munby and Russell, 1989). Such tacit knowledge stems from the construction and reconstruction of professional experience rather than the application of technical or scientific rationality (Adler, 1991; Schön, 1983, 1987). Schön suggests that this is one means of distinguishing between professional and non-professional practice.

In closing this chapter, we return to Dewey's attitude of responsibility. The desire and willingness to continuously develop and improve your personal knowledge base should be of central importance to you within your role as a professional practitioner. The purpose of reflective thinking is to enable you *to transform a situation in which there is experienced obscurity, doubt, conflict, disturbance of some sort, into a situation that is clear, coherent, settled and harmonious* ... (Dewey, 1933: 100).

REFLECTIVE ACTIVITY **14.4**

The importance of reflecting on practice

Identify the reasons why reflecting on aspects of your own experience might be important.

Discuss your response and views with a peer, colleague or your professional tutor.

List the possible consequences that might emerge if you do not reflect on aspects of your own experience.

SUMMARY OF KEY POINTS

This chapter has explored key concepts and theories associated with reflection that enables you to address the following questions.

1. What is the purpose of your reflection?

2. How can you go about doing this?

3. On what aspects of your experience and practice should you reflect?

4. To what extent should you reflect on the social and political issues that concern the children and young people with whom, and for whom, you work?

5. What criteria should you use?

You can use these questions to guide your discussions and future planning with peers, colleagues and tutors. The criteria indicated in question 5 should acknowledge the standards that you need to achieve to demonstrate effectiveness and good practice within your chosen profession. Question 4 has significance for aspects of your practice that consider the ethical and moral dimensions of your work. This should be guided by the principles, procedures and codes of ethical conduct that you need to address to exercise sound judgement when working with children and young people, their carers/guardians, personal colleagues and, where appropriate, policy-makers.

Adler, S. (1991) 'The reflective practitioner and the curriculum of teacher education', *Journal of Education for Teaching*, 17 (2): 139–50.

Altrichter, H. and Posch, P. (1989) 'Does the "grounded theory" approach offer a guiding paradigm for teacher research?', *Cambridge Journal of Education*, 19 (1): 21–31.

Argyris, C. and Schön, D. (1974) *Theory into Practice*. San Francisco: Jossey-Bass.

Boud, D., Keogh, R. and Walker, D. (eds) (1985) *Reflection: Turning Experience into Learning*. London: Kogan Page.

Brookfield, S. (1995) *Becoming a Critically Reflective Teacher*. San Francisco: Jossey-Bass.

Calderhead, J. (1989) 'Reflective teaching and teacher education', *Teaching and Teacher Education*, 5 (1): 43–51.

Cowan, J. (1998) *On Becoming an Innovative University Teacher*. Buckingham: Open University Press.

Daudelin, M. (1996) 'Learning from experience through reflection', *Organizational Dynamics*, 24 (3): 36–48.

Dewey, J. (1933) *How We Think: A Restatement of the Relation of Reflective Thinking to the Educative Process*. Boston: D. C. Heath.

Kolb, D. (1984) *Experiential Learning as the Science of Learning and Development*. Englewood Cliffs, NJ: Prentice Hall.

Korthagen, F. and Vasalos, A. (2005) 'Levels in reflection: core reflection as a means to enhance professional growth', *Teachers and Teaching: Theory and Practice*, 11 (1): 47–71.

Morrison, K. (1996) 'Developing reflective practice in higher degree students through a learning journal', *Studies in Higher Education*, 21 (3).

Munby, H. and Russell, T. (eds) (1989) *Teachers and Teaching: From Classroom to Reflection*. London: Falmer Press.

Ofman, D. (2000) *Core Qualities: A Gateway to Human Resources*. Schiedam: Scriptum.

Peterson, C. and Seligman, M. (2003) *Values in action (VIA): Classification of Strengths*. Philadelphia: Values in Action Institute (available online: **http://www.positivepsychology.org/taxonomy.htm**).

Richards, J. and Lockhart, C. (1996) *Reflective Teaching in Second Language Classrooms*. Cambridge: Cambridge University Press.

Schön, D. (1983) *The Reflective Practitioner: How Professionals Think in Action*. New York: Basic Books.

Schön, D. (1987) *Educating the Professional Practitioner*. San Francisco: Jossey-Bass.

Van Manen, M. (1977) 'Linking ways of knowing with ways of being practical', *Curriculum Inquiry*, 6: 205–28.

Appendix 1
Five priority outcomes: improvement for children's services

The Green Paper, *Every Child Matters*, proposed the introduction of a national common assessment framework as an important part of a strategy for helping children, young people and their families to achieve the five priority outcomes to:

- *Be Healthy* – This means babies, children and young people are physically healthy, mentally and emotionally healthy, sexually healthy, living healthy lifestyles, and choosing not to take illegal drugs. We also want to help parents, carers and families to promote healthy choices.

- *Stay Safe* – This means babies, children and young people are safe from maltreatment, neglect, violence and sexual exploitation, safe from accidental injury and death, safe from bullying and discrimination, safe from crime and anti-social behaviour in and out of school, and have security, stability and are cared for. We also want to help parents, carers and families to provide safe homes and stability, to support learning and to develop independent living skills for their children.

- *Enjoy and Achieve* – This means young children are ready for school, school-age children attend and enjoy school, children achieve stretching national educational standards at primary school, children and young people achieve personal and social development and enjoy recreation, and children and young people achieve stretching national educational standards at secondary school. We also want to help parents, carers and families to support learning.

- *Make a Positive Contribution* – This means children and young people engage in decision-making and support the community and environment, engage in law-abiding and positive behaviour in and out of school, develop positive relationships and choose not to bully or discriminate, develop self-confidence and successfully deal with significant life changes and challenges and develop enterprising behaviour. We also want to help parents, carers and families to promote positive behaviour.

- *Achieve Economic Well-being* – This means young people engage in further education, employment or training on leaving school, young people are ready for employment, children and young people live in decent homes and sustainable communities, children and young people have access to transport and material goods, and children and young people live in households free from low income. We also want to help parents, carers and families to be economically active.

The common assessment framework fits into *Every Child Matters*, *Youth Matters* and the *Children's National Service Framework* and is underpinned by two broad aspects of the *Every Child Matters* integrated working strategy:

1. *Workforce reform* – includes the introduction of the *Common Core of Skills and Knowledge for the Children's Workforce* to ensure all professionals have the knowledge and skills to work effectively with children and their families, and access to training when relevant. The skills and knowledge are described under six main headings:

   - Effective communication and engagement with children, young people and families;
   - Child and young person development;
   - Safeguarding and promoting the welfare of the child;

- Supporting transitions;
- Multi-agency working;
- Sharing information.

Search the websites **http://www.everychildmatters.gov.uk/deliveringservices/commoncore** and **http://www.ecm.gov.uk/workforcereform** for further details.

2. *Multi-agency working* – involves bringing professionals from different agencies together to meet the needs of children and families and to jointly agree the delivery of the actions arising from a common or specialist assessment. Information on different service models and a toolkit for practitioners are presented as the multi-agency resource online at **http://www.ecm.gov.uk/multiagencyworking**.

Undertaking a common assessment has a strong emphasis on consent and you should explain to the child and/or their parent how the information in the assessment could, or will, be shared, and seek their consent. The *Information Sharing: Practitioners' Guide* should be consulted for guidance and is available online at

http://www.ecm.gov.uk/informationsharing

A series of documents entitled *Every Child Matters: Change for Children* explain how the Children Act 2004 forms the basis of a long-term programme of change. You can download these documents from **http://www.everychildmatters.gov.uk** or

http://www.teacher net.gov.uk/publications to learn more about the National Services Framework (NSF) for the different services and professions within which you plan to work:

- *Every Child Matters: Change for Children* (Ref: DfES/1081/2004).
- *Every Child Matters: Change for Children in Schools* (Ref: DfES/1089/2004).
- *Every Child Matters: Change for Children in Social Services* (Ref: DfES/1090/2004).
- *Every Child Matters: Change for Children in Health Services* (Ref: DoH/1091/2004).
- *Every Child Matters: Change for Children in the Criminal Justice System* (Ref: DfES/1092/2004).
- *National Service Framework for Children, Young People and Maternity Services – Executive Summary* (Ref: DoH/40496/2004; also online at: http://www.dh.gov.uk/PolicyAndGuidance/ HeathAndSocialCareTopics/ChildrenServices/fs/en

Appendix 2
Dealing with disclosures

Receive

- Listen to the child.
- If you are shocked by what they are saying, try not to show it.
- Take what they say seriously.
- Accept what the child says.
- Do not ask for (other) information.

Reassure

- Stay calm and reassure the child that they have done the right thing in talking to you.
- Be honest with the child so do not make promises you cannot keep.
- Do not promise confidentiality – you have a duty to refer a child who is at risk.
- Acknowledge how hard it must have been for the child to tell you what happened.

React

- React to the child only as far as is necessary for you to establish whether or not you need to refer this matter, but do not interrogate him/her for full details.
- Do not ask leading questions.
- Explain what you have to do next and to whom you have to talk.

Record

- Make some brief notes at the time and write them up more fully as soon as possible.
- Take care to record timing, setting and personnel as well as what was said.
- Be objective in your recording – include statements and observable things rather than your interpretations or assumptions.

Support

- The child will need support through the process of investigation and afterwards.
- You will need support.
- All staff have a responsibility to recognise child abuse, ensure an appropriate referral is undertaken and co-operate with child protection procedures while working within the parameters of your own professional Code of Conduct.
- At any stage – you can consult with a duty social worker (add local numbers):
  Day time:
  Out-of-hours:
- All agencies have signed up to LCSB/ ACPC procedures that say **you** must follow agency procedures which include phoning the duty social worker.

Appendix 3

The challenge of partnership in child protection

1. Treat all family members as you would wish to be treated, with dignity and respect.
2. Ensure family members know the child's safety and welfare must be given priority but that they have a right to courteous, caring and professionally competent service.
3. Take care not to infringe privacy any more than is necessary to safeguard the welfare of the child.
4. Be clear with yourself and with family members about your power to intervene and the purpose of your professional involvement at each stage.
5. Be aware of the effects on family members of the power you have as a professional and the impact and implications of what you say and do.
6. Respect the confidentiality of family members and your observations about them, unless they give permission for information to be passed on to others or if it is essential to do so to protect the child.
7. Listen to the concerns of children and their families and take care to learn about their understanding, fears and wishes before arriving at your own explanations and plans.
8. Learn about and consider children within their family relationships and communities, including their cultural and religious contexts and their place within their own family.
9. Consider the strengths and potential of family members, as well as weaknesses, problems and limitations.
10. Ensure children, families and other carers know their responsibilities and rights, including those to services and the right to refuse services and any consequences of doing so.
11. Use jargon-free language appropriate to the age and culture of each person. Explain unavoidable technical and professional terms.
12. Be open and honest about your concerns and responsibilities, plans and limitations, without being defensive.
13. Allow children and families time to take in and understand concerns and processes. A balance needs to be found between appropriate speed and the needs of people who may need extra time in which to communicate.
14. Take care to distinguish between personal feelings, values, prejudices and beliefs and professional roles and responsibilities and ensure that you have good supervision to check that you are doing so.
15. If a mistake or misinterpretation has been made, or you are unable to keep to an agreement, provide an explanation. Always acknowledge any distress experienced by adults and children and do all you can to keep it to a minimum.

Index

Added to a page number 'f' denotes a figure and 't' denotes a table.